O8-CCO-874

WITHDRAWN

RAILROAD LAW
A DECADE AFTER
DEREGULATION

RAILROAD LAW
A DECADE AFTER
DEREGULATION

Frank J. Dooley and William E. Thoms

KRANNERT

343.73095
D72r
1994

Q

QUORUM BOOKS
Westport, Connecticut • London

Library of Congress Cataloging-in-Publication Data

Dooley, Frank.
    Railroad law a decade after deregulation / Frank J. Dooley and
William E. Thoms.
      p. cm.
    Includes bibliographical references and index.
    ISBN 0–89930–631–4 (alk. paper)
    1. Railroad law—United States. 2. Railroads—United States—
Deregulation—History. 3. Railroads—United States—History.
I. Thoms, William E. II. Title.
KF2219.D66 1994
343.7309′5—dc20
[347.30395]   94–8539

British Library Cataloguing in Publication Data is available.

Copyright © 1994 by Frank J. Dooley and William E. Thoms

All rights reserved. No portion of this book may be
reproduced, by any process or technique, without the
express written consent of the publisher.

Library of Congress Catalog Card Number: 94–8539
ISBN: 0–89930–631–4

First published in 1994

Quorum Books, 88 Post Road West, Westport, CT 06881
An imprint of Greenwood Publishing Group, Inc.

Printed in the United States of America

The paper used in this book complies with the
Permanent Paper Standard issued by the National
Information Standards Organization (Z39.48–1984).

10 9 8 7 6 5 4 3 2 1

To Our Daughters
Jan Thoms and Sarah and Anne Dooley

ACB100

Contents

Illustrations

FIGURES

Preface

Railroads, our earliest large-scale corporations, were the first American entities to be extensively regulated by government. They are less visible today than when the railroads opened the West and developed our smoke-stack industries, but as we approach the twenty-first century, our reliance on railroads is still substantial.

We have composed this book on word processors. To operate these computers, great coal trains have been running constantly from the Powder River basin in Wyoming to feed electric power plants throughout the Midwest. It is a rather indirect way of getting around to writing a book; after all, the engines do not even burn coal. Other people had to prospect and drill for oil and construct mighty diesel-electric locomotives to move this coal to the utilities. The electric industry relies on coal, and coal requires freight trains to move it. In fact, most of the railroads' profits derive from the movement of unit trains of coal.

In our home state of North Dakota, rails are responsible for the movement of the grain shipments that are vital to the economic well-being of the state. Grain also moves in unit trains and is one of the principal commodities that has stayed on the rails. Although today the railroads are preeminently carriers of bulk commodities, intermodal transportation (trailers or containers upon flat cars) has seen the return of fast scheduled freight trains to the rails. Charles Bohi, writing in the August 1993 issue of *Trains* magazine, suggested that railroads once looked to small shipments (less than carload lot [LCL]) for 10 percent of the revenue. Railroads removed themselves from the LCL business in the 1960s, but today much package freight moves by rail—but the consolidation and shipping is done by others. United Parcel Service (UPS) moves so many packages by rail (in UPS trailers carried aboard flat cars) that it is a major shipper on Conrail and the biggest single customer of the Santa Fe. On these railroads, UPS has its own dedicated trains that move coast to coast. The railroads also do a good business with steamship lines in bringing containers inland or from Pacific to Atlantic ports.

Passenger service in the United States is still somewhat of a joke. You cannot travel by train between Minneapolis and St. Louis, Cincinnati and Atlanta, or Denver and Kansas City, or for that matter, to anywhere in South Dakota, Maine, or Oklahoma. Yet Amtrak has shown steady progress in reducing costs and increasing service in its two decades of service. In addition, commuter service is thriving and a new, extensive system has been instituted in the 1990s in Los Angeles, which no one ever considered a railroad town.

Railroad labor issues, once the stuff of front-page news, have now reached a degree of cooperation, if not trust, between the carriers and the brotherhoods. Nonetheless, the forms of the Railway Labor Act still carry on an adversarial regime in labor relations. Railroading is a hazardous and stressful occupation, and, unfortunately, little has been done in studying the effects of irregular hours, twenty-four–hour operations, and dangerous working conditions upon railroaders. Compulsory arbitration mandated by the government has only been used in this industry.

Our railroad system is smaller than it has been at any time in the twentieth century. Yet what track remains is generally of good quality. Speed and safety of freight service have increased, although the number of alternate routes has diminished. Our carriers have merged, so that the industry is dominated by seven carriers: Conrail, Norfolk Southern, and CSX in the East; Burlington Northern, Union Pacific, Southern Pacific, and Santa Fe in the West. The two Canadian carriers are also present through their American subsidiaries (Soo Line, Delaware and Hudson, Grand Trunk Western, and Central Vermont); there are a few midsized carriers (Illinois Central, Kansas City Southern, and Springfield Terminal come to mind), and then there is a category known as regional railroads. Most of these are spinoffs from larger railroads, and they maintain friendly connections with their onetime parent. Then there are the true short lines or terminal switching railroads, usually a branch line now independently run by local management.

With such an expansive topic, this book could only be a survey. We speak of "a decade after deregulation," but this may be a misnomer. Railroads are still intensively regulated through the Federal Railroad Administration (FRA), an agency of the Department of Transportation. In addition, some state regulation remains, and the Interstate Commerce Commission (ICC), the oldest agency of them all, is still very much in business, although, after the Staggers Act, its effect on the day-to-day operations of railroads is minimal. Licensure of engineers has made the FRA into an agency similar to the Federal Aviation Administration in its licensing and safety function and its concern with all aspects of the industry. But the spirit of the times is for more relaxed regulation, and our text is concerned with the changes in the regulatory ethos in the past dozen years.

Our book owes its inception to many individuals. Gene Griffin, director of the Upper Great Plains Transportation Institute at North Dakota State University, has generously assisted with our research in the past three years. Particular thanks go to transportation economist Denver D. Tolliver and administrative assistant Kathy McCarthy, who kept this project going. At the University of North Dakota, Dean W. Jeremy Davis has been greatly supportive. This text has been compiled and set in type by two experts at the keyboard, our faculty secretaries, Kathy Feist and Linda Harmon.

Many friends have lent of their expertise in giving us background for the book. Paul Stephen Dempsey of the University of Denver, Kenneth L. Casavant of Washington State University, Mike Cram of Iowa State University, and Sonja Clapp of the Grand Forks, N.D., We also thank our patient editor, Arlene Belzer. State's Attorney's office have been extremely helpful. Eric Valentine, our long-suffering publisher at Quorum Books, is to be thanked for his patience and his foresight in seeing this work come to print.

RAILROAD LAW
A DECADE AFTER
DEREGULATION

1

Railroad Regulation and Deregulation

THE RISE AND FALL OF THE IRON HORSE

American railroads, our first major industrial corporations, were also responsible for the development of the geography and history of nineteenth-century America. As a result, a body of law has grown up around railroading, which has been the model for administrative and public law. The Interstate Commerce Commission (ICC), established in 1887,[1] our first administrative agency was concerned solely with the economic regulation of railroads until 1935. Railroads were the first entities to require special laws for labor-management relations, personal work-related injuries and industrial accidents, as well as hours of service.

The laws applicable to railroading reflected the concerns of the Granger movement and other shipper groups faced with a transportation monopoly. Once the river steamer had been vanquished, the railroads had no serious competition for freight or passenger traffic until the development of all-weather roads and reliable automobiles following World War I. (The electric interurban railway gave the steam railroads a run for their money, but was never a serious contender.)

Mergers and consolidations brought our great railway systems into today's recognizable configurations. The high-water mark for trackage was in 1926; although new lines have been built since then, construction has never kept pace with abandonments.[2] The development of the reliable DC-3 in the 1940s caused the decline of first-class passenger service; this decline became a rout with the placing of jet airliners in service in the 1960s. Parallel lines and branch lines fell victim to a rationalization process.[3] The railroads had left such areas as livestock, package express, and less than carload lot (LCL) shipments by 1970. A series of rail mergers in the 1960s led to the catastrophic rail bankruptcies of the 1970s.[4]

Today's railroads are privately owned corporations that have diversified throughout the transportation business. We still have no true transcontinental railroad; rather, there are four major systems in the West and three in the East. In addition, there has been a movement by the major carriers to spin off feeder lines to regional or short line railroads.[5] Passenger service is operated by Amtrak or commuter authorities and a number of privately owned recreational lines as well.[6]

Contemporary railroads function as heavy carriers of freight. Most of the traffic now moving on the rails is of two kinds: (1) bulk commodities such as coal and grain, for which there is no acceptable alternative (except barge lines for shippers and consignees lucky enough to be located on a river), and (2) intermodal traffic. The latter consists of containers or trailers that can move directly between the shipper's dock and the consignees' loading facility.

Since most time-sensitive and high-valued freight moved to truckers in the 1960s, intermodal trains are the best way in which railroads can recapture this traffic. UPS is the largest intermodal shipper on the rails, and many transpacific shipping companies have dedicated trains to move containers full of Asian products directly to North American markets—or sometimes to other ships bound for Europe, using U.S. railroads as a land bridge.

After a time of financial distress and disarray, U.S. railroading began to establish itself on a firmer economic basis during the 1980s. Although whole railroads like the Milwaukee and Rock Island disappeared, and most of the eastern railroads went into the Conrail system, what remains is healthier than rails have been since V-J Day.[7] To a certain extent, progress in railroading can be said to be a by-product of the partial deregulation of the 1970s and 1980s. This book is an account of railroading and the law at the end of the twentieth century and what part the relaxation of regulation plays in the making of the sharply altered railroad map of today.

ORIGINS OF RAIL REGULATION

When the railroads began, the individual shipper or passenger had little recourse against the rail corporation; calls for regulation resulted in a number of state agencies regulating railroads, forwarders, and warehouses within the boundaries of those (predominantly agricultural) jurisdictions. However, these attempts quickly ran afoul of the constitutional reservation of interstate commerce regulation to Congress.

Against this background, Congress enacted the Act to Regulate Commerce in 1887, which established the Interstate Commerce Commission, the first of our independent regulatory agencies.[8] ("Independent" refers to the fact that these multi-member commissions are not part of the president's cabinet, and the agency heads serve fixed terms, not dependent on the good will of the executive branch.)

To the extent that states were allowed to regulate traffic entirely within their boundaries, all states established railroad commissions, public utilities commissions, or sometimes public service commissions. Whatever their names, their missions were the same; they served to regulate monopoly power, not only of railroads, but of other utilities such as gas, electricity, telephones, and transit.

But the authority of the states was, and is, circumscribed by how much the field has been preempted by the federal government. In the case of *United States v. Colorado,*[9] the ICC's power was held to extend even to a narrow-gauge branch of the Colorado & Southern Ry. located entirely within Colorado. The 1958 amendments to the Interstate Commerce Act extended the ICC's authority to passenger train discontinuances, which had formerly been considered under state jurisdiction through the "partial abandonment doctrine."[10]

The ICC originally had but limited powers, principally in the area of policing discriminatory practices on the part of railroads, favoring certain shippers or ports. A series of amendments in 1906, 1920, 1940, and 1958 extended the ICC's authority over rails to police rates, approve mergers, regulate abandonments and discontinuances of service, regulate adequacy of service, and consider the effect of rate and service change on competing carriers or alternate modes of transportation. In 1935 the ICC received jurisdiction over the motor carrier industry, and in 1940 its jurisdiction was extended over inland waterway barge operators as well.[11] (An independent agency, the Civil Aeronautics Board (CAB), exercised similar regulatory control over the airlines from 1938 through 1984.)[12]

But while other modes were regulated in a less comprehensive fashion (agricultural commodities were exempt when they moved by barge or truck, for example), the railroads remained comprehensively regulated in all their transportation activities. Add to this the fact that railroads must build, maintain, and be taxed on their own right of way, while other carriers use facilities provided by the government, and you can understand the rails' call for competitive equity throughout the 1960s and 1970s. Although the railroad industry is still regulated (as opposed to the economic deregulation of airlines and the sunset of the CAB), there has been a considerable relaxation of the ICC's regulatory regime since the passage of the Staggers Act in 1980.[13]

DEREGULATORY LEGISLATION

By 1970 the effect of utility-type regulation on railroads had been documented and was not positive. Everywhere, the industry was in decline, in most cases not earning the cost of capital. Some railroads had disappeared; other sought relief by merger with parallel lines.

By 1970 the Burlington Northern, Seaboard Coast Line, and Penn Central were realities. Dieselization and the consolidation of freight into longer (and slower) trains had brought some savings in labor costs but not much since the costs of collective bargaining agreements were passed on with ICC approval in general rate increases. The New Haven was about to disappear when the ICC pushed it into the reluctant arms of the Pennsylvania and New York Central as a condition of their hoped-for marriage.[14] On June 21, 1970, the Penn Central conglomeration filed for reorganization under Section 77 of the Bankruptcy Act.[15] This was, at the time, the largest corporate reorganization yet undertaken. During the 1970s, most of the eastern railroads would follow the lead of the Penn Central and seek protection from their creditors in the bankruptcy courts. Lest this be considered a problem endemic only to Official Territory, it was not long before the Milwaukee and the Rock Island followed their eastern connections into reorganization.

The Rail Passenger Service Act of 1970

The high-water mark of ICC regulatory jurisdiction over railroads was the 1958 Transportation Act that gave the commission the right to overrule state commissions on the discontinuances of passenger trains. The ICC exercised this jurisdiction until 1970. At that time, the Amtrak approach was decided upon for operation of the nation's intercity trains.

The Rail Passenger Service Act, which authorized Amtrak,[16] nonetheless has several features that were harbingers of the large-scale deregulation to come. First of all, railroads that joined the Amtrak system were able to discontinue trains without permission of the ICC. Second, the ICC lost jurisdiction over the Amtrak system itself. Finally, nonreviewable discretion was given to the secretary of transportation, not the ICC, to determine the outline of the Amtrak route-map. Trains not included in the system could be discontinued without the need for regulatory permission.

Of course, if Congress did not like the results, it could always try to regain its authority, and during Amtrak's twenty-two-year history, Congress has intervened again and again. But Amtrak is now on its own, save for its dependence upon government subsidy. It was an example of what John Kenneth Galbraith called "lemon socialism"—aiding a regulated industry by unloading an unremunerative (and unwanted by the railroads) service upon the general public.

The Regional Rail Reorganization Act of 1973 (3-R Act)

Like the Amtrak law, the 3-R Act had a specialized purpose to supervise the reorganization of Penn Central and its fellow bankrupt roads in Official Territory. The vehicle was the Consolidated Rail Corporation (Conrail).[17] Much of the planning for Conrail bypassed the ICC; once again the secretary of transportation was given unreviewable discretion to map out the new rail system.

If the secretary of transportation said that a line could be abandoned, it was up to the state involved to put its money where its mouth was. If the line was to be subsidized, it could continue; otherwise, it would be discontinued without a by-your-leave from the ICC. Although since its privatization, Conrail has been treated like any other carrier, the 3-R Act extended the Amtrak deregulatory approach to freight railroading at that time.

The Railroad Revitalization and Regulatory Reform Act (4-R Act)

The 4-R Act was not a piecemeal solution to a particular problem, such as passenger service or eastern bankruptcies, as was the 3-R Act. Instead, this 1976 law was the first comprehensive attempt by Congress to reexamine the need for economic regulation of the railroad industry.[18] Congress did not yet abandon traditional regulation, but the 4-R Act made some changes to the regulatory system in the areas of maximum and minimum rates, seasonal and other such demand sensitive rates, and a zone of ratemaking freedom. Most of the achievements of the 4-R Act were overshadowed by the massive changes wrought by the Staggers Act four years later.

The 4-R Act also introduced into rail regulation the concept of market dominance. Market dominance exists when there is a lack of competition from other carriers or modes for a particular type of freight. The ICC must find that a carrier has market dominance before it can make a finding that railroad rates are too high.

The Bankruptcy Reform Act of 1978

The recodification of the bankruptcy laws, beginning with the wholesale reforms of 1978 and reenacted to cure constitutional deficiencies in 1984, contained some new provisions dealing with the reorganization of railroads.[19] Notable among them is that the Department of Transportation now has a role to play in bankruptcy proceedings, and that the ICC's abandonment role is strictly advisory. Now, it is the Bankruptcy Court who determines whether a line should be abandoned or a lease rejected. The decreased role of the ICC or state regulators was another sign of the trend in Congress to include deregulatory provisions in railroad legislation.

The Staggers Rail Act of 1980

This regulatory reform law is named for its sponsor, West Virginian Harley Staggers, a veteran of the House of Representatives, who concerned himself largely with railroad affairs during his long-term seat on the House Commerce Committee. (It was Staggers who convinced Amtrak to press its experimental TurboTrain on a tortuous mountain route over the old B&O between Washington, D.C., and Parkersburg, W.Va.)

Unlike the more famous Airline Deregulation Act of 1978, the Staggers Rail Act[20] neither deregulated the railroads nor disestablished the regulatory agency charged with their oversight. Like the companion Motor Carrier Act of 1980[21] and the Bus Regulatory Reform Act enacted two years later,[22] the Staggers Act kept the ICC in business, but substantially increased the freedom of movement for the rails. When railroaders speak of "rail deregulation," they refer to liberalized regulation following the Staggers Act and the ICC which functioned in its wake, often deregulating certain areas of rail activity on its own.

At the time of Staggers, Congress was mainly concerned with the financial health of the railroads and their ability to continue service. This was no idle fear—the Milwaukee and Rock Island, major transcontinental routes, as well as the western half of the Erie-Lackawanna had disappeared from the *Official Guide*, and salvage men were actually tearing up the track. Congress, with strong urging from President Carter, enacted the law in September 1980, stating in the preamble that the new regulatory policy stressed competition to the maximum extent possible.[23]

The Staggers law has a relaxed entry provision, which was designated to make the establishment of new short lines easier. The public convenience and necessity criterion was changed so that now the public need must only permit (not require) the establishment of a new railroad.[24] Not only does this section make it easier to salvage new short lines from the wreckage of such carriers as the Milwaukee and Rock Island, but it limits the ability of an existing railroad to challenge a certificate of public convenience and necessity. It facilitates the construction of spur lines across town to serve a shipper now served by a competing railroad, and it prohibits a railroad from preventing another line from crossing its tracks at grade. The ICC has power to arbitrate a dispute between two or more railroads pertaining to the crossing of their lines.[25]

The Staggers Act speeded up the abandonment process. If a railroad meets the burden of proof that public convenience and necessity permit abandonment, the effective date of abandonment must be within 330 days from the date the petition is filed. There are also provisions for interested parties to purchase the line, aimed at preserving the linear right-of-way for transportation or other public purposes.[26]

The principal changes made by the 1980 law were in the area of rate regulation. For the first time, within certain boundaries, railroads may charge whatever rates they choose. A rate that is compensatory (i.e., contributes to the going concern value of the carrier), is presumed to be just and reasonable. But the question of reasonableness of a rate only comes into play if the carrier has market dominance.[27]

The act also provides that carriers may contract with shippers. Within thirty days of filing a confidential contract with the ICC, the contract rate will go into effect. Although there are some provisions for challenging a rate, the main effect of the Staggers Act is that railroads may now become contract as well as common carriers. Many large-scale shipments (such as coal and grain) now move by unit trains under contract between the railroads and shippers, rather than by ICC-approved rates.[28]

At the same time the Staggers Act partially deregulated the railroads, it changed the relationship between the ICC and state regulatory agencies. While states still can regulate certain intrastate services of the railroads, in order that reregulation in the states will not undermine the national program for regulatory reform, states are required to conform to the ICC standards for regulation of railroads. If the state agency's standards are approved, the state commission may continue to regulate rail traffic within its boundaries—as long as its regulation does not constitute a burden on interstate commerce. But if the state does not correspond with federal standards, that state agency will lose its authority in rail regulation.[29]

In short, the Staggers law loosened the regulatory regime over the railroads, at the same time that it limited what states may do in the economic regulation of intrastate rail movements. Not only did the law change the federal-state balance, it also reduced the ICC's authority in many areas and gave railroads a measure of freedom in ratemaking. The ICC still stands; but the railroads have more discretion to act without having every move second-guessed by the federal agency.

REGULATION OF ENTRY

Any American citizen can start an airline. For most motor carriers, all that is needed is a demonstration of fitness. However, the construction of a railroad is a more serious matter. It requires sinking fixed costs into a private right-of-way and maintenance costs beyond that. What is more, a valley that has room for two railroads to pass through may not have enough economic activity to support the two lines. If so, both could go out of business and there would be no railroad left.

American history is full of such examples. Riders on Amtrak's Empire Service trains cannot help but notice another paralleling railroad on the west bank of the Hudson and the south bank of the Mohawk. This line, the West Shore Railroad, was built for no other purpose except to harass Commodore Vanderbilt and get him to buy the West Shore out. Legend is that Vanderbilt met with Jay Gould, the brains behind the scheme, and said he would lower his rates so as to bankrupt the West Shore. "Fine, Commodore," answered Gould. "Do you want to compete with a receiver?" Eventually, Vanderbilt capitulated and the New York Central bought the West Shore lock, stock, and redundant track.[30] Motorists on the Pennsylvania Turnpike pass through a number of narrow tunnels where the roadway shrinks from four to two lanes. These tunnels were part of the defunct Pennsylvania Central, built to persuade the Pennsylvania Railroad to buy it out. The Nickel Plate and the New York Central are within spitting distance of each other between Buffalo and Cleveland. And President Lincoln's decision to build the transcontinental railway from the banks of the Missouri, rather than the Mississippi, caused a superfluity of railroads to be built between Chicago and Omaha; the shakeout from that decision is still going on.[31]

Section 10901 of the Interstate Commerce Act provides that no railroad may extend its lines, or construct or acquire new track without a certificate of public convenience and necessity from the ICC. The term "public convenience and necessity" is not defined by the statute. Courts tend to defer to the ICC's interpretation of the language of the law. The ICC gives consideration to the interest of shippers, the creation of new markets, and the existence of rate advantages. The ICC also recognizes that no carrier has an exclusive right to occupy a particular territory. However, a new line will not be approved unless it shows promise of becoming self-sustaining in the relatively near future and will not be a burden on interstate commerce.

If a railroad is about to acquire the line of another (most often a short line acquiring a branch from a Class I railroad), the ICC will require a concurrent filing of an abandonment petition by the departing railroad along with an application for a certificate by the new carrier. A certificate is not required if the line is a mere spur line or industrial track. The ICC has spent a lot of time on the determination of what is a branch line and what is an industrial spur.[32] Until Staggers, a line was considered to be a branch line if it invaded another road's territory.

Few new railroads are being built nowadays. The last major extension in the United States was the Powder River line, built by coal-haulers Chicago & North Western and Burlington Northern in 1980. However, this section of the law has been used frequently by the ICC in licensing short line railroads to take over existing lines. The section also requires ICC approval for trackage rights over the line of another (except for Amtrak's statutory power to operate over freight railroads).

The Staggers Act changed the language of this section to say only that the ICC must grant a certificate if the public convenience and necessity "permit" rather than "require" such a new railroad.[33] The act also allows railroads to build spur lines to reach shippers served by other carriers and forbids railroads from blocking another line crossing their routes. Industrial spurs, although free from federal regulation, may be regulated by state public service commissions. In short, the Staggers law removed most of the impediments to establishing new railroads. But recent experience shows that few firms are interested in building brand-new rail lines, and most new railroads will be locally managed short lines operating over former Class I rights-of-way.

REGULATION OF RATES

Rate regulation by the ICC is but a shadow of its former self. Since 1985 the ICC has had no jurisdiction over passenger fares charged by interstate bus companies (except for suspension of a discriminatory fare or one that burdens interstate commerce) and no jurisdiction over Amtrak's fares since the mid-1970s. The ICC does have some vestigial jurisdiction over the occasional private rail carrier that is not affiliated with Amtrak or a commuter operating agency, but by and large, ICC jurisdiction is limited to passing on the reasonableness of freight rates.[34]

Prior to the passage of the Staggers Rail Act of 1980, there were few contract rates between shippers and railroads. Until 1979 the law was considered to forbid railroads from acting as contract carriers. The ICC issued a policy statement favoring contract rates that year, but it was not until passage of the Staggers law that the propriety for such rates was affirmed.

For a contract to exist between a shipper and a railroad, a carrier need only file the confidential contract and a succinct contract summary with the ICC. The contract itself is secret: only the summary is released to the public, which then has no detailed information of its terms. The only challenges permitted are by a port, claiming that the contractual relationship discriminates against that port, or by shippers, claiming that the contract impairs the railroad's ability to fulfill its common carrier obligations. For example, a shipper might claim that a railroad has all its boxcars tied up in confidential contracts, so that there are no cars available for ordinary shippers who ship under filed tariff rates.[35]

The Interstate Commerce Act requires railroads to initiate rates and to submit their tariffs to the ICC. Railroads must file a new tariff with the commission at least twenty days before it goes into effect. The commission still has investigation and suspension power over rates. However, the ICC cannot suspend a tariff unless it appears that (1) there is substantial likelihood that the protestant will prevail on the merits, (2) substantial injury will befall the protestant if the suspension is not granted, and (3) subsequent compensation will not adequately protect the protestant.[36] The ICC can, at any rate, investigate a rate without suspending it. If the proposed rate is unlawful, the ICC may cancel it. When the ICC concludes that a rate charged is unlawful, it may prescribe the maximum or minimum rate to be charged.[37] The ICC can compel refunds, establish an interim rate, or require that proceeds from a rate increase must be used for particular purposes (such as fixing up the track).[38]

Rates must be nondiscriminatory, just, and reasonable. But with regard to reasonableness, the Staggers Act only allows the ICC to review the reasonableness of rate increases if the carrier has "market dominance."[39] If traffic, such as coal or grain, can practicably move only by train, then and only then can the ICC question the justness or reasonableness of the rate. The ICC also has no jurisdiction over rate decreases unless the rail rates are below a reasonable minimum—contributing to the "going concern value" of the railroad.[40]

Because the ICC has deregulated so many commodities on its own (boxcar freight and intermodal traffic are recent examples), relatively few commodities move at tariff rates. The existence of confidential contracts means that a good deal of carriage charges are negotiated between the railroads and the shippers of bulk commodities. Economies of scale are obtained through the use of unit trains and subterminals. Although rate disapproval and suspension still remain in the Commission's arsenal of weapons, few groups except coal shippers are still heavily involved in rate protests before the commission.[41] Even fewer are cases where states are allowed to regulate rates.

REGULATION OF SERVICE

The Interstate Commerce Commission is basically concerned with rail construction and abandonments and secondarily with the provision of reasonable rates.[42] Adequacy of service is of minor concern to the ICC. Nonetheless, there have been cases wherein the commission has used its authority to compel the rail line to provide adequate car service to shippers, or to restore a certain level of utility to trackage.[43] The ICC is also concerned with the maintenance of gateways for the interchange of freight and for trackage rights by one railroad over the lines of another.

Section 11121 of the Interstate Commerce Act requires that "safe and adequate car service" be furnished to shippers.[44] In the past, the ICC has required that track be restored to a serviceable level or conditioned an abandonment upon provision of adequate alternate service.[45] This power to require adequate transportation has not been abridged but the ICC has abandoned much of this field in favor of free competition or the actions of the Department of Transportation.

SAFETY REGULATION

The Federal Railroad Administration (FRA), a unit of the U.S. Department of Transportation, is responsible for the safety of rail operations. Its concerns include the licensure of engineers, the condition of track, hours of service for railroaders, and safety condition of rolling stock. As such, it is now the primary agency involved in the day-to-day operations of railroads, although it operates in connection with state transportation agencies in track- and grade-crossing safety regulation.

The FRA establishes minimum track standards for rail carriers and classifies track according to its physical condition. From this classification, maximum track speeds are set for passenger and freight trains.[46] The FRA has its own staff of track inspectors. In states such as Utah, which have many rail miles within their borders, the state has its own track inspectors who work within FRA standards in cooperation with the FRA inspection program.

The FRA now bears the same relationship to the railroad industry that the FAA has to aviation. The resemblance is most marked in the area of licensing and drug testing of engineers and other railroaders.[47] No longer is an engineer's tenure totally dependent upon his contract or union agreement with management. Now the engineer is a licensed professional who must be tested for competence and whose license is subject to suspension.

Railroaders are subject to a twelve-hour maximum day by the Federal Hours of Service Act, also administered by the FRA. This law requires that no operating personnel may be on duty for more than twelve hours out of any twenty-four. When a crew has been on service for the statutory maximum of 12 hours, the crew is said to have "outlawed." That means that the train must stop, and a new "dogcatcher" crew must be brought out to bring the consist into the terminal. FRA's powers in this area are industrywide. On a recent visit to Colorado's Durango & Silverton Narrow Gauge Railroad, we were told that schedules had been rearranged to make sure that crews operated within the twelve-hour limit. The Federal Railroad Administration had extended its jurisdiction to tourist and recreational railroads and had recently paid an inspection visit to that isolated narrow gauge line.

Equipment used in rail service must meet FRA standards, using criteria developed in connection with the Association of American Railroads. Locomotives must be inspected by the FRA, and rolling stock must be acceptable to the FRA in order to be interchanged between railroads.

The Federal Railroad Safety Act (FRSA) was enacted in 1970 "to promote safety in all areas of railroad operations and to reduced railroad-related accidents, and to reduce deaths and injuries to persons."[48] The act specifically directs the secretary of transportation to study and develop solutions to safety problems posed by grade crossings. In addition, the secretary is given broad powers to "prescribe, as necessary, appropriate rules, regulations, orders and standards for all areas of railroad safety."[49] In 1971 the FRA, under the authority of FRSA, promulgated regulations setting maximum train speeds for different classes of track.[50] With regard to grade crossings, in 1973 Congress enacted the Highway Safety Act,[51] which made federal funds available to the states to improve grade crossings. In 1993 the United States Supreme Court held that FRA regulations do not preempt state common law claims based on a railroad's negligence with regard to grade-crossing signals, but the federal speed limits cover the entire common law field of train speed and preempted negligence claims based on a train's excessive speed.[52] Similarly, a municipal ordinance that imposed a speed limit of 25 mph on freight trains was considered to be precluded by the FRSA and regulations adopted pursuant to it.[53] A Texas law that required railroads to construct walkways along tracks was also considered preempted by the FRSA.[54]

As mentioned above, increased attention to railroad-highway grade crossings began with the Highway Safety Act of 1973, which was developed jointly by the Federal Railroad Administration and the Federal Highway Administration. The act acknowledged that crossing safety was a major problem and recommended public funding for improvements, as well as an inventory of all public crossings in the United States.[55] In the past twenty years, over $2 billion has been spent on crossings to curb "America's most preventable accident."[56] Most of this money has gone to install automatic crossing signals. Today the FHA spends about $100 million annually to buy and upgrade warning devices, clear brush, and resurface crossings.[57] This money was reauthorized as part of the Intermodal Surface Transportation Efficiency Act of 1991[58] and is allocated to each state on a formula based on rail and highway traffic density, number of grade crossings, and other factors.

In October 1992 President Bush signed into law a bill requiring the Department of Transportation to issue regulations by mid-1995 requiring additional "alerting lights" on locomotives by the end of 1997. These "ditch lights" were first developed in Canada and are another approach to the crossing-safety problem.[59] In addition, the Federal Railroad Administration is conducting research and development of high-speed trains, on a matching funds basis with the states. Currently Amtrak is involved in a five-year incremental high-speed rail project to extend electrification from New Haven to Boston. For the 1993–1998 period,[60] $982 million has been earmarked for the development of new high-speed passenger service corridors. Higher speed trains will make the elimination of grade crossings an even higher priority project.

STATE REGULATION

Grade-crossing safety is only one area where the states and federal government are both involved in regulation. Unless a function has been completely preempted by the ICC or FRA, states have regulatory powers over local aspects of railroad operations.

State regulatory agencies are of two types: (1) departments of transportation, which are usually outgrowths from traditional highway departments, and (2) public service or public utilities commissions. The latter agencies are generally concerned with utility regulation. In some states, intrastate economic regulation has been completely eliminated. Other states maintain more of an activist role. Colorado, for example, has a number of tourist-oriented recreational railroads within the state, and their fares and services have been scrutinized and regulated by the Public Utilities Commission.[61] However, the neighboring state of Wyoming has eliminated all economic regulation of railroads whatsoever.

Where a state has decided to regulate intrastate railroads, it is limited in that federal preemption has occurred in many fields—for example, abandonment and discontinuance of service. States may only regulate the intrastate aspects of railroading, and they must have their standards certified by the ICC in order to regulate railroads at all.[62]

More prevalent is the regulation of railroad safety by state departments of transportation. These agencies have responsibility for dispensing funds for branch line renewal, grade-crossing improvements, rail planning, and capital projects under the Intermodal Surface Transportation Efficiency Act (ISTEA). Many states are directly involved with commuter service, either as owner-operator or contractor.[63] Suburban commuter service is exempt from ICC regulation if the states effectively control such train service.[64] And some railroads, such as the Long Island, are owned outright by the states in which they operate.[65]

States have some regulatory power over spur and industrial tracks not regulated by the ICC. But in general, state regulation of railroads (other than in a proprietary capacity) is allowed only to the extent that the federal government has not stepped in to preempt the fields. Most regulatory endeavor is in partnership with the FRA. Track inspection is a good example of such cooperation; many states have their own state track inspectors who work with the FRA guidelines to ensure safe operation of trackage within that state's boundaries. States often intervene in ICC proceedings concerning abandonments and station closing. But, by and large, state governments are a minor factor in the totality of railroad law at the end of the twentieth century.

NOTES

1. Theodore E. Keeler, *Railroads, Freight, and Public Policy* (Washington, D.C.: The Brookings Institution, 1983), p. 22.

2. Frank J. Dooley, "The Evolution of the Short Line Railroad Industry," *Journal of the Transportation Research Forum* 31 (1990): 180.

3. William E. Thoms, "Clear Track for Deregulation," *Transportation Law Journal* 12 (1982): 183.

4. William E. Thoms, "New Rules for Bankrupt Rail," *Trains*, May 1980, pp. 28–30. ..

5. *See* Chapter 2. *See generally*, Dooley, "Evolution," pp. 180–194.

6. *See* Chapter 7. *See generally*, William E. Thoms, *Reprieve for the Iron Horse* (Baton Rouge, LA: Claitor's Pub. Division, 1973).

7. *See* Paul S. Dempsey and William E. Thoms, *Law and Economic Regulation in Transportation* (Westport, CT: Quorum Books, 1986), pp. 280–281.

8. Ibid., pp. 10–11.

9. Colorado v. United States, 271 U.S. 153, 46 S.Ct. 452 (1926).

10. Dempsey and Thoms, *Law and Economic Regulation*, p. 14. *See also* 49 U.S.C., sec. 10909 (1990).

11. Dempsey and Thoms, *Law and Economic Regulation*, pp. 17–19, 118–120.

12. Ibid., pp. 26–29.

13. Paul S. Dempsey, *The Social and Economic Consequences of Deregulation* (Westport, CT: Quorum Books, 1989), pp. 46–48.

14. Richard Saunders, *The Railroad Mergers and the Coming of Conrail* (Westport, CT: Greenwood Press, 1978), pp. 182–185.

15. Ibid., p. 295.

16. Rail Passenger Service Act of 1970, Pub. L. No. 91–518, 84 Stat. 1327 (1970), 45 U.S.C., sec. 501 (1990). *See* Harbeson, "The Rail Passenger Service Act of 1970," *I.C.C. Practitioners Journal* 38 (1971): 330.

17. Regional Rail Restructuring Act of 1973, Pub. L. No. 93–236, 87 Stat. 1010 (1974), 45 U.S.C., sec. 711 (1990). For a detailed account of the formation of Conrail *see* Saunders, *The Railroad Mergers*. Conrail has been since returned to the private sector and no longer is a recipient of federal subsidies. Conrail is now strictly a freight carrier, since the Northeast Rail Service Act of 1981 relieved it of its commuter-train responsibilities.

18. Dempsey and Thoms, *Law and Economic Regulation*, pp. 14–16.

19. Bankruptcy Reform Act of 1978, Pub. L. No. 95–598, 92 Stat. 259, 11 U.S.C., sec. 101 (1978). *See generally*, Paul S. Dempsey, Robert M. Hardaway, and William Thoms, *Aviation Law and Regulation*, 2 vols. (Austin, TX: Butterworth Legal Publishers, 1993), pp. 17:10–17:12.

20. Staggers Rail Act of 1980, Pub. L. No. 96–448, sec. 509(a), 94 Stat. 1895, 1955 (1980).

21. Motor Carrier Act of 1980, Pub. L. No. 96–26, 96 Stat. 793 (1980).

22. Bus Regulatory Reform Act of 1982, as described in Dempsey and Thoms, *Law and Economic Regulation*, pp. 117–118.

23. Thoms, "Clear Track for Deregulation," p. 212.

24. Staggers Rail Act of 1980, 49 U.S.C., sec. 10901 (d) and (e) (1982).

25. Ibid.

26. Ibid., 49 U.S.C., sec. 10904 (1982).

27. Ibid., 49 U.S.C., sec. 10701(a) (1982).

28. Ibid., 49 U.S.C., sec. 10713 (1982).

29. Dempsey, *Social and Economic Consequences*, p. 217.

30. Ibid., p. 9.

31. Currently the Burlington Northern and Chicago & North Western are the principal survivors on this route. However, the Illinois Central, Milwaukee Road, Rock Island, and a number of smaller carriers had previously served this area. Professor George Hilton of UCLA argues that Lincoln could have alleviated the oversupply of railroads in the area by establishing the starting point of the transcontinental railroad at Chicago or St. Louis. *See generally*, George W. Hilton, *The Transportation Act of 1958: A Decade of Experience* (Bloomington, IN: Indiana University Press, 1969).

32. Dempsey and Thoms, *Law and Economic Regulation*, pp. 50–52.

33. Ibid., p. 58.

34. Ibid., pp. 161–166.

35. Ibid., p. 166.

36. 49 U.S.C., sec. 10707(c)(1) (1992).

37. 49 U.S.C., sec. 10704(a)(1), (b)(1), and (c)(1) (1992).

38. United States v. Chesapeake & Ohio Ry., 426 U.S. 500, 96 S.Ct. 2318 (1976).

39. 49 U.S.C., sec. 10701(a), (b), and (d) (1992).

40. *See* Paul S. Dempsey, "Rate Regulation and Antitrust Immunity in Transportation," *American University Law Review* 32 (1983): 335.

41. Dempsey, *Social and Economic Consequences*, pp. 46–48.

42. Dempsey and Thoms, *Law and Economic Regulation*, pp. 168–183.

43. Winnebago Farmers Elevator Co. v. Chicago & N.W. Transportation Co., 354 I.C.C. 859 (1978).

44. 49 U.S.C., sec. 11121 (1992).

45. Seaboard Coast Line R.R. Co.—Abandonment between Arcadia and Port Boca Grande, Florida, 360 I.C.C. 257 (1979).

46. Dempsey and Thoms, *Law and Economic Regulation*, p. 80.

47. *See* Chapter 4.

48. 45 U.S.C., sec. 421 (1992).

49. 45 U.S.C., sec. 431(a) (1992).

50. 49 C.F.R., sec. 213.9 (1992).

51. Highway Safety Act of 1973, Title II, 87 Stat. 282, 23 U.S.C., sec. 130(d) (1992).

52. CSX Transportation, Inc. v. Easterwood, 113 S.Ct. 1732 (1993).

53. Fenton, Mich. v. Grand Trunk Western R. Co., 439 Mich. 240, 482 N.W.2d 706 (1992).

54. Railroad Commission of Texas v. Missouri Pacific R.R., 942 F.2d 179 (5th Cir. 1992).

55. Kevin P. Keefe, "On Track to Save Lives," *Trains*, August 1993, pp. 43, 46.

56. Ibid.

57. Ibid.

58. Known as ISTEA, or "iced tea" in the industry, this federal program provides aid to states for improving rail facilities, particularly those used for passenger service.

59. David J. Ingles, "Of Canadians, Ditch Lights, and Three Girls," *Trains*, August 1993, p. 6.

60. Don Phillips, "Incremental Speed," *Trains*, August 1993, pp. 12–13.

61. Colorado's short line railroads are involved in the tourist business because of the magnificent scenery and the narrow-gauge heritage of the Centennial state. Some of the lines regulated are the Durango & Silverton Narrow Gauge Railroad, the Rio Grande Ski Train, and the Cumbres & Toltec Scenic Railway. The last is actually owned by the states of Colorado and New Mexico and is operated by a railroad authority.

62. Dempsey and Thoms, *Law and Economic Regulation*, pp. 183–184.

63. *See* Chapter 7.

64. 49 U.S.C., sec. 10504 (1992).

65. *See* Chapter 3.

2

The Short Line Rail Industry[1]

Short line railroads have increasingly become an important component of the U.S. transportation system. The focus of this chapter is upon three aspects of the short line industry. First, factors underlying the development of short lines are reviewed. Second, characteristics of short lines are presented. Finally, important differences in the cost structure of Class I and short line railroads are identified.

DEVELOPMENT OF SHORT LINES

The Transportation Act of 1920 called upon the ICC to create a plan for consolidation of the nation's railroads into nineteen systems. However, the ICC feared the effect on rail employment of closing switching yards. In addition, profitable railroads opposed the consolidation plans because of proposals that they be consolidated with unprofitable railroads. Although the commission gradually backed away from the Transportation Act's consolidation mandate, the period between 1920 and 1970 is characterized as a period of decline for short line railroads. The number of short lines fell from 1,009 in 1916 to 238 in 1979.[2]

The role of short lines shifted during the 1970s. New small railroad companies were formed to take over many light density rail lines that until that time had been operated as parts of Class I rail systems. Three events are tied to this change. First, legislation establishing Conrail in 1973 provided the initial stimulus for the formation of new railroads. Second, the reorganization of the Milwaukee Road and the liquidation of the Rock Island created additional opportunities for short line creation. Finally, federal railroad deregulation legislation led to new opportunities for short line creation. The 3–R Act of 1973, the 4–R Act of 1976, and the Local Rail Service Assistance Act of 1978 all included provisions that provided operational subsidies and rehabilitation funds for light density branch lines. The Staggers Rail Act of 1980[3] created new options for communities and shippers to purchase or support rail lines identified as candidates for abandonment by Class I carriers.

Most present large Class I carriers evolved through ICC approved mergers since the 1960s. For example, mergers have led to the present Burlington Northern, CSX, Norfolk Southern, Union Pacific, Southern Pacific, and Santa Fe systems. These consolidations left the country with the largest Class I railroad systems in history. During the past decade, however, the trackage of Class I railroads has been contracting.

With deregulation in the late 1970s, Class I railroads aggressively reduced their systems. In 1978, Class I railroads owned 177,710 miles of road. By 1987, the miles of road owned by Class I carriers had fallen by 25.6 percent to 132,220 miles.[4] The downsizing of Class I railroads has been accomplished primarily via abandonment and short line sales.

Abandonment

Lines being considered for abandonment tend to be either unprofitable or only marginally profitable for their owners.[5] Historically, shippers and states have vigorously resisted rail line abandonment. The 4–R Act and the Staggers Act eased the abandonment process, imposing stringent time deadlines on the ICC for the disposition of abandonment cases. For example, unopposed abandonment applications must be approved by the ICC within thirty days. From 1970 to 1988, the ICC granted certificates of abandonment for 39,993 miles of road (see Table 2.1).

Almost 20,000 miles of track were abandoned during the 1970s. Since 1980, 20,222 miles of track have been abandoned. During the 1970s, 6 percent of the track scheduled for abandonment was restored via short line sales or rehabilitation.[6] According to Wolfe, 74 percent of the track scheduled for abandonment during the 1980s remains in service because of rehabilitation programs and short line sales. Thus, while the level of abandonment has remained high, short line sales have lessened its effect.

A few lines were taken over by states, which then proceeded to find a designated operator to run them. Twenty-six states have set up rail authorities to purchase otherwise abandoned railroads.[7] Most states have found designated operators for the service, although New York and West Virginia have also operated railroads directly.

Short Line Sales

Abandonment has been the traditional means of disposing of excess lines. More recently, Class I railroads have also been downsizing by selling or leasing track to short line operators. During the 1970s, 2,526 miles of road

Table 2.1
Miles of Road Abandoned and Miles of Short Line Created, 1970-1988

Year	Miles of Road Abandoned	Short Lines Created	
		Miles of Road	Number
1970	1,782	2	1
1971	1,287	53	2
1972	3,458	66	3
1973	2,428	414	4
1974	529	14	1
1975	708	242	1
1976	1,789	183	8
1977	2,500	900	8
1978	2,417	368	8
1979	2,873	284	8
1980	2,321	1,578	12
1981	1,342	587	10
1982	5,151	1,470	24
1983	2,454	341	15
1984	3,083	1,506	26
1985	2,343	2,620	27
1986	1,417	3,551	31
1987	818[a]	6,674	46
1988	1,293[a]	104	5
1970's TOTAL	19,771	2,526	44
1980's TOTAL	20,222	18,431	196
1970-88 TOTAL	39,993	20,957	240

Source: Frank J. Dooley, *Economies of Size and Density for Short Line Railroads*, MPC Report 91-2 (Fargo, ND: Mountain Plains Consortium, North Dakota State University, 1991), p. 10.

[a]Interstate Commerce Commission, *ICC 88—Interstate Commerce Commission 1988 Annual Report* (Washington, D.C., 1989).

were sold to forty-four short line operators (see Table 2.1). Over 18,000 miles of road were sold to 196 short lines in the 1980s. Compared with the 1970s, there was a 630 percent increase in miles of track sold and a 346 percent increase in the number of short lines created from 1980 to 1988.

Two different strategies motivate the sale or leasing of rail lines. Some sales involve the divestment of rail interests. In particular, these companies divest or pare down their systems by selling light-density branch lines. Other railroads use short line sales to establish low-cost feeder systems. In part, Class Is prefer the short line alternative because the property can be sold in its entirety. By doing so, the seller avoids the associated salvage costs and expense of selling land parcel by parcel.[8]

Divestiture may be either forced or voluntary. The liquidation sales of the Rock Island and the Milwaukee Road are examples of forced divestitures. Although these carriers were bankrupt, certain line segments within their systems remained profitable. The Rock Island and Milwaukee Road sold 2,028 and 848 miles of road, respectively, to short line operators. [9]

The Illinois Central Gulf (ICG) was perhaps the most active carrier voluntarily divesting lines. After having absorbed the parallel Gulf, Mobile & Ohio, the ICG then either abandoned lines or turned them over to twenty short lines (see Table 2.2). The ICG line sales involved high-density and presumably profitable track. These sales were not motivated by abandonment nor bankruptcy. The ICG's goal was to streamline its system, creating a core system of lines between Chicago and New Orleans, thereby making the system an attractive acquisition.[10]

Most railroads sell off lines for reasons other than divestiture. These railroads are attempting to establish low-cost feeder lines. Feeder line sales are motivated by three reasons: (1) a desire to eliminate the burdens of ownership (high operating and maintenance costs, etc.), (2) an expectation to recover some economic value from the line (sales price), and (3) a desire to preserve the benefits associated with ownership (access to traffic originated or terminated on the lines).[11]

Similar to divestiture-related sales, feeder arrangement sales and leasing arrangements are motivated by the seller's goal to maximize the economic return from the property. However, feeder line sales seek to maximize the economic return on a long-term basis rather than strictly through a one-time influx of cash as with divestiture. Thus, with feeder line sales, the seller usually will be more concerned with the short line's ability to generate and interchange traffic than it is with the selling price.

Besides the ICG, the most active railroads in short line spinoffs are the Burlington Northern (BN), Soo Line, Conrail, and CSX (Table 2.2). Between 1986 and 1988 BN sold 2,844 miles of track to eight different entities. "All these sales were designed to feed and enhance BN's remaining rail operation."[12] Over 56 percent of the track sold by the Soo Line (1,969 miles) was spun off in one sale. The sale by the Soo Line creating the Wisconsin Central

Table 2.2
Divestiture of Branch Lines by Class I Railroads, 1971 to 1988

Class I Carrier	Number of Short Line Sales	Miles of Track Sold	Average Size (in miles)
Atchison, Topeka, & Santa Fe	2	153	76.5
Burlington Northern	14	3,919	279.9
Chicago & North Western	4	1,155	288.8
ConRail	53	2,689	50.7
CSX Transportation	42	2,033	48.4
Grand Trunk Western	3	239	79.7
Guilford Transportation Co.	8	725	90.6
Illinois Central Gulf	20	3,995	200.0
Missouri-Kansas-Texas	1	2	2.0
Norfolk Southern	5	366	73.2
Pittsburgh & Lake Erie	1	32	32.0
Soo Line	13	3,469	266.8
Southern Pacific	6	560	93.3
Union Pacific	6	231	38.5
TOTAL	166	17,345	104.5

Source: Frank J. Dooley, *Economies of Size and Density for Short Line Railroads*, MPC Report 91-2 (Fargo, ND: Mountain Plains Consortium, North Dakota State University, 1991), p. 12.

Note: Summing the column values for the number of short lines created and the miles of track do not equal the total because some of the new short lines were created from lines owned by more than one Class I railroad.

is the largest short line sale to date. Conrail and CSX have spun off the most short lines, fifty-three and forty-two, respectively. The average size of short lines spun off by the eastern carriers are much smaller than those sold by western carriers (Table 2.2). The average size of short lines sold by Conrail or the CSX is approximately fifty miles. In contrast, the typical short line sale by the BN, Soo Line, and Chicago & North Western (CNW) are all over 200 miles.

The number of short lines created and miles of track sold steadily increased from 1970 to 1987 (Table 2.1). In late 1987 short line sales activity almost ceased as a result of successful legal challenges raised by rail labor unions. The unions argued that a railroad had a duty to bargain with its employees regarding the effect of a short line sale. The issue eventually reached the Supreme Court. In *Pittsburgh and Lake Erie Railroad v. Railway Labor Executives' Association*, the Supreme Court held that labor protection is not required in short line sales.[13]

While uncertainty remains over labor protection and short line sales, sales activity has resumed. To overcome concerns with short line sales, more railroads are leasing lines to short line operators. Unverified data published in *The Short Line* stated there were a total of twenty-six new short lines created in 1988 and forty-five created in 1989. Of the forty-five new 1989 short lines, thirty-four were new railroads. The other eleven railroads were existing short lines adding more roads. Fourteen of the new short lines were leased by the Norfolk Southern to new operators and ten were spun off by the CSX. Seven other Class I carriers, including the Union Pacific, Santa Fe, CNW, Conrail, Boston & Maine (B&M), and the Canadian National (CN), spun off a total of fifteen lines. Six short lines were taken over by other short lines.

A spin-off not only preserves rail service, but may actually improve it. The new owners are local or regional entrepreneurs who are more respon-sive to on-line shippers. They can provide a level of service that the former Class I carrier could not match. A survey by the ICC and Federal Railroad Administration found "a clear pattern of shipper satisfaction with both service and rates offered by the shortlines and regional railroads created after the enactment of the Staggers Act."[14] Ninety-four percent of the shippers reported that service levels had been maintained or improved. Eighty-eight percent of the shippers reported that rate levels had improved or been maintained. Similar results were reported in a survey of grain shippers.[15] Spin-off railroads can also be important mechanisms for local and regional economic development.

CHARACTERISTICS OF SHORT LINE RAILROADS

In this section, various characteristics of short line railroads are pre-sented. Because of differences by type of short line, results are reported for local, regional, and/or switching/terminal railroads.[16] To reflect changes in rail policy since 1970, results are reported for railroads created before and after 1970. Characteristics analyzed include typical firm attributes, traffic, and operating statistics. Firm attributes include number of short lines, ownership, and revenue. Traffic characteristics include principal commodi-ties hauled and density. Operating statistics are provided for miles of track, employees, employees per mile, number of interchanges, length of haul, and average speed.

Table 2.3
Short Line Railroads Classification, by Period and Type of Short Line

Type of Short Line	Before 1970	1970 & After	Overall
Regional	12	15	27
Local	144	141	285
Switching/Terminal	88	84	172
All Short Lines	244	240	484

Source: Frank J. Dooley, *Economies of Size and Density for Short Line Railroads*, MPC Report 91-2 (Fargo, ND: Mountain Plains Consortium, North Dakota State University, 1991), p. 16.

Typical Short Line Firm Attributes

In 1988, there were 484 short line railroads (see Table 2.3). Local railroads accounted for 58.9 percent of the total short lines. Over 35 percent were switching/terminal railroads, while the other 5.6 percent were regional railroads. The number of short lines created before and after 1970 are almost identical. Of the 484 short lines, 244 were formed before 1970 and 240 were formed after that year.

Sixty percent of most regional and local railroads (or linehaul short lines) are operated by private owners (see Table 2.4). Other major owners of linehaul short lines are shippers (19.6 percent) and Class I railroads (10.3 percent). The percentage of privately owned linehaul short lines rose sharply between the two periods, rising from 47.4 to 72.4 percent (Table 2.5). The number of regional and local railroads owned by shipper groups and Class I railroads fell between the two periods. The percentage of regional and local railroads owned by shipper and Class I railroads fell 14.7 and 19.3 percentage points, respectively (Table 2.5). Since 1970, there has been an increase in ownership by state and local governments and other short line railroads.

Most regional and local railroads (79.7 percent) have annual revenues under $5 million (see Table 2.5). The revenue distribution has shifted slightly between periods. Regional and local railroads created since 1970 have somewhat lower annual revenues than those created before 1970. Over 15 percent of the linehaul short lines created before 1970 have annual revenues over $10 million (Table 2.6). In contrast, only 5.9 percent of the linehaul short lines created since 1970 have annual revenues over $10 million.

Traffic Characteristics

The Association of American Railroads (AAR) Profiles database includes the top three commodities hauled by short lines. By two digit Standard

Table 2.4
Ownership Distribution for Short Lines

Type of Owner	Before 1970 (%)	1970 & After (%)	Overall (%)
Private	47.40	72.40	59.90
Shipper	26.90	12.20	19.55
Class I Railroad	19.90	0.60	10.25
Local/State Government	2.60	7.10	4.85
Other Short Line Railroad	0.00	5.10	2.55
Car Lessor	2.60	0.60	1.60
Other	0.60	1.90	1.25
TOTAL	100.00	99.90	99.95
Number of Railroads	156	156	312

Source: Frank J. Dooley, *Economies of Size and Density for Short Line Railroads*, MPC Report 91-2 (Fargo, ND: Mountain Plains Consortium, North Dakota State University, 1991), p. 17.

Note: Total does not equal 100 percent due to rounding.

Table 2.5
Gross Revenue Distribution for Short Lines

Revenue Range	Before 1970 (%)	1970 & After (%)	Overall (%)
Under $5 million	74.20	85.30	79.75
$ 5 to 9.9 million	10.60	8.70	9.65
$10 to 19.9 million	6.00	1.30	3.65
$20 to 39.9 million	5.30	3.30	4.30
Over $ 40 million	4.00	1.30	2.65
TOTAL	100.10	99.90	100.00

Source: Frank J. Dooley, *Economies of Size and Density for Short Line Railroads*, MPC Report 91-2 (Fargo, ND: Mountain Plains Consortium, North Dakota State University, 1991), p. 18.

Note: Total does not equal 100 percent due to rounding.

Table 2.6
Characteristics of Short Line Freight Traffic

Percent of Total Carloads Hauled	Top Ranked STCC Group (%)	Top Two STCC Groups (%)	Top Three STCC Groups (%)
Under 20	1.4	0.0	0.0
20.1 - 40	16.5	2.7	1.0
40.1 - 60	25.7	11.8	5.1
60.1 - 80	15.9	20.6	15.5
Over 80	40.5	64.9	78.4
Mean	66.4	82.7	89.1

Source: Frank J. Dooley, *Economies of Size and Density for Short Line Railroads*, MPC Report 91-2 (Fargo, ND: Mountain Plains Consortium, North Dakota State University, 1991), p. 18.

Transportation Commodity Code (STCC), the percentage of total carloads hauled was reported for the top three STCC groups. Most regional and local railroads are extremely dependent on three or fewer commodity groups. A single STCC group accounts for more than 80 percent of the total annual carloads for 40.5 percent of the regional and local railroads (see Table 2.6). Over 78 percent of the regional and local railroads report that the top three STCC groups account for more than 80 percent of total carloads. On average, the top STCC group accounts for 66.4 percent of a linehaul short line's annual carloads (see Table 2.6). The top three STCC groups are 89.1 percent of a typical linehaul short line's annual carloads.

The six major commodities hauled in 1988 were lumber/wood products, chemicals, farm products, pulp/paper products, coal, and nonmetallic minerals (see Table 2.7). Over 42 percent of the linehaul short lines reported that lumber/wood was one of their principal products (Table 2.7). Over 30 percent of the local and regional railroads reported that chemicals and farm products are their principal hauls. The principal commodities hauled were quite similar for linehaul short lines created before and after 1970.

Density of traffic is calculated by dividing the total carloads handled by the miles of track. Densities were calculated for regional and local railroads created before and after 1970. Densities for switching and terminal railroads are not directly comparable with linehaul railroads.

Regional and local railroads created before 1970 have higher average densities than those created since 1970. The average density for regional railroads fell 76.9 percent, from 499.9 cars per mile to 115.4 cars per mile (see Table 2.8). The average density for local railroads fell 75.6 percent, from 446.9 cars per mile to 108.9 cars per mile.

Table 2.7
Commodities Hauled by Short Lines

Commodity	Percent of Linehaul Short Lines Hauling		
	Before 1970	1970 & After	Overall
Lumber/Wood Products	42.9	37.2	40.1
Chemicals	24.4	37.8	31.1
Farm Products	17.3	42.9	30.1
Pulp/Paper Products	28.2	24.4	26.3
Coal	26.9	17.3	22.1
Nonmetallic Minerals	17.9	21.8	19.9
Food/Kindred Products	14.1	17.3	15.7
Clay/Glass/Stone	10.9	12.2	11.5
Primary Metal Products	9.6	6.4	8.0
Hazardous Materials	6.4	6.4	6.4
Waste/Scrap	5.8	5.1	5.4
Metallic Ores	6.4	3.2	4.8
Petroleum/Coal Products	5.8	3.8	4.8
Transportation Equipment	2.6	4.5	3.5
Fabricated Metal Products	1.3	1.3	1.3
Textile Mill Products	0.6	0.6	0.6
Machinery, Except Electric	0.6	0.6	0.6
Misc. Mixed Shipment	0.6	0.6	0.6
Ordnance	0.6	0.0	0.3
Rubber/Misc. Plastics	0.6	0.0	0.3
Furniture/Fixtures	0.0	0.6	0.3
Number of Railroads	156	156	312

Source: Frank J. Dooley, *Economies of Size and Density for Short Line Railroads*, MPC Report 91-2 (Fargo, ND: Mountain Plains Consortium, North Dakota State University, 1991), p. 20.

Table 2.8
Short Line Mean Traffic Density

Type of Railroad	Mean Density			Paired T-Test
	Before 1970	1970 & After	All Short Lines	
Regional	499.9	115.4	286.3	-2.25*
Local	446.9	108.9	276.0	-5.65*
Regional and Local	451.3	109.6	277.0	-6.06*

Source: Frank J. Dooley, *Economies of Size and Density for Short Line Railroads*, MPC Report 91-2 (Fargo, ND: Mountain Plains Consortium, North Dakota State University, 1991), p. 21.

Note: The * denotes a statistical difference between the pre- and post-1970 means at the 95 percent level of significance.

Table 2.9
Changes in Traffic Mix

Commodity	Average Carloads per Mile		Percentage Decrease	Paired T-Test
	Before 1970	1970 & After		
Lumber	313.43	146.46	53.6	-1.83*
Chemicals	293.14	157.60	46.2	-1.10
Farm Products	261.69	50.87	80.6	-2.31**
Pulp and Paper	446.23	162.48	63.6	-2.28**
Coal	589.05	218.53	62.9	-3.01**
Nonmetallic Minerals	226.82	79.45	65.0	-1.96*
Food/Kindred Products	168.10	67.79	59.7	-2.59**
Clay/Glass/Stone	398.43	69.55	82.5	-1.25
Primary Metal Products	722.51	120.44	83.3	-2.97**

Source: Frank J. Dooley, *Economies of Size and Density for Short Line Railroads*, MPC Report 91-2 (Fargo, ND: Mountain Plains Consortium, North Dakota State University, 1991), p. 22.

Note: The * and ** denote a statistical difference between the pre- and post-1970 means at the 90 and 95 percent level of significance, respectively.

Average density varies widely, depending upon the commodity hauled by the railroad. Pre- and post-1970 densities were calculated for the nine principal commodities hauled by linehaul short lines (see Table 2.9). The density is not a commodity-specific density. Rather it is the firm density for railroads hauling at least 10 percent of a specific commodity. The mean traffic density declined for all nine of the principal commodities (Table 2.9). The differences in the mean densities between linehaul short lines created pre- and post-1970 were statistically significant for all of the commodities except chemicals and clay/glass/stone.

The largest decline in absolute terms was for primary metal products. For linehaul short lines formed before 1970, the mean density for those hauling at least 10 percent primary metal products was 722.5 cars per mile (Table 2.9). For linehaul short lines created since 1970, the mean density for primary metal products fell over 602 cars per mile, to 120.4 cars per mile. The lowest absolute density, 50.87 cars per mile, was for farm products hauled by linehaul short lines created since 1970. In relative terms, the mean density for the nine principal commodities fell by an average of 66.4 percent. The percentage decline ranged from 46.2 for chemicals to 83.3 percent for primary metal products. Most short line railroads operate as freight carriers only; however, a small but growing number of carriers are in the excursion passenger business, or "recreational railroading," as well.[17]

Operating Statistics

Linehaul short lines created since 1970 are longer than those formed before 1970. The difference in means for miles of road is statistically significant at the 95 percent level of confidence for regional, local, and all short lines (see Table 2.10). The mean miles of road increased 77.2 percent for regional railroads, from 391.3 miles to 693.6 miles. For local railroads, the mean miles of track rose from 41.6 miles to 60.6 miles, an increase of 45.8 percent. The difference in mean miles of road is not statistically different for switching/terminal railroads.

All types of short lines created since 1970 employ fewer people on average than are employed by short lines formed before 1970. The difference in means for the number of employees is statistically different at the 95 percent level of confidence level for all but regional railroads, which is significant at the 90 percent level (Table 2.10). The mean number of employees fell by 42.7 percent for regionals, 60.9 percent for local, and 92.5 percent for switching/terminal railroads. For railroads created since 1970, the typical regional and local lines employ 304 and 13.5 persons per mile, respectively.

The average number of employees per mile has fallen for all types of short lines. The difference in the mean number of employees per mile for pre- and post-1970 short lines is statistically significant at the 95 percent

Table 2.10
Comparison of Pre- and Post-1970 Short Lines

Item/Years	Regional	Local	Switching/ Terminal	All Short Lines
Miles of Road				
Before 1970	391.33	41.57	22.80	52.00
1970 & After	693.60	60.62	23.87	87.32
Overall	559.26	51.00	23.32	69.51
Paired T-Test	2.58**	2.82**	0.22	2.54**
Employees				
Before 1970	530.58	34.54	108.21	86.50
1970 & After	304.00	13.51	8.12	31.63
Overall	404.70	24.03	61.86	59.55
Paired T-Test	-2.05*	-4.40**	-4.83**	-4.10**
Men per mile				
Before 1970	2.10	1.06	5.77	2.77
1970 & After	0.45	0.39	0.85	0.54
Overall	1.18	0.73	3.49	1.67
Paired T-Test	-2.37**	-4.48**	-5.50**	-6.22**
Interchanges				
Before 1970	7.42	2.16	3.82	3.02
1970 & After	13.07	1.87	1.76	2.53
Overall	10.56	2.01	2.81	2.77
Paired T-Test	1.57	-1.62	-4.57**	-1.41

Source: Frank J. Dooley, *Economies of Size and Density for Short Line Railroads*, MPC Report 91-2 (Fargo, ND: Mountain Plains Consortium, North Dakota State University, 1991), p. 24.

Note: The * and ** denote a statistical difference between the pre- and post-1970 means at the 90 and 95 percent level of significance, respectively.

level of confidence for all types of short lines (Table 2.10). The mean number of employees per mile fell by 78.6 percent for regional, 63.2 percent for local, and 85.2 percent for switching/terminal railroads. The mean number of employees per mile for railroads created since 1970 is 0.45, 0.39, and 0.85 for regional, local, and switching/terminal railroads, respectively. When contrasting pre-1970 to post-1970 created lines, the number of employees per mile for regional and local railroads is almost the same. Before 1970, the

Table 2.11
Interchanges with Other Railroads

Number of Interchanges	Regional (%)	Local (%)	Switching/ Terminal (%)	All Short Lines (%)
Created Before 1970				
1	0.0	48.6	25.0	37.7
2-5	50.0	45.1	54.5	48.8
> 5	50.0	6.3	20.5	13.5
Number of Railroads	12	144	88	244
Created 1970 & After				
1	0.0	58.9	58.3	55.0
2-5	33.3	36.9	39.3	37.5
> 5	66.7	4.2	2.4	7.5
Number of Railroads	15	141	84	240
All Short Lines				
1	0.0	53.7	41.3	46.3
2-5	40.7	41.0	47.1	43.2
> 5	59.3	5.3	11.6	10.5
Number of Railroads	27	285	172	484

Source: Frank J. Dooley, *Economies of Size and Density for Short Line Railroads*, MPC Report 91-2 (Fargo, ND: Mountain Plains Consortium, North Dakota State University, 1991), p. 25.

typical regional railroad employed almost twice as many employees per mile as the typical local railroad.

The change in the number of interchanges has varied by type of short line. The difference in the mean number of interchanges is only statistically significant for switching/terminal railroads (Table 2.10). The mean number of interchanges for switching/terminal railroads fell from 3.82 to 1.76. The mean number of interchanges increased from 7.42 to 13.07 for regional railroads. There was little difference in the mean number of interchanges for local railroads.

While the mean number of interchanges has not varied significantly for pre- and post-1970 short lines, more short lines created since 1970 have only one interchange. Almost 38 percent of the short lines created before 1970 had only one interchange (see Table 2.11). For short lines formed since 1970, 55.0 percent have only one interchange. Over 40 percent of the switching/terminal railroads have only one connection, suggesting that many terminal railroads have been created since 1970.

Table 2.12
Speed Limits on Short Lines

Timetable Speed	Short Line's Total Main and Branch Line Track Mileage (in %)			
	< 25 miles	25-100 miles	> 100 miles	All Short Lines
< 10 MPH	53.3	35.3	16.5	23.3
11-25 MPH	42.3	42.8	29.8	33.7
26-40 MPH	2.8	18.0	37.2	30.4
> 40 MPH	1.6	3.9	16.6	12.6
TOTAL	100.0	100.0	100.1	100.0
Number of Railroads	139	125	55	319

Source: Frank J. Dooley, *Economies of Size and Density for Short Line Railroads*, MPC Report 91-2 (Fargo, ND: Mountain Plains Consortium, North Dakota State University, 1991), p. 26.

Note: Total does not equal 100 percent due to rounding.

The average length of haul is less than 150 miles for 44 percent of all short lines.[18] This includes mileage traveled on other railroads as part of a joint movement. The average length of haul is 150 to 500 miles for 26 percent of the short lines, 500 to 1,000 miles for 16 percent, and over 1,000 miles for the remaining 8 percent. The distribution is similar for all three types of short lines.

Timetable speeds on main and branch line trackage are relatively slow for over half of the short lines surveyed by the U.S. Department of Transportation (DOT) (Table 2.12). The distribution of timetable speeds varies by size of short line. Over 95 percent of the short lines with less than 25 miles of track operated at speeds of less than 25 miles per hour. In contrast, almost 54 percent of the short lines with more than 100 miles of track operated at speeds over 25 miles per hour.

Slow timetable speeds are more of a potential problem for longer short lines. Shorter short lines can complete service over their lines even when they move at speeds under 25 miles per hour. However, limited timetable speeds on longer short lines implies "that the current condition of track and structures may hamper economical operations on those carriers."[19]

SOURCES OF COST SAVINGS

By their very nature, short lines have a more flexible cost structure than Class I railroads. In this section, information highlighting the differences between Class I and short line labor costs is provided. The three major sources of cost savings are labor, equipment, and maintenance of way.

Labor

High rail labor costs are a major reason underlying the recent growth of short lines in the United States. As a result of lower labor costs, short lines may be able to continue operating profitably over light-density rail lines when Class Is can no longer do so. Labor costs are especially critical for light-density branch lines. In 1982 Class I rail labor costs for train crews, locomotives, freight cars, and maintenance of way were estimated to equal 49.2 percent of total operating costs on light-density lines. Short line rail labor costs may be appreciably lower than Class I rail labor costs as a result of less restrictive work rules, smaller crew consists, and lower wage rates.

The labor characteristics of short lines are compared to those of the Burlington Northern (BN). The BN is a good reference carrier for short line comparisons because it still operates a considerable amount of branch lines. In addition, BN is one of the carriers aggressively attempting to sell portions of its light-density lines.

Tolliver and Dooley[20] collected primary data from forty-eight short line railroads. In addition to various railroad characteristics, information was obtained about employment levels, job classifications, wage rates, and benefit packages. Similar information for the Burlington Northern was obtained from R-1 annual reports.

Job Classifications and Work Rules

There are four major differences between short lines and Class I carriers in the areas of rail labor work rules and job classifications. The first difference is the scale of the work force. Second, is the number of job classifications. Third, is the distribution of employees among the classifications. Fourth, is the utilization of job classifications, particularly regarding train and engine crews.

First, the size of the labor force differs between Class Is and the typical short line. In 1987 total employment for Class I railroads (excluding Amtrak and Auto-Train) was 248,526 persons or 1.88 employees per mile of track. In comparison, the typical short line formed since 1970 had 31.6 full-time workers, or 0.54 employees per mile of track (Table 2.11). Thus, when controlling for size, the typical short line railroad's per mile work force is only 29 percent of a Class I railroad's.[21]

The second major difference between short line and Class I railroads is the number of job classifications. Class I railroads may have contracts with up to nineteen different unions. Work rules generally segregate work duties

Table 2.13
Short Line Work Force

Employee Classification	Percent of Short Lines with Employees in Classification	Mean Number of Employees on a Short Line in Classification
Train Crew	95.0	4.4
Administration	82.5	2.2
Maintenance of Way	57.5	6.6
Mechanical	40.0	3.4
Clerks & Freight Handlers	35.0	2.6
Communications & Signals	27.5	1.2
Yard Crew	15.0	4.0
Shop Crafts	10.0	2.0

Source: Frank J. Dooley and Denver D. Tolliver, *A Comparison of Short Line and Class I Labor Costs in North Dakota*, UGPTI Report No. 73 (Fargo, ND: North Dakota State University, 1989), p. 10.

by union, preventing employees from performing duties outside their classification.

The number of job classifications for short lines is difficult to determine. Most short lines do not distinguish between job classifications. As a result, a direct comparison between job classifications for short line railroads and Class I railroads cannot be made. However, short line operators reported that they group their employees among eight general job classifications.

Class I railroads obviously have employees from all job classifications. None of the short lines, however, had employees in all the job classifications. The three most common job classifications reported by short line railroads were train crews (95.0 percent), administration (82.5 percent), and maintenance of way (57.5 percent) (see Table 2.13). No other job classification was reported by more than 40 percent of the short lines.

The third major difference between short line and Class I rail labor is the distribution of employees among job classifications. While short line and BN job classifications are not directly comparable, several broad categories do match up. The major difference in the distribution of employees concerns the category of train and engine crews. At the close of 1986, Burlington Northern's train and engine crew work force comprised 34.0 percent of all BN workers (see Table 2.14). In comparison, the typical short line classified almost 53 percent of its workers as train and engine crew employees.

Utilization of job classifications is the final difference between short line and Class I railroads. Short lines can succeed with fewer job classifications for three reasons. First, employees perform more than one type of duty.

Table 2.14
Employment on Burlington Northern and Short Line Railroads

Job Classification	Burlington Northern (%)	Typical Short Line (%)
Train & Engine Crews*	34.0	52.6
Maintenance of Way	22.5	20.9
Executive/Professional/Administrative	20.3	15.8
Maintenance of Equipment	17.8	5.4
All Other	5.4	5.3
TOTAL	100.0	100.0

Source: Frank J. Dooley and Denver D. Tolliver, *A Comparison of Short Line and Class I Labor Costs in North Dakota*, UGPTI Report No. 73 (Fargo, ND: North Dakota State University, 1989), p. 11.

*Includes both road train and yard crews.

Second, short lines contract out some of the less routine work. Finally, strict Class I work rules are relaxed on short lines.

Short line job classifications are somewhat misleading because employees typically do several types of work. For example, it is not unusual for a short line employee to operate a train, repair track, and make sales calls. Owners and employees may both benefit from the less structured system of job classifications. Many short line owners feel that the lack of strict job classifications leads to operational flexibility and large cost savings. According to the owners, the employees also benefited by being encouraged to perform a variety of tasks. The owners feel that employees are more satisfied with their work because their jobs are less tedious and more interesting. This observation has not been corroborated by short line employees.

Short lines are able to decrease the number of job classifications by contracting some types of work out to other firms. The types of work most frequently contracted are track maintenance (60.4 percent), car and engine repairs (52.4 percent), and equipment repairs (35.4 percent). This is consistent with the low percentage of short lines reporting employees for these types of job classifications. Contracting out may also allow the short line to avoid the associated fixed costs for items such as track maintenance and repair equipment or car and locomotive shops. Approximately 8 percent of the short lines contracted out administrative/clerical services and 6.3 percent contracted communications.

Finally, most Class I railroads believe that antiquated work rules restrict their operations. Until progress in the early 1990s, many trains operated

Table 2.15
Wage Differential between Burlington Northern and Short Line Railroads

Employee Classification	Average Hourly Wage Rates		Wage Rate Ratio (%)
	Burlington Northern*	Typical Short Line	
Train Crew*	$25.00	$10.10	247.5
Administration	19.77	13.01	152.0
Maintenance of Way	18.00	8.85	203.4
Mechanical	17.00	10.49	162.1
Yard Crew	25.00	12.06	207.3

Source: Frank J. Dooley and Denver D. Tolliver, *A Comparison of Short Line and Class I Labor Costs in North Dakota*, UGPTI Report No. 73 (Fargo, ND: North Dakota State University, 1989), p. 11.

*Calculated from ICC Wage Forms A and B. Wages include straight time actually worked, overtime, time paid but not worked, constructive allowances, vacations, and holidays. Service hours are actual hours worked at straight pay and overtime rates.

with four- or even five-man crews. Some crews even included firemen and brakemen although trains are diesel powered and often do not pull cabooses. In contrast, the average crew consist on a short line is only 2.13 workers.

Wages and Benefits

Three major differences exist between the wages and benefits for short line and Class I employees. First, the absolute wage scale is much lower for short line than BN employees. Second, the method of payment for the two types of employees differs. Finally, benefit packages are less attractive for short line employees.

First, short line hourly wage scales are much lower than comparable Burlington Northern (BN) wage scales. Average hourly wage rates for short line labor range between $8.85 and $13.01 per hour (see Table 2.15). Hourly wage rates for similar job classifications on the BN were calculated from ICC Wage Forms A and B. On average, BN labor receives between $17 to $25 per hour. Expressed as a ratio, the typical BN hourly wage rate is between 152 and 247 percent as much as that of the typical short line employee (Table 2.15).

Second, perhaps a more important distinction between the two types of rail labor is the difference in the method of payment. Short line employees are paid on an hourly basis. Overtime is paid on the basis used in most industries, time-and-a-half. The typical work day for a short line employee is 8.26 hours.[22]

Class I rail labor's total salaries are extremely complex to calculate. Class I train and engine crews are paid on a dual basis of distance traveled and length of time on duty. Their standard work day is eight hours or a run of 108 miles. This sets a minimum flat payment for all runs, even those that require less than eight hours or 108 miles.

The calculation of overtime is also complicated as it is a function of mileage and time. Overtime payments for Class I train and engine crews may vary according to factors that influence train speed such as track condition, traffic, or geography of the area. In general, overmiles (miles run more than 108 miles per day) are paid on a flat rate per mile. Overtime is paid on an hourly basis at time-and-a-half.

The calculation of Class I train and engine crews' salaries is also complicated by work rules resulting in additional compensation for several factors not related to work. Payment is received for items such as deadheading, terminal delays, and held-away-from-home terminal. The salary cost for items other than straight pay and overtime is estimated to equal 23 percent of total pay.[23]

Fringe benefits are the final major difference between short line and Class I employees. As a percentage of annual salary, the average fringe benefit package of BN employees' was over twice that of short line employees. In 1986 BN's employees fringe benefits were estimated to be 35.56 percent of their total salary.[24] A comparable figure for short lines was 16.96 percent.

Class I employees have attractive comprehensive benefit plans. The fringe benefits offered to short line employees are much more limited. According to survey results, benefits vary somewhat from short line to short line with larger firms offering more benefits. The most commonly offered benefits were health insurance, railroad retirement, and dental insurance—offered by 76.2, 57.1, and 35.7 percent of all short lines, respectively. Other fringe benefits offered by fewer short lines (between 10 and 25 percent) included life insurance, paid vacation, profit sharing, pension plans, bonuses, paid holidays, and unemployment insurance.

Equipment and Maintenance of Way

The cost structure of short line railroads is also more flexible because of equipment and maintenance of way. "A small railroad can maintain a less costly inventory of freight cars and locomotives, fitting that inventory to its unique traffic needs. In addition, small operators can more closely control expenditures on each segment of rail line, maintaining the track for the specific volume and nature of local traffic rather than conforming to generalized maintenance standards common to Class I carriers."[25]

Table 2.16
Typical Short Line Freight Diesel Locomotives

Locomotive	Horsepower	Axles	Weight (pounds)	Fuel Efficiency[*]
GP9	1750	4	258,000	114.6
GP38-2	2000	4	260,000	123.0
GP40-2	3000	4	270,000	163.7
SD40-2	3000	6	385,000	163.7
C40-8	4000	6	400,000	190.0

Source: Frank J. Dooley, *Economies of Size and Density for Short Line Railroads,* MPC Report 91-2 (Fargo, ND: Mountain Plains Consortium, North Dakota State University, 1991), p. 34.

[*]Gallons per hour, assuming that the locomotive is in Run 8 (top speed).

It is difficult to compare locomotive requirements for local and regional railroads versus Class I carriers. Each type of railroad uses different types of locomotives for their linehaul carriage. Locomotives vary in horsepower, axles, tractive effort, etc. (see Table 2.16).

A second difference is the cost of the power. A direct comparison is difficult to make between used and new equipment. Local and regional railroads almost exclusively purchase used locomotives. Class I railroads are more likely to purchase new or rebuilt locomotives. An additional factor complicating the locomotive cost is the associated fuel and maintenance cost. A locomotive with a higher purchase price may be cheaper to operate.

Among the types of locomotives favored by local railroads are GP7s, CF7s, and GP9s. All of these units have low horsepower, are nonturbocharged, and are simple to operate and maintain. In November 1989, a typical operating GP7 or CF7 ranged in price from $65,000 to $80,000. The GP9s, which have more power, cost around $90,000 for an operating unit to $150,000 for a rebuilt unit.

Class I carriers have sold many of the smaller locomotives from their fleets. However, recent changes in Class I locomotive demand and purchasing practices have led Class I carriers to purchase used equipment. This has driven locomotive prices up and reduced the availability of certain units. Thus, new local railroads may find it more difficult to find power in the future.

With larger traffic levels, larger networks, and perhaps larger budgets, regional carriers have a wider range of suitable locomotives to choose from, including 6–axle units. In addition to the smaller units mentioned above, regional railroads use GP35s, GP38s, GP40s, and SD40s. Regional railroads' costs for used locomotives ranged from $85,000 to $115,000 for a GP30 to

$400,000 to $500,000 for a GP40. A used SD40, the Class I industry standard for many years, ranged from $100,000 to $250,000. The price for a recently rebuilt SD40 is between $500,000 and $800,000. There is also a growing shortage of medium-sized locomotives. A lack of medium horsepower units has caused Class Is to keep older units. In addition, Class I carriers are increasingly purchasing used medium locomotives to be remanufactured.

The Class I railroads use a variety of locomotives. For linehaul purposes, the most recent purchases by Class Is have been of high power and high tractive effort locomotives. The typical price of a SD60, C40-8, GP60, or B40-8 ranges from $1.1 to $1.5 million.

Maintenance of way costs are also difficult to standardize, being subject to several variables. Maintenance of way costs are influenced by the type and weight of rail, average speed, track curvature, traffic density, roadbed and soil characteristics, bridges and structures, and other factors. Thus, estimates of annual normalized maintenance of way costs vary widely.

According to the U.S. Department of Transportation, the average annual maintenance of way (MOW) expense for a short line railroad is $10,236 per mile. (The average annual MOW expense ranged from $3,368 to $29,068 per mile.) The wide range in MOW cost is explained in part by the variation in traffic density and timetable speeds for short lines. In addition, the U.S. Department of Transportation estimate may include deferred maintenance cost.

Normalized maintenance of way costs were estimated using a comprehensive economic-engineering model at the Upper Great Plains Transportation Institute (UGPTI).

Normalized maintenance of way (NMOW) is an idealized concept or standard. It denotes the annualized sum necessary to maintain a track at some predefined level. NMOW cost may never agree with actual track expenditures during a given year. Actual expenditures are subject to budgetary constraints and management priorities. In the short-run, carriers can (and do) defer normalized maintenance. However, over a longer period of time, the cumulative effects of deferred maintenance will require rehabilitation of the line, or will lead to its abandonment.[26]

The UGPTI model considers the physical requirements and costs of ties, ballast, rail, bridges, crossings, switches, inspection, signals, spot maintenance, snow removal, vegetation removal, signing, and miscellaneous costs.

The average annual NMOW cost per mile on light density branch lines is $8,880 per mile under Class I ownership.[27] Under short line ownership, the NMOW cost for the same line is $7,100 dollars per mile.[28] The short line MOW cost is 20 percent less than the Class I carrier cost. The primary reason for lower short line MOW costs are lower tie installation and ballast costs as a result of lower labor costs. Short line NMOW cost savings are offset by lower rail and materials costs for Class I carriers. In addition, Class I labor is more productive as Class I carriers use more specialized, high-cost equipment.

SUMMARY AND CONCLUSIONS

Since the mid-1970s, Class I railroads have been attempting to rationalize their rail networks by either abandoning or selling their light-density branch lines. Since 1970, almost 40,000 miles of road have been abandoned. During the same time, 240 new short lines operating almost 21,000 miles of track have been created.

Short lines created since 1970 are much different from short lines created before. The typical short line created since 1970 is longer, but employs fewer people than the earlier created short lines. On average, a short line formed since 1970 is 87.3 miles long and employs 31.6 people. In contrast, the average short line formed before 1970 is only 52 miles long, but has 86.5 employees. Thus, the average number of employees per mile of track has fallen from 2.77 to 0.54, or 80.5 percent.

Compared with Class I trunk lines, most short lines operate over light-density lines. In addition, short lines formed since 1970 have a much lower average traffic density than those created before. The pre-1970 average density for local and regional railroads was 451.3 cars per mile. Since 1970 the average density for local and regional railroads has fallen by 75.7 percent to 109.6 cars per mile.

In conclusion, the spin-off of short lines by Class I carriers has created a short line industry with two distinct segments. As a whole, pre-1970 short lines are viable small railroads. In contrast, many of the short lines created since 1970 operate over lines that were at best marginally profitable for their former Class I owners. As such, the economic success of the new short lines is closely related to their ability to control costs, especially labor, and provide improved service.

Class I railroads reported that they may sell an additional 17,265 miles of track by 1994. The characteristics of these potential short lines are most likely similar to those of short lines created since 1970. Given the lower traffic densities on these lines, public policies and private decision making must recognize that the new short lines will require a more flexible cost structure to operate economically.

NOTES

1. Adapted from Frank J. Dooley, *Economies of Size and Density for Short Line Railroads*, MPC Report 91-2 (Fargo, ND: Mountain Plains Consortium, North Dakota State University, 1991).

2. Harvey Levine and Craig Rockey, *Statistics of Regional and Local Railroads* (Washington, D.C.: Association of American Railroads, 1988), p. 67.

3, Staggers Rail Act of 1980, 94 Stat. 1895 (1980).

4. *Railroad Facts 1988* (Washington, D.C.: Association of American Railroads, 1988), p. 42.

5. Jon H. Mielke, "Short Line Railroad Creations: Terms of Sale, Impacts on Viability, and Public Policy Implications," *Journal of the Transportation Research Forum* 29 (1988): 138.

6. Eric K. Wolfe, "Status of the Local & Regional Railroad Industry," paper presented at the Second American Railroad Conference, Chicago, IL, September 21–23, 1988.

7. Levine and Rockey, *Statistics*, p. 77.

8. Mielke, "Short Line," p. 138.

9. Ibid.

10. Apparently, the divestment strategy was successful. In March 1989, ICG was sold to Prospect Groups, Inc., and its name was changed to Illinois Central Transportation Co.

11. Mielke, "Short Line," p. 138.

12. Ibid.

13. Pittsburgh & Lake Erie R.R. v. Railway Labor Executives' Association, 491 U.S. 490, 109 S.Ct. 2584 (1989). *See also* Chapter 5.

14. U.S. Department of Transportation, Federal Railroad Administration, *A Survey of Shipper Satisfaction with Service and Rates of Shortline and Regional Railroads* (Washington, D.C., 1989).

15. Frank J. Dooley and Julie M. Rodriguez, "Rail Service Levels for Grain Shippers Under Class I and Short Line Ownership," *Journal of the Transportation Research Forum* 29 (1988): 86.

16. A regional railroad is one with 350 miles or more of track and/or revenues greater than $40 million. Switching and terminal railroads identified themselves as such. All other short lines are local railroads.

17. Edward A. Lewis, *American Shortline Railway Guide*, 3d ed. (Milwaukee, WI: Kalmbach Pub. Co., 1986), pp. 2–3.

18. U.S. Department of Transportation, Federal Railroad Administration, *Deferred Maintenance and Delayed Capital Improvements on Class II and Class III Railroads*, A Report to Congress (Washington, D.C., 1989).

19. Ibid.

20. Denver D. Tolliver and Frank J. Dooley, "Short Line Rail Labor Costs," *Research in Changing Environments, Proceedings of the 23rd Canadian Transportation Research Forum* (Regina: University of Saskatchewan Press, 1988), pp. 1–15.

21. Dooley, *Economies of Size*, p. 28. In addition to size, the scale of the work force is related to the density of traffic, the presence of powerful labor organizations, and other variables.

22. Frank J. Dooley and Denver D. Tolliver, *A Comparison of Short Line and Class I Labor Costs in North Dakota*, UGPTI Report No. 73 (Fargo, ND: Upper Great Plains Transportation Institute, North Dakota State University, 1989).

23. Ibid.

24. Ibid.

25. U.S. Dept. of Transportation, *Deferred Maintenance.*

26. Denver D. Tolliver, *The Benefits and Costs of Local and Regional Railroads,* UGPTI Report No. 80 (Fargo, ND: Upper Great Plains Transportation Institute, North Dakota State University, 1989).

27. Ibid.

28. Ibid.

3

Railroad Rationalization and Restructuring

From the Civil War through World War II, railroads were the dominant carriers of passengers and freight in North America. After V-J Day, the availability of nonrationed gasoline and access to air carriers provided a choice for travelers, many of whom opted for alternatives to passenger trains. The growth of interstate highways after the Korean War led to a shift of freight traffic from railroads to motor carriers. That, coupled with a downsizing of heavy industry and the movement of what remained from the northeastern "rust belt" to the southern "sun belt," led to a decline in railroad profitability.[1]

By the 1970s several large carriers were bankrupt. The federal government established Amtrak to take over most railroad passenger service,[2] and commuter traffic was spun off to state authorities.[3] The decline of northeastern rail traffic and the subsequent bankruptcies of most carriers after the disastrous Penn Central merger led to the establishment of Conrail, originally a government-supported outfit, to take over freight service in that region.[4]

Following the passage of the Staggers Act in 1980,[5] railroads found it easier to exit markets, abandon or spin off trackage, and to contract with large shippers for the movement of bulk commodities. The 1980s were a period of economic resurgence for most railroads; after the Milwaukee and Rock Island liquidations, there have been few large-scale mainline abandonments. It appears that, although we have fewer rail lines than at any time during the twentieth century, those that remain are in far better economic condition.

ABANDONMENT

Abandonment is a term of art that refers to a railroad's discontinuing all use of a particular line of track. If no other carrier is providing service over the line, the abandoning railroad will be free to tear up the track and use it somewhere else. Since few, if any, businessmen are willing to construct a new railroad on the old right-of-way, abandonment is a serious step. Once a railroad is abandoned, it is gone. For this reason, Congress and the ICC have placed restrictions on a railroad's ability to abandon its line.

One problem for the railroads has been the maintenance (including paying property tax) on redundant and excessive track. Two-thirds of all freight traffic today operates over only one-fifth of the rail system, while 10 percent of the total trackage accounts for only 0.5 percent of the traffic. Railroads have used abandonment proceedings to rid themselves of these lines.

Railroad Abandonment Procedures

Prior to the enactment of the Staggers Act of 1980,[6] a railroad had the burden of proving that the public convenience and necessity permitted the abandonment.[7] The ICC had to balance the burden to the carrier of continued service with the adverse effects on shippers and local communities. The burden of proof was on the railroad to show that public convenience and necessity would allow the discontinuance, and there were a lengthy set of procedural requirements designed to ensure that the railroad had considered all alternatives before ending service. The commission had power to deny or delay the abandonment.

The ICC has had plenary jurisdiction over rail abandonments since the 1926 case of *Colorado v. United States.*[8] In that proceeding, the Supreme Court of the United States held that the regulatory power of the commission extended to the abandonment by the Colorado & Southern Railway of a narrow-gauge branch line located entirely in Colorado. The Court said, inter alia, that "The power to make the determination (to give the ICC abandonment authority) inheres in the United States as an incident to its power over interstate commerce. The making of this determination involves an exercise of judgement upon the facts and to exercise thereon the judgment whether abandonment is consistent with public convenience and necessity. Congress conferred such powers upon the Commission."[9] So even intrastate abandonments come within ICC jurisdiction.

The commission can condition abandonments upon the provision of alternate service or improving alternative routes. Usually, an abandonment petition is brought by the railroad, but occasionally it may be brought by another party (such as a highway department which covets the right of way). Usually, abandonment means that the railroad is free to remove the tracks and use the land underneath for other purposes (or to sell it). However, in many cases the line was built on easements or fees subject to defeasance, whereupon the land reverts to the underlying landowner. The latter case is problematic for continuing the linear right-of-way or using it for other purposes.

The Staggers Rail Act placed a stringent timetable on the commission's disposition of abandonment appeals. Railroads must submit to the commission a diagram of their routes, indicating the lines that are potentially subject to abandonment. The act provides that, if the application is unopposed, the ICC must approve the abandonment within 30 days.[10] If the commission concludes that public convenience and necessity permit the abandonment, it has 90 days to issue a certificate that permits the abandonment within 120 days after the application is filed.[11]

Disposition of the Right-of-Way

Within ten days after the abandonment is published in the *Federal Register*, any person may offer to pay the carrier a subsidy for the continuance of the rail service, or offer to buy the line. The ICC must postpone issuance of the abandonment certificate when a financially responsible person has offered financial assistance and it is likely that the assistance is equivalent to the difference between revenues and avoidable cost, or when an interested party has agreed to acquire the line. If the line is to be sold, and the parties fail to agree on the amount of the compensation, they may submit the question to the ICC for determination.[12]

A carrier (usually a short line) that has purchased a rail line from an abandoning carrier (usually a Class I) may not discontinue service on the line for two years after the sale nor sell it to another carrier (except the original railroad) within five years of the sale.[13] The statute is silent about what happens when the acquiring carrier simply runs out of money. In any case, the Bankruptcy Reform Act of 1978 gives a the federal Bankruptcy Court, rather than the ICC, ultimate authority over disposition of an insolvent debtor railroad's assets—including abandonment of lines.[14]

Once the ICC decides upon abandonment, it is required to find whether the right-of-way is useful for public purposes, including highways, power lines, mass transit, or recreational facilities. If the commission so finds, disposition of the right-of-way is held up for 180 days while an attempt is made to find a buyer who will take possession of the intact linear right-of-way.[15]

Since 1916 the U.S. railway network has slimmed down from 254,000 miles to less than 145,000 miles. Although the large-scale abandonments of the 1970s have passed, track is still being abandoned at the rate of 2,000 to 3,000 miles each year.[16] As of 1991, 3,245 miles of abandoned railroad have been preserved and converted into hiking or biking trails. Wisconsin has some 555 miles of ex-railroad "public access linear parks," Michigan has 369, and Washington 361, including the 145-mile John Wayne Pioneer Trail, the longest rail-to-trail conversion in the country (formerly the mainline of the defunct Milwaukee Road).[17] Typically, a local or state agency acquires the right-of-way for recreational purposes. Sometimes the original ballast is left behind and becomes the trail surface; other times asphalt, wood chips, or other surfaces are used. Tunnels usually present no particular problem (except for lighting); the derailed bridges generally are modified with wooden decks. (One of the few interstate trails is the former Northern Pacific bridge over the Red River, between Grand Forks, N.D., and East Grand Forks, Minn.; the states involved have constructed a bikeway with fenced-in railings where the Winnipeg Flyer once steamed.)

The National Trails System Act provides for rail-banking (holding a right-of-way for possible future railroad use while allowing interim use as a recreational trail). Since 1990 the U.S. Supreme Court has upheld the constitutionality of this law, and, in Missouri, a court favorably ruled on the conversion of the former Missouri-Kansas-Texas 200–mile St. Louis Line, which will be the nation's longest rail trail.[18] Rail-banking has the potential for keeping the linear property intact, forbidding remaindermen (such as adjoining farmers) from taking possession and fencing or cultivating the land, thus destroying the uninterrupted linear nature of the property. Experience in constructing the Los Angeles Metro rapid transit system (which essentially replicates the old Pacific Electric Railway), shows the tremendous expense involved in reconstructing a once abandoned rail system from scratch.

Discontinuance of Passenger Trains

Since 1958 the Interstate Commerce Commission has had jurisdiction over the discontinuance of interstate passenger trains and appellate jurisdiction over states' refusal to grant rail discontinuance petitions.[19] Under ICC review, the number of passenger trains fell by 60 percent between 1958 and 1970, at which time only 360 intercity trains were left.[20]

Passage of the Rail Passenger Service Act of 1970 transferred most of the remaining intercity trains to Amtrak, which immediately halved the number of trains operating and consolidated parallel routes.[21] Those railroads remaining outside of the Amtrak system were left within the jurisdictional ambit of the ICC. One by one, these railroads either discontinued service or joined with Amtrak at a later date.[22]

Commuter trains remained within ICC jurisdiction; however, section 10504 of the Interstate Commerce Act exempts suburban rail systems from ICC jurisdiction if the carriers' fares are subject to the authority of the governor of the state in which the line operates.[23] The language of the statute refers to "local public body," meaning commuter rail authority. At this writing, all commuter trains are operated on behalf of state transportation authorities. Sometimes, as in the case of New York or Pennsylvania, the state itself provides the service; in most cases Amtrak or a freight railroad operates the trains in contract with the state authority (see Chapter 7).

What jurisdiction over passenger train discontinuance remains with the ICC is vestigial—the occasional private train operated outside the Amtrak system and not part of a commuter rail network.

SHORT LINE SALES

In the beginning, all railroads were short lines.[24] Our first railroad, the Baltimore & Ohio, had great ambitions (catch that word "Ohio"), but started running between Baltimore and Ellicott Mills (now Ellicott City), Maryland, a distance of thirteen miles. Our second common carrier, the Strasburg, built 4.5 miles of track in Pennsylvania and never exceeded that length. The B&O grew to over a thousand miles, and New York's short lines were hammered by the redoubtable Commodore Vanderbilt into the mighty New York Central system, but many short lines like the Strasburg remained independent, untouched, and unwanted by the major carriers. The merger movement of the 1960s dealt mainly with consolidating the big guys; the little fellows were pretty much left alone.

The 1970s saw a massive change in the face of railroading, and the red-brick Blaine Mansion on Washington's Embassy Row that houses the American Short Line Railroad Association became a power center in transportation policy. The phenomenal growth in short line formation was a consequence of the bankruptcy of the large east-west carriers. A trustee in bankruptcy has the power to reject a lease, and many nonoperating landlords suddenly found themselves back in the railroad business. For example, the Providence and Worcester Railroad was chartered in 1845 and began operating between its namesake cities in New England in 1847. In 1890 it was leased to the New York, New Haven & Hartford Railroad. When Penn Central absorbed the New Haven in 1969, it refused to assume the P&W lease. The P&W, stuck with maintaining a railroad that nobody else wanted, began operating independently in 1973, and in the last twenty years has expanded, now operating most of the freight lines of its onetime tenant New Haven.[25]

The 1970 bankruptcy petition of Penn Central, the largest corporate bankruptcy in American history, was responsible for the birth of Amtrak and, later, Conrail[26] but also spawned a host of short lines. Conrail's predecessors[27] had operated about 25,000 miles of track (19,000 of these were Penn Central lines), of these less than 15,000 are operated by Conrail today. Much of the remainder is now operated by short lines. The Rock Island filed for bankruptcy in 1975 and shut down completely in 1980. The Milwaukee Road filed for bankruptcy in 1975. It shut down everything west of Miles City, Montana, in 1980, and in 1982 retreated east to Ortonville, Minnesota. At the time the Soo Line took over what was left—the Milwaukee was down to 3,100 miles, down from a prebankruptcy system of 10,500 miles.[28] Class I railroads took over some of the better lines of the Rock Island; new short lines were formed to take over the rest.

Lines rejected by Conrail were offered to local communities for operation by a "designated operator." In many cases, they were the foundation for the creation of short line railroads throughout the East and Midwest. Many of these original operators are still in business, and new short lines are being formed. Following Conrail's lead, several other major railroads divested themselves of low-density lines. The Illinois Central and Burlington Northern have been foremost in this movement, but the other major western lines are now following this policy. Divestiture was made easier by the Staggers Act abandonment procedures. Short lines often have less-expensive terminal operations and are free of restrictive union agreements. They have local management and are able to work well with local shippers for traffic that larger railroads tend to ignore. The Class I railroads often maintain good relations with short lines that essentially feed that one carrier. Burlington Northern has such a relationship with the Montana Rail Link and the Red River Valley and Western. Some short lines, like the Strasburg, make their bread and butter from tourist passenger operations and freight is a sideline, but the run of the mill short line exists to haul a few commodities to a connection with a Class I friendly carrier. For a more detailed exposition of the short line movement, refer to Chapter 2.

MERGERS AND CONSOLIDATIONS

ICC approval has been required since 1920 for one rail carrier to acquire another.[29] This requirement involves merger, consolidation, or acquiring control of another railroad through stock ownership, management, or otherwise. In addition, commission approval is sometimes required when a noncarrier seeks to acquire control of a carrier.[30] If the takeover is deemed by the ICC to be consistent with the public interest, the transaction is exempt from antitrust laws.

The Railroad Merger Movement

Until 1960 the ICC's policy was to favor end-to-end mergers or mergers of weak railroads, rather than parallel mergers, which would diminish competition. In 1960 the parallel Erie and Lackawanna were allowed to merge, because they were financially weak carriers. The same year, the Norfolk & Western, a strong coal-hauler in Virginia, was allowed to acquire the parallelling Virginian Railway because operating efficiencies were persuasive.[31] In 1963, the Seaboard Air Line and Atlantic Coast Line were allowed to merge. This was a departure from the ICC precedent inasmuch as they were both large, prosperous, competing railroads.

The merger movement continued in full force throughout the 1960s. The Norfolk & Western expanded from a regional carrier to a major east-west railroad by acquiring the Nickel Plate, leasing the Wabash, and buying the connecting Sandusky line from the Pennsylvania Railroad. The Chesapeake and Ohio took control of the parallelling Baltimore & Ohio and Western Maryland to create the Chessie System, named for the sleepy cat who adorned its advertising. The emergence of the Chessie and N&W systems created a regional imbalance, with onetime giants Pennsylvania and New York Central feeling left out of the party. These two longtime rivals sought to merge too, and in 1968 the ICC, after requiring the parties to take the hapless New Haven under their wing, allowed the Water Level Route and the Standard Railroad of the World to consolidate as the Penn Central Railroad.[32] Penn Central absorbed the New Haven in 1969 and filed for bankruptcy the following year. By virtue of the Regional Rail Reorganization Act of 1973, Penn Central was joined by fellow bankrupts Erie-Lackawanna, Reading, Lehigh Valley, Lehigh & Hudson River, and Central of New Jersey into the eastern colossus known as Conrail. Originally a government ward, Conrail became privately traded and now is a profitable concern.

The Northern Lines were consolidated into the Burlington Northern in 1970, when the ICC approved the merger of the Burlington, Northern Pacific, Great Northern, and Spokane, Portland & Seattle, incidentally driving the final nails into the coffins of the Milwaukee and Rock Island. The Burlington Northern then acquired the Frisco Lines in 1980 and is now the longest railroad in the country. In 1994, the Burlington Northern merged with the Santa Fe. Meanwhile, Chessie and the Seaboard merged to form CSX, with a parallel coordination of the Norfolk & Western with the Southern Railway. Acquisition of the Western Pacific and Missouri Pacific by the Union Pacific brought us the rail map that we have today. After ICC disapproval of the Southern Pacific–Santa Fe merger, the beleaguered SP was finally absorbed by the Rio Grande. Today, 86 percent of revenue ton-miles and 93 percent of the industry's profits are held by the following carriers:

East: Conrail
            CSX
            Norfolk Southern

West: Burlington Northern
            Union Pacific
            Santa Fe
            Southern Pacific[33]

ICC Procedure in Rail Mergers

The ICC must determine that the merger of two or more Class I carriers is in the public interest. That phrase has been interpreted as "compatible, or at least not contradictory or hostile to the public interest." Congress has specified that the ICC must take into account the following:

the effect of the transaction on the adequacy of transportation to the public

the effect of including or excluding other carriers to the transaction

total fixed charges that result from the proposed transaction

the interest of carrier employees (see Chapter 5)

whether the proposed transaction would have an adverse effect on competition within the region

It was the last factor that caused the ICC to disapprove of the parallel Southern Pacific–Santa Fe merger. [34] The ICC must consider antitrust laws in its analysis of whether the public interest is satisfied by the merger.[35] The Interstate Commerce Act allows the ICC to impose conditions on the merger; these might protect competing carriers (by requiring gateways to remain open), require inclusion of carriers (such as the New Haven in the Penn Central merger), or require labor protection for displaced employees (see Chapter 5). In addition, the ICC has required trackage rights to be made available to competing carriers. When the Union Pacific–Western Pacific merger was allowed, the merged carrier was required to allow the Rio Grande to operate over its tracks between Pueblo and Kansas City, and the Southern Pacific to operate between St. Louis and Kansas City.[36]

Although the ICC is instructed to follow antitrust policy in its approval or disapproval of mergers, it is not required to follow the same sort of reasoned analysis that the Justice Department would make.[37] The Staggers Act, mindful of how the Rock Island was left to languish for over a decade while the ICC haggled over the details of UP's merger bid, contains stringent time deadlines. A merger of control of two or more Class I railroads must be decided in not more than thirty-one months.[38] Other transactions of regional or national transportation significance must be decided within ten months; other mergers must be decided within six months. The 4-R Act had already established an alternate procedure for mergers, where the initial analysis of the proposed transaction is to be made by the secretary of transportation. The ICC is then directed to give due weight and consideration to the secretary's report.[39] The intent of both statutory requirements is to speed up the ICC's deliberative processes and allow railroads to plan for a merged or separate future.

GOVERNMENT OPERATION OF RAILROADS

Federal Ownership

During the Reagan administration, the federal government relinquished what equity ownership it had in U.S. railroads. The Panama Railroad was transferred, along with the Panama Canal Company, to the Republic of Panama as part of the Panama Canal Treaty. The Alaska Railroad was transferred to the state of Alaska[40] and Conrail was privatized.[41] Even the U.S. Department of Transportation's test track in Pueblo, Colorado, was conveyed to the Association of American Railroads, an industry trade association.

The federal government still owns some preferred shares in Amtrak and directs the subsidies and some policies of that company through the Federal Railroad Administration. Although the federal government actually controlled all the railroads during World War I, we have bucked the worldwide trend and have resisted the urge to nationalize our railroads. State ownership, however, is prevalent throughout the country.

State Ownership

"Statelization" is the process by which a state becomes involved in the ownership or operation of a common-carrier railroad. The process was accelerated by the Regional Rail Reorganization Act of 1973,[42] the Railroad Revitalization and Regulatory Reform Act of 1976,[43] and the Local Rail Service Assistance Act of 1978.[44] Federal funds made available by these acts provided an incentive for states to develop rail plans and policies, and get around state laws and constitutional provisions prohibiting investment of public funds in private enterprises.

State operation of lines has been in the following areas: commuter lines, shor tline railroads, and strategic main lines.

State ownership of commuter railroads began with the purchase of the Long Island Railroad by the State of New York in the 1960s. The Northeast Rail Service Act of 1981[45] divested Conrail of the responsibility for commuter services, which were taken over by the states along the Northeast Corridor. Of these, New York (Metro–North Commuter Railroad), New Jersey (NJ Transit) and Pennsylvania (SEPTA) got into the railroad business directly, owning and operating the commuter lines. Other states have contracted with private railroads or Amtrak to run the services (see Chapter 7).

Most states have some involvement in short line railroading. In many cases, state and local governments have picked up branch lines that a Class I railroad has dropped. Few states (West Virginia is a notable exception) operate the railroads directly; most look for a designated operator to run the line, or possibly the state leases the entire railroad to a private carrier. In Vermont, the Rutland Railroad was bankrupt and about to be liquidated. The state acquired the railroad in 1960 and has leased it to two carriers: the Green Mountain Railway and the Vermont Railway.

Few states have the wherewithal to operate mainline railroads. However, the state of Alaska is a major operator, as the Alaska Railroad was transferred to the state government from the U.S. Department of Transportation in 1984.[46] Alaska railroaders are state employees, and the company is run directly by the state department of transportation. South Dakota, faced with the breakup of the Milwaukee Road, acquired the former transcontinental mainline from Minnesota to Montana and leased it to Burlington Northern; the state rail authority also has acquired segments of other railroads and leased them to designated operators. Other than the Milwaukee, South Dakota had no transcontinental railroads passing through the state; abandonment of that line would have meant disaster for the agricultural producers of that state. Kyle Railways also operates the westernmost part of the old Rock Island mainline for the states of Kansas and Colorado.

Recently there has been an effort by the Southern Pacific and Santa Fe to spin off their lines in the Los Angeles, San Francisco, and San Diego areas to local transit authorities for commuter service. The Metrolink system in Los Angeles has been built on these lines, with freight railroads contracted to operate cargo service on the routes. The Southern Pacific has offered California its "Coast Line" between San Francisco and Los Angeles as a route for high-speed passenger trains. If accepted, this would make California the most intensive state railroad operator.

Foreign Ownership

Unlike airlines and steamship companies, there are no prohibitions against foreign ownership of U.S. railroads. Foreign capital built many of our railroads; it is said that the Chicago & North Western Railway has left-track running because of British influence in the construction of that line.

Today the only substantial foreign ownership in American railroading is by the major Canadian railroads. The Canadian National Railway (a Crown corporation) owns the Grand Trunk Western, Central Vermont, and Duluth, Winnipeg & Pacific railways; the Canadian Pacific (privately owned) operates the Soo Line and Delaware and Hudson railroads and operates them along with its Canadian system as part of a transcontinental line, CP Rail (see Chapter 8). The CP system incorporates what is left of the old Chicago, Milwaukee, St. Paul & Pacific Railway.

BANKRUPTCY

Railroad Bankruptcy Procedures

Since 1979 railroads in reorganization have been governed by the new Bankruptcy Code. Amended again in 1984 to correct certain constitutional infirmities, the Act has governed all reorganization plans of insolvent debtors since its effective date of October 1, 1979. Railroads that previously had filed for reorganization (such as the Milwaukee and Rock Island) were governed under old Section 77 of the 1898 Bankruptcy Code.[47]

Subchapter IV of Chapter 11 deals with the reorganization of railroads. The Department of Transportation selects a panel of five persons, one of whom the bankruptcy court will choose to be a trustee. With regard to railroad bankruptcies, the court and trustees have dual loyalties: they must take into account the interest of the public, as well as that of the debtor railroad's estate, its stockholders, and creditors.[48]

Except for abandonment cases, a railroad in reorganization is still subject to state and federal regulation, particularly that of the ICC. However, the ICC now has only advisory authority over the abandonment of railroad lines. The trustee, if she decides to abandon a portion or all of the railroad, must file an application for abandonment, but the court will tell the ICC when the deadline is for its report, and that report is merely a recommendation to the bankruptcy court, which has the final say in the matter.[49]

A trustee in bankruptcy takes possession of all property of the railroad, protecting it from creditors at the same time that she is supposed to be operating it for the public. If she chooses to petition for abandonment, all the court must find is that abandonment is: (1) in the best interest of the estate, (2) is essential to the reorganization plan, and (3) is consistent with the public interest. However, no removal of track may take place until the time for filing appeals has been exhausted.[50]

Except for the public interest, labor, and abandonment provisions, railroads in reorganization are treated similarly to other corporate bankruptcies. The trustee must come up with a reorganization plan, which might include abandonments or transfer of lines to other railroads. The old section 77 did not authorize liquidation of a railroad under reorganization. The reorganization court would dismiss the petition for reorganization, and a state receivership would generally follow. Now if the railroad cannot be successfully reorganized, the railroad must be liquidated within five years and its assets sold or otherwise disposed of, with the proceeds going to the secured creditors.[51]

Bankruptcy and Transportation[52]

Bankruptcy is a constitutional right, and Congress has been charged by the Constitution with the establishment of a uniform system for achieving it.[53] However, the states can establish their own schedules of exemptions (property which the debtor may keep out of the assets available to creditors). The purpose of the bankruptcy laws is that debtors can seek protection from their creditors, at the same time that an orderly system is set up for paying the creditors' claims. All the great transcontinental railroads (except for Jim Hill's Great Northern) were built with debt financing. Most of them eventually defaulted, and the railroads were operated by trustees in bankruptcy. The trustee had the duty of operating the railroad for the benefit of shippers and passengers, and preserving the assets of the railroad company for the benefit of creditors. This sounds contradictory, and many of these reorganizations took a long time. The longest on record was forty-two years for the Pittsburgh, Shawmut & Northern—long enough for a young lawyer to serve until retirement age in the reorganization of a single railroad. In most cases, the original stockholders who built the railroads received nothing for their investment. This reorganization problem was dealt with by limiting railroad reorganizations to five to ten years in extraordinary proceedings.[54] We sadly tell our law students that they can no longer count on making a lifetime career out of reorganizing only one railroad.

Railroads were not only the first major U.S. corporations, but provided some of the most spectacular bankruptcy proceedings. The failure of the Penn Central system was the largest corporate bankruptcy in U.S. history.[55] Created from two barely solvent mainline railroads in the northeast, with the insolvent New Haven thrust upon them like an unwanted stepchild, the Penn Central debacle brought down with it most of its connecting lines in the East.[56] However, the Penn Central's estate was disposed of outside the bankruptcy process. Instead, Congress opted for two statutory solutions: (1) the Rail Passenger Service Act,[57,] which set up Amtrak as a government-sponsored railroad to operate intercity passenger trains, and (2) the Regional Rail Reorganization Act,[58] which set up Conrail to take over the operations of the freight railroads in the northeast (Penn Central plus its bankrupt connections).

Rather than being liquidated, the railroad assets of Penn Central and the other bankrupts were folded into the Consolidated Rail Corporation—Conrail. Originally Conrail operated with a heavy government subsidy (used in large part to rehabilitate the track). Having been returned to the private sector (the creditors of the bankrupt railroads received stock in Conrail), the big consolidated network is now the preeminent carrier in the Northeast.

The later bankruptcies of the Rock Island and Milwaukee Road ended in the liquidation of both carriers, although legislation was passed to ease the effect on employees. Most of the Milwaukee was abandoned, and what was left was sold to the Soo Line, now owned and operated by the Canadian Pacific. The Rock Island Line was a mighty sad road, and most of it is gone, although some parts are operated by short lines such as Iowa Interstate and Kyle Railways.[59]

By contrast, airlines have been shut down and liquidated by bankruptcy courts without any corresponding congressional response. There are some differences between air and rail bankruptcies: any new airline can fly in to replace a bankrupt competitor, while no one is going to build a new railroad once one has been ripped up. An important difference between airline and rail reorganization is the treatment of labor contracts. Although both carriers are subject to the provisions of the Railway Labor Act, the bankruptcy laws provide greater protection for rail workers. Railroaders can only change their contracts by mutual consent using the provisions of Section 6. In the airline industry, it is possible to reject a collective bargaining agreement, although the duty to bargain for a new contract remains.[60]

DIRECTED SERVICE ORDERS[61]

The ICC can use directed service orders as a way of responding to emergencies that have snarled rail traffic.[62] These are orders by which the ICC orders one railroad to operate over the lines of another. The railroads can later solve their dispute over who pays for what; the important part is to keep the traffic moving. Directed service orders were used on a small scale in the early days of ICC regulation, in cases where a bridge was out or a line was blocked. More recently, these orders have been used in the case of mainline railroads that became insolvent and stopped operating. When the Rock Island shut down in 1980, the Kansas City Terminal was ordered to provide service over the Rock's lines until the property could be liquidated in an orderly manner. When the bankrupt Delaware and Hudson ceased operations, the ICC ordered directed service operations by the Susquehanna Railroad until the Canadian Pacific could take possession of the line.

Section 11123 of the Interstate Commerce Act provides that if the Commission finds that there is an emergency requiring immediate action, it may take a number of steps, including suspending car-service rules and requiring joint use of terminals and a "reasonable distance" of mainline track. In other words, the ICC can order a railroad to use another line's cars or engines to move the traffic.[63]

Section 11124 states that when a carrier cannot transport the traffic offered to it, the Commission may direct the handling, routing, and movement of its traffic over another railroad. The railroads are supposed to work out the financial arrangements, but if they cannot, the ICC will do it for them.[64]

Finally, extensive directed-service powers were given to the commission by Section 11125, which directs transportation over one railroad by another when the first carrier cannot handle traffic because it has been abandoned by court order or has simply given up without any regulatory approval.[65] It is by this provision that the massive directed-service operations of the Rock Island and Delaware and Hudson were ordered.

The law also provides for the takeover of a line whose "cash position makes its continuing operation impossible."[66] This was the situation of the Rock Island when the line was shut down. The railroad performing directed service does not make any changes in the operation of the inactive line. It hires the same workers under their existing collective bargaining agreements. Directed service orders will remain stopgap, temporary emergency measures.

NOTES

1. Paul S. Dempsey, *The Social and Economic Consequences of Deregulation* (Westport, CT: Quorum Books, 1989), p. 19.

2. Paul S. Dempsey, "The Dark Side of Deregulation: Its Impact on Small Communities," *Administrative Law Review* 39 (1987): 445, 450–452.

3. William E. Thoms, "Is the Clock Running Down for U.S. Commuters?" *Trains*, October 1983, p. 30.

4. William E. Thoms, "Clear Track for Deregulation," *Transportation Law Journal* 12 (1982): 183, 201–206.

5. Pub. L. No. 96–448, 94 Stat. 1895 (1980). *See* Thoms, "Clear Track," pp. 211–215.

6. Paul S. Dempsey and William E. Thoms, *Law and Economic Regulation in Transportation* (Westport, CT: Quorum Books, 1986), pp. 58–59.

7. Colorado v. United States, 271 U.S. 153, 46 S.Ct. 452 (1926).

8. Ibid.

9. Seaboard Coast Line R.R. Co.—Abandonment between Arcadia and Port Boca Grande, Florida, 360 I.C.C. 257 (1979).

10. 49 U.S.C., sec. 10903 (1992).

11. 49 U.S.C., sec. 10904 (1992).

12. 49 U.S.C., sec. 10905 (1992).

13. 49 U.S.C., sec. 10905(e)(4) (1992).

14. Dempsey and Thoms, *Law and Economic Regulation*, pp. 291–293.

15. 49 U.S.C., sec. 10906 (1990).

16. Dan Cupper, "Rails to Trails: History Underfoot," *Trains*, May 1991, pp. 24–25.

17. Ibid.

18. Preseault v. Interstate Commerce Commission, 494 U.S. 1, 110 S.Ct. 914 (1990).

19. William E. Thoms, "Regulation of Passenger Train Discontinuance," *Journal of Public Law* 22 (1973): 103, 108–131.

20. Ibid., p. 131.

21. Ibid., pp. 131–136.

22. William E. Thoms, *Reprieve for the Iron Horse* (Baton Rouge, LA: Claitor's Pub. Division, 1973), pp. 69–71.

23. 49 U.S.C., sec. 10504 (1992).

24. Edward A. Lewis, *American Shortline Railway Guide*, 3d ed. (Milwaukee, WI: Kalmbach Pub. Co., 1986), p. 2.

25. Ibid., pp. 176–177.

26. Ibid., pp. 2–3.

27. Penn Central, Erie-Lackawanna, Lehigh Valley, Lehigh Hudson River, Reading, and Central New Jersey.

28. Lewis, *American Shortline*, pp. 2–3.

29. 49 U.S.C., sec. 11343 (1990).

30. 49 U.S.C., sec. 11343(a) (1990).

31. Dempsey and Thoms, *Law and Economic Regulation*, p. 219.

32. Ibid., p. 225.

33. Dempsey, *Social and Economic Consequences*, pp. 147–149.

34. Ibid., pp. 158–159.
35. Ibid., pp. 151–152.
36. Ibid., pp. 153–154.
37. Dempsey and Thoms, *Law and Economic Regulation*, pp. 217–225.
38. Ibid., pp. 230–231.
39. Ibid., pp. 232–233.
40. Alaska I Railroad Transportation Act of 1982, Pub. L. No. 97–468, 96 Stat. 225, 45 U.S.C., sec. 1201 (1982).
41. Conrail Privatization Act, Pub. L. No. 99–509, 45 U.S.C., sec. 1301 (1986).
42. Pub. L. No. 93–236, Title IV, 87 Stat. 1070, 45 U.S.C., sec. 701 (1990).
43. Pub. L. No. 94–210, Title VIII, 90 Stat. 125 (1976).
44. Pub. L. No. 95–607, 92 Stat. 3059 (1978).
45. 45 U.S.C., sec. 1101 (1982).
46. *See* 45 U.S.C., sec. 1201 (1982).
47. William E. Thoms, "New Rules for Bankrupt Rails," *Trains*, May 1980, pp. 28–30.
48. Ibid.
49. Ibid.
50. Ibid.
51. Ibid.
52. From Paul S. Dempsey, Robert M. Hardaway, and William Thoms, *Aviation Law and Regulation*, 2 vols. (Austin, TX: Butterworth Legal Publishers, 1993), pp. 17:11–17:12. Reprinted with permission. Published and copyrighted 1993 by Butterworth Legal Publishers, a division of Reed Publishing (USA), Inc.
53. Ibid., p. 17:2.
54. Ibid., p. 17:3.
55. *See* Joseph R. Daughen and Peter Binzen, *The Wreck of the Penn Central* (Boston: Little, Brown, 1971).
56. Penn Central, Erie-Lackawanna, Lehigh Valley, Lehigh Hudson River, Reading, and Central New Jersey.
57. 45 U.S.C., sec. 501 (1990).
58. 45 U.S.C., sec. 701 (1990).
59. To date, the Rock Island has been the largest railroad liquidated in the United States. Portions have been taken over by state governments with short line railroads designated to operate them.
60. 45 U.S.C., sec. 156. *See* McClain, "Bankruptcy Code Section 1113 and the Simple Rejection of Collective Bargaining Agreements: Labor Loser Again," *Georagetwon Law Review* 80 (1991): 191.
61. This section is adapted from William E. Thoms, "Those Directed Service Orders," *Trains*, September 1981 (Copyright 1981 by Kalmbach Publishing Co., reprinted with permission).
62. 49 U.S.C., sec. 11123–11125 (1990).
63. 49 U.S.C., sec. 11123 (1990).
64. 49 U.S.C., sec. 11124 (1990).
65. 49 U.S.C., sec. 11125 (1990).
66. Ibid.

4

Legal Issues Affecting Railroad Employment

RAILROAD RETIREMENT[1]

Railroad employees are the only private-sector employees not covered directly by Social Security, but rather by a separate plan that actually predates Social Security.[2] The system has been changed over the years, and it was restructured by the Railroad Retirement Act of 1974 to place the Railroad Retirement System (RRS) on a sound financial basis. Railroads were the first industry of significant size in which a seniority system of employees encouraged long and continuous service from skilled workers. The promise of pension upon retirement or disability sealed the fate of most railroad workers who literally spend their life working on the railroad.[3]

The Railroad Retirement Trust Fund boasted a surplus of $7.6 billion in 1989. It will be seventy-five years before a possible shortage of funds is foreseeable.[4] Railroad Retirement taxes are currently 21 percent of wages, with 16.9 percent paid by the carriers and 4.1 percent paid by the employees.[5] Railroad Retirement is used today to define the second tier of the Act, which in fact allocates one-quarter of its payments to pay tier-one benefits not covered by Social Security.[6] That equals $500 million and combined with the regular $1.8 billion tier-two payments, the annual cost of tier-two payments is $2.3 billion.[7] This amount is expected to double by 2015, even though the number of beneficiaries is expected to be reduced by 50 percent.[8] This is a problem because the future employment levels are critical to the continued solvency of the system.[9]

The system, despite its $7.6 billion surplus, will be faced with paying a bill of $31 billion in already accrued annuities, and if the railroad industry disappears, no one entitled to annuities will be paid.[10] If the employers would shoulder half of the burden, then they would have to pay a tax rate of 22.1 percent as opposed to the current 16.1 percent [11] If the employees were to shoulder half of the burden, then their taxes would increase from 4.9 percent to 10.9 percent and mean 10 percent less take-home pay.[12] If current beneficiaries were asked to shoulder half of the burden, it would mean a 22 percent reduction in benefits.[13] A workable solution would be to make them share the load, one-third each. However, all attempts to revise the system to that form have been rejected and opposed politically.[14] It appears as though the competition between the railroads and other transportation industries will intensify, and any increase in the payroll taxes will place the railroads at a greater disadvantage because the other industries already pay less for employee pension benefits.[15] The central problem with Railroad Retirement is that Congress has promised benefits that the system may not be able to cover.[16] Their revenue sources are "directly dependent upon the health of the railroad industry, which is mature and is in decline as far as employment is concerned."[17] With Social Security, there are always strong industries, such as computers, to cover declining industries like textiles.[18] Unfortunately, the railroads have no such growth on the horizon and although the second tier of the Railroad Retirement System enjoys a $7.6 billion surplus the future does not look bright.[19]

Title I of the Railroad Retirement Act of 1974 replaces the Act of 1937. The new act provides all retirement and survivor benefits as respects employees with ten or more years of railroad service who retire after December 31, 1974. Section Four of the act states that benefits will be payable to their spouses and survivors. Those benefits will include a Social Security component equivalent to what would be paid under the Social Security Act upon the basis of the employee's combined railroad and nonrailroad service, as well as an additional "staff" component based on the employee's railroad service along with certain cost-of-living adjustments. Most career railroad employees retiring under the new act will receive somewhat more benefits than they would have received under the old formulas.

Title II of the act provides for benefits payable to beneficiaries who retired before January 1, 1975. Their benefits, however, would be adjusted and payable under Title I and cover both past railroad and nonrailroad employment. The only difference is that the "staff" component is paid under the guidelines from the Act of 1937 to preserve the dual benefits some retirees may have been receiving.

The act, therefore, has developed a two-tiered system to pay railroad retirees. The first tier was based on the old system and paid retirees under the guidelines of the Social Security Act for railroad and all other employment. The second tier is new, and it pays for only past railroad employment under the guidelines set out in the Railroad Retirement Act.

The new two-tier model created a relationship between the RRS and the Social Security System (SSS) that had never existed before. There were people who in the past were recovering dual benefits; they will continue to do so if they were collecting those benefits before October 31, 1974. However, from now on, there will be no new railroad retirees collecting dual benefits. The phasing out of dual benefits is hoped to keep the RRS out of bankruptcy. Everyone who retired after December 31, 1974, collects retirement benefits based on this two-tier system. Accordingly, the work that was done outside the railroad will be covered under the Railroad Retirement Act according to Social Security Act guidelines and will not be covered by Social Security itself. If the phasing out of dual benefits did not occur, it was projected that the RRS would have been bankrupt by 1981.

The computation of annuities under the Railroad Retirement Act of 1974 follows according to the two tier model mentioned previously. An employee's regular annuity (monthly benefit payable, on the basis of an employee's compensation, to an employee, spouse, or his survivors either due to retirement or disability) would consist of two parts: a past service Social Security component computed according to Social Security guidelines for both railroad and nonrailroad service minus any actual Social Security the employee was earning; and a future staff component paid strictly on railroad service before January 1, 1975.

The past service component consists of two parts as well. One part would be a computed amount according to the Railroad Retirement Act for all service through December 31, 1974, minus the amount of that same railroad service under Social Security guidelines. The second part is $1.50 for each of the employee's ten years of service before 1975, and $1.00 for each year in excess of ten years before 1975, which would be allowed for all employees who work for the railroad after January 1, 1975.

The future staff benefits would be equal to 0.5 percent of the employee's average monthly compensation after 1974 added to $4 times the amount of service after 1974. This amount, as well as the second part of the past service component, will be subject to cost-of-living adjustments according to the Consumer Price Index from September 30, 1986, to the September 30, in the year preceding when the employee's annuity began to accrue or September 30, 1980, whichever came first. For employees who were collecting annuities before January 1, 1975, they will continue to collect, but under these new guidelines. Each of them received four automatic cost-of-living adjustments, June 1, 1977, June 1, 1978, June 1, 1979, and June 1, 1980.

On top of all this, employees who are entitled to it will continue to receive dual benefits and supplemental annuities ranging from $23 to $43 per month. Spousal and survivor annuities will be adjusted so they have their annuities calculated under the same tier-two model. They will also be allowed to continue to receive dual benefits if they had previously done so. When both spousal and employee annuities are being collected, there will be a combined maximum of $1,200 (per month) or 90 percent of the employee's taxable earnings, whichever is larger. There is also a minimum amount set out by the new act. A combined annuity must never be less than what it would have been on December 31, 1974 under the old act. There is a similar minimum provided for the Social Security portion of the annuity paid to railroad employees under the new act. Most spousal and survivor annuities will increase, but they are at least guaranteed that they will not decrease. Most survivors under the old Act received 110 percent of what they would have made under Social Security. Under the new act, a survivor could make up to 130 percent of what he would have made under Social Security.

The Railroad Retirement Act takes the place of both Social Security and company pensions. It is portable within the railroad industry, so as to enable the railroader to take a vested pension with him from job to job. It is designed to reward persons who have given a life's career to the railroad industry, by singling them out for special retirement treatment.

DRUG TESTING IN THE RAILROAD INDUSTRY[20]

Historical Background

Recognition of alcohol and drug problems began as early as the 1830s, manifesting itself in railroad-adopted programs prohibiting the use and possession of "ardent spirits" on company property. Company-sponsored drug prevention programs, the most common being Rule G,[21] were largely unsuccessful in stopping the drug and alcohol abuse prevalent within the railroad industry at the time.

Original Rule G formulations were directed strictly at curtailing alcohol abuse, but later, as the use of drugs increased in society, the railroads amended their Rule G provisions to extend to the prevention of drug use on the job. For the most part, Rule G regulations were followed by employers and employees alike; however, there was a minority of employees who did not comply with the provisions. A major problem with the implementation of Rule G was its reliance on the subjective view of management and co-workers as to whether or not the employee in question exhibited the characteristics of being under the influence. Supervisors were educated to spot things such as slurred speech, impaired gait and motor functions, blood shot eyes, and the smell of alcohol on the employee. This technique was not always accurate and, more importantly, was often ignored. Also, since Rule G partially relied on a co-worker referral system, which tended to be subjected to the natural unwillingness on the part of these co-workers to report other employees to management, the problem of drug and alcohol abuse persisted. This unwillingness to report other employees is commonly referred to as the "conspiracy of silence." The "conspiracy of silence" doctrine has been viewed as "the single most substantial obstacle to the solution of the alcohol and drug problem."[22] Implementation of Rule G continues on today as one of many programs directed at prevention of drug and alcohol use on the job.

A more recent creation of the railroad industry, designed to cope with the drug and alcohol problem, has been the implementation of employee assistance programs (EAPs). An EAP is more of an employee-centered rehabilitation program than a drug or alcohol prevention program per se. The focus of the EAP is twofold. First, the program aims to elicit compliance with Rule G—provides counseling designed to allow the employee to recognize their problem and rectify their behavior before a Rule G violation occurs. Second, counseling is offered and recommended after a Rule G violation has taken place.

Bypass agreements, a by-product of the increase in power of the unions, became a common method used by by railroad employers to curb the drug and alcohol problem among employees. "Bypass agreements are collective bargaining agreements that encourage employee support of Rule G through substitution of rehabilitation for punishment."[23] Indicative of bypass agreements and other similar programs are that they are implemented only after a Rule G violation has already occurred. Once again reliance is placed on co-workers to refer an employee using drugs or alcohol to counseling and treatment, with the idea that if the employee participates in the program he or she will not be punished. This usually only applies to a first time offender. However, if the employee refuses to join the program, discipline will ensue. A bypass agreement differs from an EAP in two distinct ways. First, a bypass agreement is a program developed out of an agreement between the railroad management and the employee's union allowing for employee input and is more representative of employee concerns than is an EAP which is implemented by the management alone. Second, a bypass agreement promotes rehabilitation rather punishment after a violation has occurred, whereas an EAP will punish as well as rehabilitate the employee following a violation. "These agreements are referred to as 'Rule G bypass agreements' and mark the single most important development in this field since the institution of employee assistance programs in the early 1970's."[24]

The first bypass agreement became effective in November 1980. Overall, the program was considered a success. Numerous referrals were received to the employee assistance program, but surprisingly, most of these referrals were self-referrals rather than co-worker referrals. "This experience suggests that bypass programs may break the 'conspiracy of silence' through the expression of peer concern and resulting self-referrals, rather than co-worker reporting.[25] Although this first attempt was considered a success by the Federal Railroad Administration (FRA), they remain skeptical, stating the test sample used might not be all that accurate because the railroad that implemented the experimental program already had a high level of safety prior to implementation of the program.

Yet another railroad-sponsored program, Operation Red Block,[26] was implemented by the Union Pacific Railroad in April 1984. This program was developed prior to the implementation of federal regulations. Its focus is on informing and educating both supervisors and employees on the deadly effects of alcohol and drug use on the job. Also known as companion agreements, these programs are implemented when an employee is found to be in violation of the rule by a management official. "The employee is disciplined [generally dismissed] but is offered a probationary reinstatement on the condition that the employee first complete counseling or treatment. Like bypass agreements, companion agreements are generally limited to first offenses.[27]

Federal Proposals of 1983

The FRA, aware of, and in response to, the drawbacks of the programs previously described, issued an Advance Notice of Proposed Rulemaking (ANPRM) on June 30, 1983, in an effort to combat the drug and alcohol problem through federal mandates. The goals of the proposed rulemaking were immediate response, national implementation, and uniformity. In addition to the opinions and comments requested from interested parties, the FRA based its ANPRM conclusions upon a previous testing program in which it had participated: the Railroad Employee Assistance Program (REAP).

The FRA, along with representatives from management and railroad labor unions, conducted tests to determine the scope of the alcohol and drug problem on the railroads and the effectiveness of the employee assistance programs. They then outlined potential changes in the program that might be more beneficial. The report noted that a conservative estimate of monetary damage caused as a result of alcohol and drug use by employees on the job was $2 million. Furthermore, "fewer than 4% of the problem drinkers were served by employee assistance programs, and the programs did not include elements directed at the two-thirds of on-the-job drinkers who are not 'problem drinkers.' "[28] The report was critical of the railroads' lack of treatment and uniformity in application of its drug use programs once a violation had been established. Even to the exclusion of the persistent problem of nondetection, the FRA noted that railroads were inconsistent in punishing violators and although employees might initially be terminated for a violation, a substantial number were later recalled; even those dismissals that initially were called final. Furthermore, initial dismissal for noncompliance of the company's alcohol and drug use rules were only "about one in 250."[29]

Federal regulation of the railroads is by no means a new idea. Federal regulation dates back to the 1890s and is premised on the belief that it is mandatory in the interests of safety. Unlike other transportation fields, including the airlines, motor carriers, and commercial marine carriers, already subject to more direct federal regulation, railroads had historically been regulated to a lesser extent. However, railroads, having a direct impact on the communities and states through which they pass, make federal regulation an appropriate instrument to promote uniformity of rules, including rules prohibiting alcohol and drug use by railroad employees on company time.

While still in the promotional stage, the FRA solicited comments and suggestions from railroad management, union representatives, and interested others. Discussion centered on the following alternatives:

Federal Rule G

"Railroad employees involved in safety-sensitive functions would be prohibited from (1) reporting for duty or remaining on duty while under the influence of alcohol or drugs, (2) possessing alcohol or drugs while on duty, or (3) using alcohol or drugs while on duty. In addition, such a rule could specify a period prior to work, such as four or eight hours, during which abstinence would be required."[30]

At the close of discussion, it was settled that a Federal Rule G provision would be repetitive of the current private Rule G provisions already in place. The difference between a Federal Rule G and the private Rule G provisions is the enforcement provisions. The Federal Rule G enforcement would fall on the railroads rather than the individual employees involved. Some of the same problems affecting private initiatives, such as continuation of the conspiracy of silence, would remain a source of conflict. Also, practical considerations, such as an inadequate personnel force to adequately enforce the rule against the railroad, decrease the effectiveness of this sort of federal program.

Mandatory Testing Programs

Random drug testing was discussed but later rejected and not included in the Final Rule issued in 1985. This proposal was met with a wide range of opinion. Various employee organizations were adamantly opposed to the idea of random testing. They claimed that this type of testing program would have the effect of working as an affront to the employee's dignity, but more importantly, random testing would be a deep intrusion into the lives of the employees without requiring the railroad's administration to have reasonable suspicion of misconduct prior to testing. Furthermore, concern over the accuracy of the actual testing procedures and possible consequences of taking the testing out of the realm of collective bargaining, which traditionally governed employee and employer disputes over such testing, was a major factor in its eventual rejection in the Final Rule of 1985.

On the other hand, a random drug testing program would have been a nondiscriminatory manner for enforcing compliance with the railroad's drug and alcohol prohibition rules, thus eliminating complaints of harassment. Also, the tests would have provided results more reliable than the system of visual observations currently relied upon by the railroad. Interestingly enough, these very same concerns and opinions were expressed prior to the Final Rule of 1988, which adopted random testing. During the 1983–1985 discussions, testing was primarily reserved for occasions when reasonable suspicion arose. These occasions arose when a supervisor had a suspicion that an employee was under the influence, or the employee failed his operational tests, or following an accident in which the employee is involved.

Supervisory Observations and Co-Worker Certification

Several of the proposed regulations of the FRA did nothing more than require enforcement by the railroads to the programs they were already privately implementing. Among these programs were random supervisory observations of employees and education of co-workers in techniques to spot signs of drug and alcohol impairment. In actual application of this program, supervisors and responsible employees, such as conductors or engineers, would be required to certify in writing, at the beginning and end of a tour of duty, that to the best of their belief and knowledge no employee was under the influence. The result of these non- or less-activist approaches by the Federal government was to allow each railroad to establish programs complementary to their various operating styles.

Other Possible Approaches

Based on comments and suggestions gathered from the ANPRM in 1983, and again in 1984, the FRA made public a Notice of Proposed Rulemaking (NPRM).

FRA proposes rules to (i) prohibit the use of alcohol and drugs in railroad operations, (ii) require toxicological testing of employees following major accidents and incidents, (iii) require pre-employment drug urine screens for applicants for certain positions, (iv) authorize the railroads to require employees to cooperate in breath and urine tests administered by or for the railroad in certain circumstances that would be deemed to constitute just cause for testing, (v) require the railroads to institute policies that will encourage the identification of employees troubled by alcohol and drug abuse, and (vi) institute improvements in the accident/incident reporting system that will assist in better documenting the extent of alcohol and drug involvement in train accidents. These measures are designed to facilitate the control of alcohol and drug use in railroad operations and thereby prevent accidents, injuries, and property damage.[31]

Final Rule of 1985

By 1985, the year the first Final Rule was announced, the FRA had made several decisions regarding previously mentioned policy options. While reinforcing private implementations of Rule G, the FRA declined to adopt a federal Rule G. Nor did the FRA find it appropriate to employ random testing or impose off-duty restrictions on alcohol consumption. While some areas of the railroad system might be benefited by such a program in general, the need was not present to implement such a program on a comprehensive scale. Nor did the FRA feel that federal mandatory disqualification or licensing requirements were appropriate.

As a method of dealing with the alcohol and drug problem, the FRA developed a three-part program. First, continued cooperation with railroad labor organizations and the railroads in promoting and refining existing voluntary programs was seen as fundamental to the success of prohibition of drug and alcohol use on the railroad system. These voluntary programs educate railroad workers to the extent of the problem and its detrimental effects, not only on the safety of the railroad, but the community as well. Second, the FRA would issue regulations aimed at prohibiting drug use by Hour and Service Employees and impose an obligation on the railroad management to assure compliance with the regulations. Regulation would also require testing of railroad workers both prior to employment as a part of their preemployment physical and after the occurrence of a major accident. Better reporting of accidents involving employees under the influence of drugs or alcohol would also be required.[32]

Final Rule of 1988

Between 1985 and 1988 the FRA realized that changes in society, including an increased use of drugs and decreased effectiveness of detection by visual observation, made it increasingly necessary to employ random drug testing. Furthermore, all programs in existence as of 1988, whether they were those of the railroad or the FRA, had not effectively dealt with the problem, and the public was still at risk. The FRA began to see random testing as the only available and viable alternative not yet being used.

The FRA determined that the confidentiality measures utilized by their random program would eliminate possible constitutional issues, and accuracy of the test results would be guaranteed by following guidelines published by the Department of Health and Human Services (HHS).

While the FRA stated that the risk created by drug and alcohol abuse on the job could no longer be tolerated, the FRA refused to go so far as to say that surveillance could be used during off-duty times. The rule is premised on the idea that since all employees would be on notice of potential for testing at any time, they would thus be deterred from taking drugs off the job as well as on the job.

Supervising evaluations and volunteer-only programs, while having an effect on some individuals, do not on others. Perhaps because of more serious addictions or for other reasons, some just do not respond to these programs and instead go out of their way to further conceal their problems.

It is to these people that the FRA hoped to reach through its random drug testing program.

"The rule allows railroads to develop and submit plans providing for testing at anytime [an] employee is lawfully on duty."[33] Two requirements apply to this rule. First, the employee must be on duty in order to get notice of the testing, and second, the testing must be done within the period of time allowable for the Hours of Service Act. These requirements minimize the possibility of employees excusing themselves from work on the days that they know the test will be given. The goal of random testing is deterrence and detection. For the most part, detection is accomplished by either the voluntary programs already in existence or by the random selection process.

In cases where a test is deemed positive, an employee is subject to discipline as laid out in his or her collective bargaining agreements. The employee may not return to work unless a negative test sample is submitted and a rehabilitation program is completed. Even after returning to work, the employee will be required to complete rehabilitation programs and be periodically tested for a period no longer than sixty months. However, the railroad does not have to retain an employee who has been found in violation of the rule. If an employee refuses to submit to the test, they are then subject to a ninety–day suspension.

The FRA stated that this program would not be applicable to small railroads because it would not be unfeasible or economical to do so. Also, most small railroads don't operate on tracks that pose a hazard to others. Railroads of fifteen covered employees and less were considered to constitute a small railroad and were thus excluded.

Congressional Enactments

In the years after the FRA implemented their alcohol and drug program, Congress made a series of attempts to pass legislation that would have modified the regulations then in place. The proposed new legislation was greatly influenced by the large number of major accidents caused by drug and alcohol use of employees in the transportation industry. The *Exxon Valdez*, spilling hundreds of thousands of gallons of oil into waters surrounding Alaska, and the Conrail accident in Chase, Maryland, were the most famous such incidents. In the direct aftermath of these accidents, Congress moved to get bills such as the Railroad Drug Abuse Prevention Act of 1989 passed.

The stated goals of this legislation were: (1) to cover all safety sensitive employees rather than merely hands-on employees; (2) to apply to all train accidents, not just major ones; (3) to require rehabilitation for first offenders; and (4) to require testing for supervisors.

This bill did not pass when originally submitted because the Senate wanted a program aimed at all modes of transportation, not just railroads.

Since the inclusion of industries such as airlines, motor carriers and marine carriers was not forthcoming, the Senate declined to pass the bill.

The bill finally was the Omnibus Transportation Employee Testing Act of 1991. This bill, often cited here as the Drug Abuse Prevention Act, amended 45 U.S.C. § 431 by adding a new section. This bill was passed largely out of the concern that the FRA regulations weren't as complete or effective as they should be. For instance, the FRA didn't include random alcohol testing, just random drug testing, even though statistics show one in seven employees used alcohol. This bill also provided better constitutional protection.

The legislative history demonstrates Congress' desire to make changes in the FRA's regulations where needed, including expanding the number of drugs for which employees are tested once appropriate testing procedures are developed. There is also a general trend of expanding the realm of whom may be considered a covered employee for the purposes of testing.

While leaving existing regulations intact except as inconsistent with the new statute, the secretary of the Department of Transportation has instructions to require "railroads to conduct pre-employment, reasonable suspicion, random, and post-accident testing of all railroad employees responsible for safety-sensitive functions."[34] The new statute also provides for disqualification or dismissal for a length of time if the employee is found to be impaired by alcohol while on duty, or drugs whether it be on or off duty. Most of the new legislation is concerned with safeguarding privacy on the dependability of tests to ensure that employees' constitutional rights aren't violated. Rehabilitation programs are required for all safety-sensitive employees and encouraged for all railroad employees.

Who is Covered?

All regulations passed by the FRA are applicable to "covered employees." Covered employees are those employees who perform services subject to the Hours of Service Act (45 U.S.C. § 61–64(b)) while on duty. According to the Hours of Service Act, employees deemed to be covered are those employees that are "actually engaged in or connected with the movement of any train, including hostlers."[35] Among those previously considered to be covered were train and engine crews, yard crews, hostlers, train order and block operations, dispatchers, and signalmen.

The FRA, while not specifically mentioning categories of employees, states that its provisions "extend to all employees engaged in functions bearing directly on the safety of rail operations."[36] More recent additions of employees covered by the act include those responsible for inspections of maintenance of railroad track and structures, those who work with rolling stock, those who handle the paperwork for shipment of hazardous materials, on-board service personnel on passenger trains, and others affecting safety. On-board personnel would probably be held to include conductors because they are often the ones in direct charge of other employees during the trip, and they are responsible for making vital safety decisions involving the movement of the train.

With the broad definition supplied by both the FRA and the Hours of Service Act, those covered can be expanded fairly easily at a later date if the need were to arise.

Implementation of Private Railroad Initiatives

While the federal regulations preempt state law dealing with the same subject matter, they do not preempt state criminal laws punishing reckless conduct that results in loss of life or property. Nor do they preempt state laws that do not place an undue burden on interstate commerce and those that involve a local hazard. Unlike the preemption of state laws, the federal regulations specifically advocate that the railroads continue their own voluntary programs and even allow for railroads to increase the scope of the current federal regulations as they apply to the individual railroad.[37]

The underlying rationale for the involvement of the federal government in regulating railroad testing procedures was the view that the voluntary programs employed by the railroads were not sufficient to deal with the alcohol and drug problems. However, taken in conjunction with the federal regulations, volunteer programs are vital to the increased educational awareness of the employees and prohibition of alcohol and drug use on the job.

Implementation of private railroad initiatives often result in litigation based on claims of either violations of an individual's constitutional rights or violations of collective bargaining agreements. Litigation is usually brought with the notion that the addition of drug screening during the periodic physical violated the employee's collective bargaining agreement. Disputes involving collective bargaining agreements are handled procedurally by the Railway Labor Act (RLA). The RLA, which governs labor-management relations for both the airlines and railroads, provides for the orderly settlement of disputes between labor and management to prevent disruptions of transportation and strikes. The RLA classifies disputes as major or minor and, depending on their individual categorization, they are dealt with differently.

A 1989 United States Supreme Court case, *Consolidated Rail v. Railway Labor Executives' Association*, involving an addition of drug testing to the previously required periodic physical exams, which typically only included urine testing for sugar, albumin, and occasionally drugs, is a good example of the delineation between major and minor disputes. If a dispute is classified as major, the RLA requires a lengthy process of mediation and dispute resolution. While this mediation is taking place, the court is in essence freezing the actions of the parties until final resolution of the dispute. The obvious result of a delay of this sort in a situation involving postaccident testing is a loss of evidence—in this case, the decrease of the individual's blood-alcohol level or percentage of controlled substances found in the blood below detectable limits.

On the other hand, when a dispute is classified as minor, the parties are subject to mandatory and binding arbitration either through the National Railroad Adjustment Board or by an adjustment board chosen by the parties. While arbitration is occurring, the court will prevent strikes by labor, and management, being under no obligation to maintain the status quo, may proceed with testing. In other words, in a situation involving post-accident testing, the employer may go ahead and test the employee immediately following the accident over the employee's objections. From the perspective of the employer, the most favorable result would be for a dispute to be deemed minor, and the reverse is true for the employee.

Decisions as to what is or is not a minor dispute are predicated on a finding of whether the proposed change of an agreement goes to only part of an agreement already in existence, or rather, whether it adds a completely new provision to the agreement. If found to go to only part of the agreement between the parties, and is arguably justified, then the parties must submit to arbitration.

Note, for example, the following: In 1984, two railroads—Burlington Northern Railroad Company and Norfolk & Western Railway Corporation—added urinalysis drug screens to their required periodic physical. Previously, these physicals included urinalysis testing, but only for sugar and albumin. The addition to the periodic physical exams was deemed a minor dispute. Based on the past practices of the company to require such testing occasionally, the current use of urine testing during physicals, and the prior implementation of this sort of testing, the court concluded that this was a minor dispute and not a material departure from the agreement of the parties, and thus a matter for decision for the board. All the court must decide is whether it is "arguably justified by the implied terms of its collective-bargaining agreement (i.e., the claim is neither obviously insubstantial or frivolous, nor made in bad faith.)"[39]

Future additions by railroads to the federal scheme of drug and alcohol regulations will be subject to the same scrutiny. Possible areas of contention could arise with addition of employees not subject to the Hours and Service Act, and addition to the type of drugs tested for; that is, other than the five specified in the federal regulations.

In contrast to the result in the Seventh and Eighth Circuit Courts of Appeals cases involving Burlington Northern and Norfolk & Western railroads, a Third Circuit case involving an almost identical drug screening program implemented by Conrail was held to be a major dispute. Periodic medical exams given by Conrail included drug screening only if the doctor had reasonable suspicion of drug use or if the employee had previously been found in violation of the antidrug regulations. The Third Circuit held that the addition of drug screening to employees for whom there was no reasonable suspicion of drug use was a departure "so far from past practices as to change the terms of their agreement,"[40] and hence the court concluded this was a major dispute. The Supreme Court resolved this dispute between the circuits by declaring that the dispute was "minor." The Supreme Court noted that the efforts by Conrail had not been insubstantial in the past, and the expansion of its medical exams to include drug screening without the requirement of prior suspicion of drug use was not an extenuated break from past practice and thus constituted only a minor dispute. In settling the conflict between the circuits, the Supreme Court had in effect authorized the addition of drug screening to periodic physicals in the railway industry.

The more a new drug prevention program is in line with past efforts or can be argued as such, the courts will classify the dispute as minor and allow the implementation of the program while awaiting further review. The courts are more willing today to allow for new and different drug prevention programs to be implemented in the railroad industry than they previously had been.

Constitutional Issues Related to Drug Testing Programs

Although the FRA supports the railroads in their implementation of drug and alcohol testing above and beyond the minimum base level set by the federal government, this does not provide the railroads with protection from claims by employees that such programs are violations of their constitutional rights. The Constitution provides that certain constitutional cases may not be brought against a private party. However, where a showing can be made that the federal government and the private actor have a sufficient nexus of activity between them, then those constitutional issues may be raised against the private actor. This doctrine is referred to as State Action. Government involvement must be shown before constitutional protection, state or federal, can be extended to private employers (railroads).[41]

Once state action has been found, a challenge to the private employer's drug testing program can be made through the search and seizure provision of the Fourth Amendment, self-incrimination under the Fifth Amendment, the due process clause of both the Fifth and Fourteenth amendments, the equal protection clause of the Fourteenth Amendment, and finally, the elusive right of privacy—a right not explicitly stated in the Constitution.

Drug testing, done by either blood or urine tests, has been challenged under the Fourth Amendment's protection against unreasonable searches and seizures.[42] The United States Supreme Court has already classified both blood and urine testing to be searches for the purpose of the Fourtth Amendment. In determination of whether something is or is not an unreasonable search and seizure, two things must be shown: (1) that a search has occurred, and (2) whether that search was unreasonable or not.

Reasonableness is determined by balancing the "nature and quality of the intrusion on the individual's Fourth Amendment interest" to the government's interest that requires such an intrusion.[43] Cases involving searches completed without warrants have been found to satisfy this standard when based on reasonable suspicion or individual suspicion. This result is based on the recognition that evidence would be lost (drop in blood alcohol levels) if a search warrant was required. Hence, application of the Fourth Amendment has been denied even when warrantless searches are employed in the following circumstances: (1) where the industry is a "pervasively regulated industry" and, consequently, an individual's expectations of privacy are lowered; (2) where the government interest is compelling, as it is in railroad safety; and (3) in cases of "special needs," where use of warrant and probable cause searches are just not viable.

The Fifth Amendment self-incrimination clause, applicable any time the government seeks to impose criminal liability on an individual, has been severely limited by the U.S. Supreme Court. The Court has stated on several occasions that there must be a substantial hazard of self-incrimination and evidence taken in the form of a blood test, normally considered physical evidence, is not the type considered protected by the Fifth Amendment; that is, testimony or communicative evidence. The result of these rulings has been to place an almost complete ban against invocation of the Fifth Amendment to prevent imposition of blood or urine testing.

Due process concerns arise in two situations: (1) when there is lack of adequate notice to the employee prior to the test being given, or (2) when an employee has been terminated without a hearing. Challenges to a testing program brought under the due process clause are decided on a case-by-case method. These decisions are based on a very lenient standard of review because of the substantial public purpose toward which the testing provisions are directed. "Program requiring accurate testing methods, chain-of-custody measures, and procedures allowing an employee to contest the results will likely withstand due process challenges."[44]

Few drug test challenges have been brought on the basis of the test being a violation of the individual's right to privacy. The U.S. Supreme Court, based on past decisions, does not feel that the right to privacy is an effective limit on the government's ability to gain personal data on individuals. Furthermore, the Court appears likely to hold that the government interest of safety outweighs the individual right to nondisclosure.

Rule Today

Every year on March 1, the railroad must submit a report to the FRA listing, among other things, the number, type, and result of drug tests given that year pursuant to either FRA regulations or private Rule G provisions. The federal regulations, while only imposing a minimum standard for drug tests, do not preclude the railroads from imposing stricter tests. Compliance with federal regulations is required of all who participate in either the industry or are covered employees. However, railroads are given the majority of the responsibility for ensuring that the rules are followed. "Railroad[s] must exercise due diligence to assure compliance."[45] Employees are also held responsible for compliance to the rules, and their consent is deemed to be provided by their mere participation in the railroad industry. Enforcement of the rules is either by the FRA or the railroads; there is no private right of action.

Prior to any drug testing program, the employees must be informed that the company has begun to implement drug programs. Also, prior to any individual drug test, the employee involved must be given notice not only of the administration of the pending test but also the basis on which the test is to be administered.

While the regulations prohibit any employee from coming to work or remaining at work while intoxicated (level .04 BAC [Blood Alcohol Content] or above), they do not allow for regulation of alcohol consumption of an employee off-duty. This is not true as far as controlled substances are concerned. Since controlled substances are illegal under state laws, in general, the railroad may prohibit their use even while off-duty because of the potential for residual effects hampering the employee's work performance. However, where controlled substances are prescribed by a medical officer, with knowledge of the nature of employee's duties at work and with a reasonable good faith belief that medication will not adversely affect the employee while on duty, the employee may be permitted to work. Drugs tested for include: marijuana, narcotics, stimulants, depressants, and hallucinogens.

Where a test result comes back positive, the employee must be removed from covered service and given notice of such removal. The employee may request a postsuspension hearing. Despite testing positive, employees can be eligible to return to work after being evaluated by an EAP counselor and after having completed a rehabilitation program, when an EAP counselor finds the employee fit to return to work. The employee must test negative for drugs prior to returning to work and will be subject to followup testing and further rehabilitation efforts. If, on the other hand, the employee refuses to take a drug test when instructed to, the employee will be subject to a nine-month disqualification period. The railroad is free to impose harsher sanctions, but the employee can request and must be granted a postsuspension hearing.

The regulations delineate the various incidents in which postaccident testing is appropriate. These are as follows:

1. Major train accident: A major train accident is considered one in which a fatality occurs, or a hazardous material spill occurs resulting in either $50,000 damage to property, reportable injury, or evacuation

2. Impact accident: An impact accident occurs where there is $50,000 worth of property damage to railroad property or a reportable injury

3. Fatal train accident: A fatal train accident occurs where an injury resulting in death occurs to an on-duty railroad employee, and

4 Passenger train accident: Any accident involving a passenger train qualifies as a passenger train accident.

However, accidents involving grade crossings do not become subject to testing unless there is independent reason to believe that drugs or alcohol were involved. For any of these types of accidents, the railroad officials at the scene of the accident are required to make a good faith determination as to whether a test is required for the accident in question based on the above stated criteria. Once it is determined that testing is required, each employee assigned to the crew of any train involved in an accident must be tested. Testing is to be done at any independent medical facility with a medical review officer present and done according to very explicit guidelines.

Railroads are given authorization to test for reasonable cause, which is determined by visual observations of the supervisory staff. Reasonable cause can be found when reasonable suspicion exists (1) after a train accident, (2) an incident has occurred, or (3) following procedural violations. If the test is not implemented within eight hours of a finding of reasonable cause, the railroad is barred from administering the test.

Preemployment drug screens may be used for all persons applying for a position involving covered service. These tests should be given in connection with the preemployment medical exam where feasible.

The federal regulations authorize the implementation of random drug testing. Any program involving random drug testing must utilize objective, neutral criteria. In other words, each employee has a "substantial equal statistical chance of being selected within a specified time frame."[46]

Employees are subject to random testing only during the time while the employee is at work. Notice need only be given after the employee reports for duty and then only "so far in advance as is reasonably necessary to ensure the employee's presence at the time and place set for testing."[47] Testing must occur during the employee's regular work day, and he/she may not be held overtime to complete testing. Random testing is done for the following drugs: marijuana, cocaine, PCP, opiates, and amphetamines.

Finally, the regulations require that the railroad provide programs to facilitate the identification of troubled employees, to provide opportunity for counseling, and to foster employee participation. Basically, all that is required is a continuation of the already existing programs implemented by the railroads themselves.

Advances in the area of drug and alcohol abuse have been extensive in the railroad industry. However, room for further expansion has not been precluded and in fact is mentioned with approval in both the new congressional enactment and the FRA regulations. Collective agreements, as well as constitutional considerations, will impose the greatest obstacles on expansion of testing in the future.

LICENSING OF LOCOMOTIVE ENGINEERS

The railroad engineman, the eagle-eyed driver of the iron horse, remained an unlicensed professional during the first century and a half of railroading. Although there were apprenticeship programs worked out with the unions, generally engineers were promoted from the ranks of firemen.[48] As the diesel locomotive came into general use, the fireman, who tended no fires, was eventually phased out. Many railroads rely on locomotive simulators for training new engine-cab employees. Despite the trend for regulation of professions charged with public safety, including licensing of pilots by the FAA and certification of mariners by the Coast Guard, the engineer, who does all his work on private property, was considered to be a private citizen whose qualifications were set by the employing railroad. In short, a railroad engineer was a person who had convinced a railroad to hire him or her as an engineer.

Few careers carry as much responsibility as that of a passenger engineer. A fullyloaded mtrak train may carry upward of 400 riders; despite the best efforts, it takes over a mile to stop a train traveling at full track speed. Nonetheless, impairment of engineers was treated as a company matter; being drunk at the throttle was something like being inebriated in the office; you could lose your job, but you wouldn't go to jail for it.

All this has changed with licensing of engineers by the Federal Railroad Administration, an agency of the Department of Transportation.[49] On June 22, 1988, President Reagan signed into law the Rail Safety Improvement Act of 1988, which provided that the Department of Transportation can fine individuals for willful violations, and may even, after notice and opportunity for hearing, bar individual workers from performing safety-sensitive duties.[50] A rule establishing minimum qualifications for engineers was issued by the FRA on June 19, 1991, and became effective on September 17 of that year. It requires railroads to have a process for evaluating prospective operators of locomotives and determining that they are competent before they can drive an engine.[51]

Passage of the Rail Safety Improvement Act came as a surprise to the railroad industry. The previous three Congresses had failed to approve bills calling for little more than funding authority for ongoing railroad safety projects. It was generally thought that the disastrous Amtrak-Conrail wreck at Chase, Maryland, in 1987 , in which Conrail engineer Ricky Gates was found to be operating his engine under the influence of drugs, had a part in the passage of the tougher rules for railroaders.

Actual licensure still remains in the hands of the employing carrier. Each railroad must have a certification program that includes: (1) a procedure for qualifying engineers, (2) a designation of the classes of service that will be used, (3) a procedure for evaluating the prospective engineer's past safety record, (4) tests for sight and hearing. (5) a training program, (6) a procedure for knowledge testing, (7) skill testing, and (8) a procedure for monitoring operational performance.[52]

Each railroad had to submit its procedures and standards to the FRA by November 15, 1991. The FRA certifies the programs that meet its standards. There are three classes of service: train service engineers, locomotive servicing engineers (hostlers), and student engineers.[53] The effect of these regulations is to place engineers in a similar position to other transportation employees with regard to occupational licensing. The principal difference is that the railroads, not a government agency, do the certification.

THE FEDERAL EMPLOYERS LIABILITY ACT

An injured railwayman cannot look to state worker compensation plans for maintenance during his disability. Instead, his remedy is a tort action under the Federal Employers' Liability Act (FELA).[54] Recovery for injuries to railroad workers under FELA is limited to actions for on-the-job injuries. The railroad industry is unique in requiring a lawsuit or settlement before workers are compensated for their work-related injuries.

Originally passed in 1908, FELA was considered a model statute for its time.[55] New York had yet to pass the first state workmen's compensation law, and the general constitutionality of worker's compensation was not established until 1917.[56] FELA has evolved into a fault-based compensation system that provides the exclusive remedy for railroaders injured while engaged in interstate commerce.[57] FELA departs from traditional tort-based remedies in that it does away with both the fellow-servant rule and the doctrine of assumption of risk, and replaces the common law principle of contributory negligence with of a rule of comparative negligence.[58]

Although a fault-based system, FELA departs from the fault principle inasmuch as if employer negligence played any part, no matter how small, in producing the injury, the case must go to a jury.[59] Recoverable damages include lost wages, medical expenses, estimated future earnings, and payment for pain and suffering.[60] These are questions for a jury and are rarely set aside for excessiveness.[61]

There is no "cap" or upper limit on damages recoupable by a FELA action. However, between 1979 and 1987, between 19 percent and 33 percent of FELA cases that went to trial ended with a defense verdict, where the employee got nothing.[62] Of course, most FELA cases are settled without a trial. The railroad plaintiff's bar handles most FELA cases on a contingency basis similar to most personal injury suits (with one-third of the judgment a common basis), and the act and its jurisprudence have given rise to firms, expert in railroad tort law, who specialize in FELA suits. Nonetheless, recoveries are still capricious and unpredictable.[63]

Supporters of FELA are mostly of the "if it ain't broke, don't fix it" camp. They contend that the FELA encourages safety in an inherently hazardous industry, that state workers' compensation systems are overburdened and do not fully compensate employees for their injuries, that 85 percent of railroad employee injury claims are settled without the necessity for the injured worker to hire a lawyer, and that abolition of FELA will have but a small effect on the caseload of federal courts.[64]

Proponents of tort law reform on the railroads cite the high transaction costs of FELA actions (both the contingency fee paid to plaintiff's counsel and the defense costs incurred by the carriers, and the unacceptable zero outcomes of a defense verdict). Because the statute requires the injured party to charge railroad fault in the accident, labor unions often tell their members to say as little as possible about the cause of an accident except that "the extent of the carrier's fault is undetermined at this time."[65] Rail management cites increased FELA transaction costs (and the occasional high-priced award) as a factor placing them in an unfavorable position vis-á-vis their highway, water, and air transportation competition. Rail management currently favors repeal of FELA in favor of a less costly compensation system. The inadequacy of state workers' compensation systems could be avoided by creating a no-fault compensation system with more generous standards, applicable to railroad employees currently covered by FELA.[66]

In 1993 the Third Circuit U.S. Court of Appeals declared that wholly emotional injuries stemming from job-related stress are compensable under FELA. A Conrail dispatcher in Philadelphia alleged that, by requiring him to work under unreasonably stressful conditions, the railroad breached its duty to provide a safe workplace. The court agreed, saying that a train dispatcher's duties carried such pressure that insomnia, fatigue, and depression were predictable outcomes. The railroad knew about the unhealthy environment but did nothing to improve the situation, and thus was held liable. This case was the first in which FELA was held to compensate for totally psychological injuries.[67]

Rail unions and the plaintiff's bar support retention of the existing FELA system, and Congress has several times considered proposals for reform. Until such reforms are enacted, however, the federal district courts will be the exclusive remedy for suits by injured railroaders against their employers.[68]

NOTES

1. The authors thank Michael Paul, Esq., for his work in researching this section.

2. Frank Wilner, ["The Railroad Retirement System: Its Past, Present, and Future," *Transportation Practitioners Journal* 56 (1989): 218

3. Ibid., p. 220

4. Ibid., p. 219

5. David M. Cawthorne, "Board Finds Rail Retirement Fund Sound, But Says Changes in Financing Needed," *Traffic World*, September 17, 1990, p. 19.

6. Wilner, "Railroad Retirement," p. 249.

7. Ibid.

8. Ibid.

9. Ibid., p. 253

10. Ibid.

11. Ibid.

12. Ibid.

13. Ibid.

14. Ibid., p. 254.

15. Ibid.

16. Ibid., p. 252.

17. Ibid.

18. Ibid.

19. Ibid.

20. This section was written by Patricia Ibister, law student at the University of North Dakota, under a stipend provided by the Burtness Trust.

21. Rule G is the Association of American Railroads' Standard Code of Operating Rules prohibition against employee drug use and reads: "The use of alcoholic beverages or narcotics by employees subject to duty is prohibited. Being under the influence of alcoholic beverages or narcotics while on duty, or their possession while on duty, is prohibited." George E. Warner, "The Ratification of the 'Special Needs' Analysis to Employer Substance Abuse Testing: Skinner v. Railway Labor Executives' Association, 109 S.Ct. 1402," *Hamline Law Review* 13 (1990): 167, 170; citing 48 Fed. Reg. 30724, 30732 (1983) (Advanced Notice of Proposed Rulemaking).

22. 48 Fed. Reg. 30723 (1983) (Advanced Notice of Proposed Rulemaking).

23. Haberberger, "Reasonable Searches Absent Individualized Suspicion: Is There a Drug-Testing Exception to the Fourth Amendment Warrant Requirement After Skinner v. Railway Labor Executives' Association," *University of Hawaii Law Review* 12 (1990): 343, 351–352.

24. 48 Fed. Reg. 30723 (1993) (Advanced Notice of Proposed Rulemaking).

25. Ibid.

26. 49 Fed. Reg. 24252 (1984) (Advanced Notice of Proposed Rulemaking).

27. Ibid.

28. 48. Fed. Reg. 30723 (1983) (Advanced Notice of Proposed Rulemaking).

29. Ibid.

30. Ibid.

31. 49 Fed. Reg. 24252 (1984) (Advanced Notice of Proposed Rulemaking).

32. The FRA's final rule prohibits on-the-job use, possession, or impairment by alcohol or any controlled substance, mandates postaccident toxicological testing after certain serious accidents and incidents, authorizes railroads to require breath and urine tests on reasonable cause, requires railroads to adopt policies to aid in the indentification of troubled employees, provides for preemployment drug screens, and requires more complete reporting of alcohol and drug involvement in train accidents. FRA also issues miscellaneous amendments necessary to implement the new regulatory program. 50 Fed. Reg. 31508 (1985) (Final Rule).

33. 53 Fed. Reg. 47102, 47112 (1988) (Final Rule).

34. 45 U.S.C., sec. 431(r)(1)(A) (1992).

35. 45 U.S.C., sec. 61(b)(2) (1992).

36. 53 Fed. Reg. 47107 (1988) (Final Rule).

37. This part prescribes minimum federal safety standards for control of alcohol and drug use. "This part does not restrict a railroad from adopting and enforcing additional or more stringent requirements not inconsistent with this part," 49 C.F.R., sec. 219.1(b) (1991).

38. 491 U.S. 299, 109 S.Ct. 2477 (1989).

39. Ibid., 491 U.S. at 310.

40. Consolidated Rail v. Railway Labor Executives' Association, 109 S.Ct. 2477 (1989). Betty J. Christian and Janice Barber, "Employee Drug Testing in the Transportation Industry: Private Initiatives and Government Imperatives," *George Mason University Law Review* 12 (1990): 561, 566.

41. Factors taken into consideration are "whether the activity of the government and the private actor are so intertwined for their mutual benefit that the private actor should be subjected to constitutional limitations," Burton v. Wilmington Parking Authority, 365 U.S. 715, 81 S.Ct. 856 (1961); "appearance of government approval, past and present aid given by the government, and the public nature of the facilities," Evans v. Newton, 382 U.S. 296, 86 S.Ct. 486 (1966); "(1) whether the income of the private employer is derived from government funding, (2) whether regulation of the employer is extensive and detailed, (3) whether the services provided by the private employer are traditionally the exclusive prerogative of the government, and (4) whether the relationship between the private employer and the government can be characterized as symbiotic," Rendell Baker v. Kohn, 457 U.S. 830, 102 S.Ct. (1982), cited from Haberberger, "Reasonable Searches," p. 356.

42. Skinner v. Railroad Labor Executives' Association, 489 U.S. 602, 618 (1989). Blood testing involves extracting body fluids by penetration of the body, while urine is the intrusion into a bodily activity otherwise held to be private, consequently both are searches. 49 Fed. Reg. 24252 (1984) (Advanced Notice of Proposed Rulemaking).

43. Haberberger, "Reasonable Searches," p. 343.

44. Ibid., p. 366.

45. 49 C.F.R., sec. 219.05 (1991).

46. 49 C.F.R., sec. 219.601 (1991).

47. 49 C.F.R., sec. 219.601(41) (1991).

48. William E. Thoms, "The Vanishing Fireman," *Loyola Law Review* 14 (1967): 125.

49. Gerri Hall, "Rail Safety Improvement Act of 1988: Wrought from the Wreckage of Chase," *Federal Bar News and Journal* 36 (1989): 87.

50. Ibid.

51. Ibid.

52. Qualification for Locomotive Engineers, 49 C.F.R., sec. 240 (1991).

53. 49 C.F.R., sec. 240.107 (1991). *See also* 49 C.F.R., sec. 240.223 (1991).

54. Rule C. No. 60–100, 35 Stat. 65 (1908) (codified as amended at 45 U.S.C., sec. 51–60 (1988).

55. Thomas E. Baker, "Why Congress Should Repeal the Federal Employers' Liability Act of 1908," *Harvard Journal on Legislation* 29 (1992): 79, 80.

56. Ibid.

57. New York Central R.R. v. Winfield, 244 U.S. 147, 37 S.Ct. 546 (1917).

58. Baker, "Why Congress," p. 82.

59. Rogers v. Missouri Pacific R.R., 352 U.S. 500, 77 S.Ct. 443 (1957).

60. Baker, "Why Congress," p. 84.

61. Ibid.

62. Ibid., p. 100.

63. Arnold I. Havens and Anthony A. Anderson, "The Federal Employers' Liability Act: A Compensation System in Urgent Need of Reform," *Federal Bar News and Journal* 34 (1987): 310, 313.

64. Baker, "Why Congress," p. 87 (citing Steven G. Gallagher, Counsel Federal Courts Study Committee).

65 .J. H. Blount and J. E. Dvorak III, *Justice for the Injured Railroad Worker (And How to Achieve It)* (Griffith, IN: Justice Publishing Co., 1987), p. 3.

66. Baker, "Why Congress," pp. 116–119.

67. Consolidated Rail Corp. v. Gotshall, 62 L. W. 4609, 114 S.Ct. 2396 (1994).

68. For a recent comprehensive review of the Federal Employers' Liability Act, *see* Transportation Research Board, *Compensating Injured Railroad Worlers Under the Federal Employers' Liability Act* (Washington, D.C.: National Academy Press, 1994).

5

Labor Protection on the Railroads[1]

Labor protection arrangements in the railroad industry were a lingering souvenir of the short-lived nationalization of the rails during World War I.[2] The Transportation Act of 1920 called upon the Interstate Commerce Commission (ICC) to create a plan for consolidation of the nation's railroads into a limited number of systems.[3] The ICC, however, feared the resulting effect on rail employment of closing switch yards and terminals. Gradually, the ICC backed away from the Transportation Act's consolidation mandate and in 1934 began to attach labor protection conditions to those mergers that it approved.[4]

In 1936, faced with the reality of ICC-mandated labor protection, railroad management met with its unions to forge the Washington Job Protection Agreement. The Washington Agreement became the basis of most modern labor protection arrangements in railroad consolidations. The essential provisions of the Washington Agreement included compensation for dismissed employees, allowances for those displaced from higher positions, and payment of moving expenses entailed in taking jobs in new locations.[5] Eighty-five percent of the nation's railroads eventually signed this agreement.[6] Although the railroads would have preferred not to address labor protection conditions at all (since the burden of compensating the laid-off workers rests with the carriers), both they and their unions decided to work out an agreement themselves rather than have one imposed upon them by the ICC.

As evidenced by the Washington Agreement, labor and management, working together, were able to establish labor protection provisions on their own. Until 1939, however, a question remained as to the ICC's authority to impose labor protection conditions under its mandate, which required consideration of the public interest in mergers. This issue was resolved in *United States v. Lowden*,[7] when the Supreme Court held that the ICC could require labor protection along the lines of the Washington Agreement without specific statutory authority.[8] Following this decision, the ICC began to impose conditions modeled. after the Washington Agreement.

JOB PROTECTION MANDATED BY THE ICC

When Congress considered the Transportation Act of 1940,[9] its major concerns were depression and unemployment.[10] Consolidation plans then before the ICC would possibly affect 200,000 to 400,000 railway jobs, most of which were held by men between the ages of 45 and 60, whose chances of reemployment were slim.[11] The Transportation Act therefore imposed a statutory obligation on the ICC to provide labor protection in merger cases. The Interstate Commerce Act[12] was amended to provide that in the case of a railroad merger, all employees of such railroads must be placed in no worse position in relation to their employment after the merger had taken place.[13] In addition, this protection was to be afforded to such employees for a minimum of four years from the effective date of the final action by the ICC. Thereafter, measures were taken to prevent railroad mergers from aggravating another economic recession.

The ICC mandated additional standards for employee protection in a series of railroad merger cases. The leading case arose from the 1952 consolidation of the passenger stations in New Orleans, and as a result, these requirements became known as the "New Orleans Conditions." In the *New Orleans Union Passenger Terminal Case*,[13] the ICC had to decide what job protection should be afforded railroad workers affected by railroad mergers.[14] The ICC determined that railroad workers should be afforded the protection set forth in the Washington Agreement, which granted railroad employees a payment from the railroad for the decrease in income arising from a job change caused by a railroad merger.[15] The Washington Agreement also provided for the reimbursement of moving expenses, loss suffered in the sale of a home, and a provision prescribing rates for displaced employees.[16]

The ICC in *New Orleans*, however, placed two limitations on the Washington Agreement. The first limitation was that employee benefits should be reduced to the extent the employee received compensation from other employment or unemployment insurance.[17] The second limitation on the Washington Agreement required employees adversely affected by a consolidation prior to May 17, 1952 (four years from the date of the ICC's order approving the New Orleans Union Passenger Terminal Merger) to receive as a minimum the major protections afforded by the Oklahoma conditions. The Oklahoma conditions differed from the Washington Agreement in that: (1) employees received 100 percent protection under the Oklahoma conditions whereas under the Washington Agreement, the amount of payment was contingent upon years of service, and (2) the Oklahoma conditions went into effect on the date of the commission's order and continued for four years, whereas the payments under the Washington Agreement went into effect from the date of the adverse effect and continued for a maximum of five years.[18] If the total amount received under the Oklahoma conditions was less than those provided by the Washington conditions, however, the employee received compensation according to the Washington Agreement. Therefore, the *New Orleans* conditions judicially enacted many economic protections for employees affected by mergers.

During the 1960s, many railroads, often long-time competitors, decided to merge. Some of their reasons included: (1) the economics of scale resulting from a larger system, (2) the economics of running long freight trains over long distances in the diesel age, (3) the elimination of duplicate facilities, and (4) an attempt to compete with the trucking industry. Assuming that the ICC would require labor protection in mergers, many of the post-1960 consolidations included voluntary labor protection agreements arranged by the carriers and the brotherhoods. This sort of agreement was viewed by rail management as insurance for withdrawal of labor's opposition to the merger before the ICC and the courts. For example, in the Norfolk & Western, Penn Central, and Burlington Northern mergers, the carriers voluntarily agreed to reduce jobs only by attrition,[19] which in effect guaranteed some employees lifetime jobs.

THE RAIL PASSENGER SERVICE ACT OF 1970

The promised savings from the great railroad mergers of the 1960s failed to materialize. Many of the newly merged railroads later filed for reorganization in bankruptcy court. By the end of the decade, most railroads were engaged in mass cost-cutting efforts. The labor-intensive passenger train became a scapegoat for the rails' woes. Air competition and the completion of the interstate highway system boded ill for private operation of passenger trains.[20] In response to the flood of petitions that were filed to discontinue passenger train transportation, the ICC threatened to approve the end of all intercity rail passenger service.[21] Under the threat of a national transportation crisis, Congress passed, and President Nixon signed, the Rail Passenger Service Act of 1970.[22] This act established the National Railroad Passenger Corporation (Amtrak) to take over the operation of the nation's intercity passenger trains.[23] The act also directed those railroads that were being relieved of their passenger burden to provide labor protection to their furloughed passenger trainmen.[24]

The railroads and their unions were unable to agree upon a voluntary labor protection plan under the Rail Passenger Service Act.[25] Perhaps this impasse was due to the fact that the issues were too big, or perhaps each side felt that it might benefit from a government-imposed settlement. In any event, the secretary of labor, as authorized under the act, determined the extent of the labor protection provisions that were then to be made part of any contract between Amtrak and the participating railroads.[26]

The labor protection provisions imposed by the secretary of labor were based upon the Washington Agreement, although greatly expanded. For example, the burden of proof was shifted from the worker to the railroad to prove that the assumption of passenger service by Amtrak was not the cause of the employee's misfortune.[27] Moreover, instead of four years of labor protection, the period was increased to six, its base date being the time of employment displacement.[28] A displaced worker was also given the option of taking a lump-sum settlement in lieu of a monthly dismissal allowance. In addition, moving benefits were further expanded, and in no case could the benefits be less than those provided under the Interstate Commerce Act.[29] Although this protection was offered to employees of the railroads involved with the Amtrak takeover, Amtrak itself was responsible for labor protection of its own employees.[30]

The Rail Passenger Service Act dealt only with Amtrak's assumption of rail passenger service and the private railroads' discontinuance of passenger trains. The ICC has, however, applied the employment protection provisions provided for in the Rail Passenger Service Act of 1970 along with the New Orleans conditions to subsequent mergers.[31] For instance, in *New York Dock Railway v. United States*, the New Orleans conditions as well as the Railroad Passenger Service Act were applied to the merger of two small Class III terminal railways in New York City.[32] The Second Circuit expanded the provisions under the Rail Passenger Service Act of 1970 to include the Appendix C-1 provisions, but denied any double recovery or pyramiding of benefits.[33] The provisions set forth by the Second Circuit thus became known as the *New York Dock* conditions and were significantly more protective of railway labor interests than any previously imposed single set of conditions.[34]

THE REGIONAL RAIL REORGANIZATION ACT OF 1973

When the Penn Central merger lost its luster, the railroad filed for bankruptcy, taking six other connecting Eastern railroads with it. Relief from passenger losses was not enough, and in 1976 Conrail emerged as the government-sponsored major freight carrier in the Northeast. Section III of the Regional Rail Reorganization Act of 1973 (Reorganization Act) brought Conrail into being.[35] The Consolidated Rail Corporation (Conrail) was designated to be a private company, incorporated under the laws of the state of Pennsylvania, rather than as a federal agency.[36] The Reorganization Act authorized Conrail to, among other things, acquire rail properties and operate rail service over such properties.[37] The act was necessitated by the bankruptcies of seven eastern railroads, caused by deferred maintenance, truck competition, and heavy debt load due to merger and acquisition costs.[38] Subchapter V authorized $250 million for labor protection, reimbursing Conrail and its predecessors for displacement allowances, and job protection payments made pursuant to the same subchapter.[39]

Subchapter V, the most expensive labor protection provision in U.S. history, was designed to curry labor's support for the creation of Conrail to incorporate and replace the seven bankrupt railroads in the Northeast. It extended to all employees of Conrail and its predecessors the labor protection already enjoyed by most employees of the Penn Central and Erie Lackawanna Railroads under their own merger agreements.[40] This meant that employees of other bankrupt eastern lines (Central of New Jersey, Reading, Pennsylvania–Reading Seashore Lines, Lehigh & Hudson River, and Lehigh Valley) would either receive Conrail jobs or receive equivalent labor protection to that received by Penn Central and Erie Lackawanna railroaders. Subchapter V provided all Conrail employees with five years seniority with the predecessor railroads job protection until age 65.[41] This protection included a monthly displacement allowance equal to the average 1974 monthly salary, increased to reflect general wage hikes; a severance benefit of up to $20,000 in lieu of continued employment; and certain fringe and relocation benefits.[42]

Where was the money to come from? The Conrail law contained appropriations to pay for the initial burst of job protection claims, but that money soon was all spent. The Staggers Act of 1980 appropriated an additional $235 million for subchapter V benefits, but made it clear that after that money was gone, Conrail would have to fund the benefits from its own revenues.[43] During the first five years of Conrail's existence, it was a significant drain on the federal treasury, depending upon annual bailouts of hundreds of millions of dollars. Conrail, however, did become profitable in the 1980s[44] and was returned to the private sector.

The benefits sounded generous, but in theory, the expense for labor protection would be short term and limited for Conrail. Older trainmen would bump those with less than five years of service, and those displaced workers would not be eligible for any benefits. Employees might quit and enter another line of work or move away from the railroad. However, by doing so, they would no longer be eligible for displacement allowances. What Congress did not foresee was the decline in Conrail's traffic to the point where the normal attrition process would not work fast enough to reduce labor protection costs. If Conrail were to bear the labor protection costs itself, it would not pay Conrail to cut the work force, since the employees would still be paid the same amount to not work.

SPECIAL LABOR PROTECTION STATUTES

The tide in favor of railroad employee benefits began to turn against furloughed workers with the liquidation of the Chicago, Rock Island &

Pacific Railroad (Rock Island Line) and the reorganization of the Chicago, Milwaukee, St. Paul & Pacific Railroad (the Milwaukee Road), two large midwestern lines.[45] Congress responded with two restructuring laws, including labor protection terms less generous than the ICC would have given to former employees of both lines.

The Milwaukee Railroad Restructuring Act[46] provided that former employees of the Milwaukee were entitled to 80 percent of straight-time salary for up to three years or a lump-sum payment not to exceed $25,000.[47] Similar labor protection provisions for Rock Island employees were called for in the Rock Island Railroad Transition and Employee Assistance Act of 1980 (RITA).[48] Apparently, a Conrail solution was considered to be too expensive, and Congress did not wish another expensive bailout for railroads.

While the Milwaukee was restructured (and eventually sold to the Soo Line, albeit with over two-thirds of its trackage abandoned), the Rock Island was liquidated with its tracks either torn up or sold to other railroads. The Rock Island reorganization court refused to implement the labor protection provisions of RITA.[49] The bankruptcy court reasoned that claims for such protection would become senior against the estate of the Rock Island.[50] Since a trustee in bankruptcy is supposed to preserve the railroad's estate for the benefit of creditors, the court concluded that imposing labor protection liens would amount to an unconstitutional taking of the creditors' property. The bankruptcy court's decision was upheld on appeal by the United States Supreme Court.[51]

THE NORTHEAST RAIL SERVICES ACT OF 1981

In 1981 President Reagan vowed to cut domestic spending, including transportation subsidies. Office of Management and Budget Director David Stockman was insisting that the President eliminate all funding for both Conrail and Amtrak. Labor protection provisions, which seemed merely humane during the Carter years, seemed like a raid on the treasury to the new administration and a Republican senate. Rail labor's strength was ebbing and the brotherhoods were unable to match the collective bargaining gains of workers in some nontransportation industries.[52] The relative political strength of labor had diminished as unions now represented a mere 17 percent of the industrial work force.[53] In addition, the economic strength of railway unions had diminished, due in part to the decline of their industry. Also, the mood in Congress had changed. Lifetime protection could not be expected by railroad employees since most laid-off workers in other industries had only unemployment compensation funds for security. Labor protection had never been a broad statutory guarantee, but rather had been pieced together for the benefit of employees affected by a particular merger or governmental program (such as Amtrak).

The immediate concern of Congress in 1981 was to stem the flow of red ink resulting from Northeast Corridor (Boston/Washington) operations by Conrail. Conrail was losing a great deal of money operating commuter trains, and the loss was being made up by the taxpayer. Furthermore, the Reagan administration wanted Conrail sold to the private sector. Conrail was the landlord of the Northeast Corridor, and Amtrak was the tenant on the busiest stretch of railroading in North America. Thus, Conrail, a freight railroad, found itself running a multitrack electrified railroad used mostly by Amtrak and commuter passenger trains. Transferring this passenger-oriented electric railroad to Amtrak, it was assumed, would bolster Conrail's financial health. As part of the effort to make Conrail profitable for eventual sale to the private sector, Conrail was excused from the passenger business beginning in 1982; its suburban trains were to be transferred to Amtrak or to commuter authorities.[54]

Amtrak, which was established to run passenger trains, employed no engineers or conductors as late as 1981. Amtrak relied on contracting railroads to provide employees on a cost-plus basis for Amtrak trains. Amtrak would then pay the railroads their costs plus a small profit. In addition, Conrail had been established to run freight trains, but it owned much of the track where Amtrak ran. Even in the Northeast Corridor, when ownership of the tracks was transferred from Conrail to Amtrak,[55] Conrail employees were still used on Amtrak passenger and commuter trains operated by local transit authorities.

The Northeast Rail Services Act (NERSA),[56] part of the Budget Reconciliation Act of 1981,[57] provided for direct Amtrak operation of intercity trains with its own employees rather than those of Conrail or other freight railroads.[58] NERSA also authorized Amtrak to establish a subsidiary called "Amtrak Commuter" that would operate the suburban trains formerly operated by Conrail.[59] Amtrak Commuter, however, never came into existence; the states preferred to operate their own commuter trains.[60]

When NERSA provided for the elimination of Northeast Corridor passenger trains from Conrail's responsibility, Conrail was relieved of many of its labor protection costs,[61] for with such an albatross around its neck, no one would buy the government-owned carrier.

Along with this restructuring, NERSA directed the secretary of labor to devise a new labor protection provision that would provide termination allowances not to exceed $25,000 per employee.[62] Either an employee would be offered a permanent position with Conrail or the railroader would receive a separation allowance of up to $25,000 to help him or her get a new start elsewhere.

NERSA also specified the manner by which Conrail could eliminate certain fireman and brakeman positions.[63] The government was to pay for lump-sum severance payments made by Conrail to employees who accepted termination, up to a maximum of $25,000. These benefits, however, were limited to $215 million for fiscal year 1982 and $185 million for fiscal year 1983.[64] Furthermore, NERSA mandated the establishment of a central hiring roster consisting of former Conrail, Milwaukee, and Rock Island employees for preferential hiring by other railroads.[65] The new law also relieved Amtrak of many labor protection costs arising from Title V of the Conrail law.[66]

Government provisions for labor protection were the result of a long history of federal involvement in railroad labor policy, ICC policies encouraging rail consolidation, and congressional concern about unemployment and politically savvy rail unions.[67] In addition, the specter of a rapidly increasing number of unemployed middle-aged men concentrated in former railroad communities, unable to find work elsewhere, has probably continued to haunt Congress.

It is clear, however, that what Congress gives, Congress may take away. If a congressional statute gave lifetime job protection to rail employees, it is apparent that Congress may modify or eliminate such protection by statute. Congress is also no longer as fearful of the political power of rail unions as it once was. Organized labor now contains less than 15 percent of the work force and enjoys limited support outside its ranks.[68] The public sentiment appears to regard some railroaders, unfairly though it may be, as holding sinecures, and public perceptions are often the basis for legislative policy. The labor protections of NERSA were much less favorable than those in previous laws, inasmuch as they were limited in amount ($25,000) and duration, and future transactions will have much less concern for the fate of rail workers, as large-scale layoffs become more commonplace in the industrial scene.

THE ALASKA RAILROAD TRANSFER ACT

The Alaska Railroad was one of two railroads completely owned and operated as a public carrier by the federal government (the Panama Railroad being the other).[69] In 1985 the Alaska Railroad was sold to the state of Alaska and now operates as a wholly owned state corporation.[70] Transfer of employees to the state of Alaska was handled differently than the other railroad transactions, since these railroaders were federal civil servants, not private employees. Nonetheless, a form of labor protection was stipulated in the Alaska Railroad Transfer Act of 1982.[71] The state of Alaska was required to conclude a labor agreement with the railroad unions, retain all former federal employees (except officers) for two years after transfer at no diminution of wages, and to give priority of hire to furloughed Alaska Railroad employees.[72] In addition, a lump-sum severance option was also required.[73]

The Alaska Railroad benefits seem much less comprehensive than the earlier protective conditions but are in line with the vastly reduced labor protection provided by NERSA. They do not provide lifetime job protection nor generous severance allowances. It should be remembered, however, that the change on the Alaska Railroad is merely an intergovernmental transfer, not a merger. Full scale operation of freight and passenger service have continued with no layoff of railroaders following the transfer to the state.

LABOR PROTECTION AND SHORT LINE RAILROADS[74]

Ex Parte 392

Since 1985 the commission has refused to impose labor protection on acquisition cases other than mergers or consolidations.[75] The Staggers Rail Act gave the ICC the authority to exempt a railroad transaction from the requirements of the act when ICC regulations are not necessary to carry out the policies of Congress. The fundamental purpose of the exemption process was to allow the ICC to grant exemptions from the act where deregulation would be consistent with the policies of Congress.[76] Under *Ex Parte 392*, the ICC provided an abbreviated procedure for noncarriers to acquire railroads.[77] Labor protective provisions were not imposed in these cases.[78]

The ICC's decision in *Ex Parte 392* led to an acceleration in the number of short line sales. Frustrated with the failure of years of nationwide labor-management bargaining to reduce labor costs, many of the nation's Class I railroads turned to short line sales. Other railroads tried to lease rail lines to non-union subsidiaries or subsidiary lines that already had a labor contract more favorable to management. For example, Guilford Transportation leased the entire Boston & Maine, Maine Central, and Delaware & Hudson railroads to the Springfield Terminal, a former trolley line in New England, with a labor contract more favorable to rail management than the national agreements.

In response, rail labor brought two general issues regarding labor protection in short line spin-offs before the courts. First, must a selling carrier bargain about labor protection in an *Ex Parte 392* sale or alternatively are union agreements binding on the new carriers? Second, may a carrier enjoin a strike over labor protection in an *Ex Parte 392* sale?

The question of labor protection in short line sales became murky due to conflicting decisions between federal courts of appeal. *In Railway Labor Executives Association v. Pittsburgh & Lake Erie Railroad Company*, the Third Circuit held that rail unions must be included in the negotiations of line sales to new operations.[79] This decision directly conflicted with later opinions in the Eighth and Seventh Circuits. The Eighth Circuit Court upheld the Burlington Northern's spin off of lines to the Montana Rail Link.[80] The Seventh Circuit followed the Eighth Circuit in allowing the Chicago & North Western's attempt to sell its Duck Creek lines.[81] On June 21, 1989, the

Supreme Court of the United States decided the matter as far as the Pittsburgh and Lake Erie sale was concerned.[82] However, because of the special facts of that case, many of the issues concerning labor protection in short line sales remain unresolved.

The P&LE Case

Pittsburgh and Lake Erie (P&LE) was a steel-hauling short line railroad serving points in Ohio and western Pennsylvania. Once a part of the mighty New York Central System, the "Little Giant" went its own way as an independent line after the formation of Conrail. Part of its business was handling overhead traffic for the Baltimore & Ohio, bypassing B&O's own lines. The B&O began upgrading its own trackage and avoiding the P&LE route with its merger into the Chessie System.

As the fortunes of the steel industry declined, so did those of the P&LE.[83] The railroad's owners found a willing buyer, P&LE Rail Co. (Railco), a subsidiary of Chicago & West Pullman Transportation Corporation. Railco, however, was unwilling to take on the burden of P&LE's labor contracts. While the railroad would remain, only 250 of P&LE's 750 employees would be offered jobs with Railco.

The Railway Labor Executives Association (RLEA)[84] claimed that this transaction was one affecting rates of pay, rules, and working conditions under the Railway Labor Act.[85] The RLEA indicated its willingness to negotiate all aspects of the matter, including the decision to sell the railroad.[86] The P&LE indicated a willingness to discuss the matter, but noted that bargaining was not required because this was a sales transaction governed by the Interstate Commerce Act.[87] The company claimed that the Section 6 notices posted by the unions (proposing changes in wages, work rules, and working conditions) were invalid since this transaction was preempted by the ICC.[88]

On August 19, 1987, the RLEA sought to enjoin the P&LE from going forward with the sale of the line. On September 15, 1987, the unions went on strike. The district court denied the railroad's request for an injunction ending the strike, on the grounds that the Norris–LaGuardia Act (NLGA)[89] prohibited most injunctions in labor disputes.[90]

Subsequently, on September 19, 1987, Railco filed a notice of exemption pursuant to *Ex Parte 392*, which exempted Railco from the ICC's labor protection requirements.[91] None of the unions had requested labor protection from the ICC. On October 8, the district court ruled that the ICC's preemption of the issue negated the duty that P&LE had to bargain with the unions over the sale. In addition, the district court held "that the NLGA did not forbid the issuance of an injunction under such circumstances."[92]

The Third Circuit Court of Appeals reversed.[93] The court did not share the belief that the Interstate Commerce Act and the Railway Labor Act were on a collision course. Specifically, the court held that the ICC's intervention did not void the NLGA's prohibition on labor injunctions.[94]

On remand, the district court held that although the railroad did not have a duty to bargain with its employees over the decision to sell the property, it did have to confer with the unions over the sale's effect on the employees.[95] The court went on to rule that the status quo provision of the Railway Labor Act must be satisfied before the sale could be consummated despite ICC approval of the transaction.[96] The court then granted the unions' request to enjoin the sale and the Court of Appeals affirmed.[97]

The Supreme Court reversed and in doing so may have set a precedent for no labor protection in short line sales.[98] The Court, through Mr. Justice White, spoke of the interaction of three statutes—the Interstate Commerce Act (ICA), the Railway Labor Act (RLA), and the Norris–LaGuardia Act (NLGA).[99]

Without disregarding the RLA's duty to bargain or the NLGA's hostility to injunctions, the Court found that the RLA did not authorize an injunction against the proposed sale.[100] Working to harmonize the various statutes, the Court's decision was grounded on several considerations.

The Court first noted that the RLA speaks of a "change in agreements."[101] In this case, however, the sale did not of itself change a labor agreement. Moreover, the original agreement between P&LE and the unions did not contemplate any such sale. As such, the P&LE was under no obligation to serve Section 6 notices upon the unions.

Second, the Court rejected the RLEA's argument that the posting of Section 6 notices by the union required the railroad to preserve the status quo.[102] The majority stated:

[W]e are convinced that we should be guided by the admonition . . . that the decision to close down a business entirely is so much a management decision that only an unmistakable expression of congressional intent will suffice to require the employer to postpone a sale of its assets pending the fulfillment of any duty it may have to bargain over the subject matter of union such as were served in this case. Absent statutory direction to the contrary, the decision of a railroad employer to go out of business and consequently to reduce to zero the number of available jobs is not a change in the conditions of employment forbidden by the status quo provision of § 156.[103]

Finally, the Court's construction of the RLA noted the necessity of avoiding conflicts between the RLA and the ICA.[104] The court found that the ICC has plenary jurisdiction over rail transactions. Nothing in the Railway Labor Act deals specifically with an employer going out of the railroad business. Since the collective bargaining agreement is silent concerning sale of the railroad, the unions cannot stop the sale by posting notices.

Although the railroad did not have to bargain with the union over its sale of the business, there does remain a limited duty to bargain over the effect of the sale upon employees. The Court did state, however, that obligation ceased when the sale was closed after the ICC's *Ex Parte 392* exemption became effective.[105] The Court remanded the case to the Third Circuit as to whether or not the Court of Appeals should have lifted the injunction against the strike.

So *P&LE v. RLEA*, which had the effect of halting short line spin-offs, was finally decided for management.[106] However, the *P&LE v. RLEA* holding is limited to the facts of a special situation and is not necessarily applicable to the spin-off of short line railways. There are at least five reasons that *P&LE v. RLEA* may not resolve other cases involving labor protection in short line sales.

First, the P&LE was not a sale involving the spin-off of part of the railroad. The P&LE was being sold intact—as is. In contrast, most short line spin-offs involve the sale of light density branch lines by a Class I railroad to a friendly connecting company.

The fact that this was a proposal by the railroad to get out of the railroad business altogether was very important to the Court.[107] Footnote 17 suggests that a different result may be reached in a partial line sale.[108] In footnote 17, the Court distinguished *Railroad Telegraphers v. Chicago & N.W.R. Co.*[109] from the present case. The Court noted that "a railroad's proposal to abandon certain single-agent stations and hence abolish some jobs was a bargainable issue."[110] It is arguable that Telegraphers would control in the case of a partial line sale.

Second, P&LE was not maintaining any contractual or other relationship with the new company. The P&LE stockholders planned to take the proceeds from the sale and exit from the railroad business. In contrast, many of the spin-off short lines are closely affiliated with their parent Class I. It is not uncommon for short lines to rely on a Class I for their freight car supply or services such as tariff filings.

Third, the unions had not requested ICC labor protection from the ICC (possibly believing the action to be futile under current policies of the ICC). Though they are not required to ask for labor protection, they may so petition.

Fourth, there still is a limited and undefined duty to bargain with unions over the effect of a sale. With a seller that is an ongoing railroad, the employees who worked the discarded lines can displace other employees on the seller's network. Thus, the effect on other current employees may be enough to require full-scale bargaining when a railroad wishes to continue operating but spin-off an unprofitable branch line.

Finally, the unions' Section 6 notices were served after the P&LE's agreement with Railco had been settled.[111] *P&LE v. RLEA* does not address the case where a union serves a Section 6 notice anticipating a future sale.

The Court stated: "We address the duty to bargain about the effects of the sale only in the context of the facts existing when the unions' notices were served. We do not deal with a railroad employer's duty to bargain in response to a union's § 156 notice proposing labor protection provisions in the event that a sale, not yet contemplated, should take place."[112]

In summary, *P&LE v. RLEA* probably will not be the last word on labor protection for railroad employees in short line situations. Thus, other than allowing the Little Giant to sell its lines, issues surrounding labor protection and short line sales remain unresolved.[113]

The Supreme Court's P&LE decision dealt with the sale of an entire railroad. However, the P&LE fire sale approach is not the ordinary railroad spinoff wherein unwanted branches are sold to a newly formed carrier and the mainline railroad continues with a slimmed-down system.

Two U.S. courts of appeals have now held that P&LE applies to partial line sales. In a proceeding involving the Chicago & North Western, the Eighth Circuit upheld its sale to the Dakota, Minnesota & Eastern Railroad of C&NW's granger lines without the necessity of bargaining with unions.[114] The court stated that the Railway Labor Act did not require the railroad to bargain over the sale of the branch lines, and thus the C&NW did not have to post Section 6 notices, or to maintain the status quo on the lines after the Interstate Commerce Commission had given its approval of the takeover. Although the railroad does not have to bargain over the sale, there is a residual duty to bargain about the effects of the sale on its employees, and such a duty is a "major dispute" that requires the Section 6 route of notice, meeting, and conferring.[115]

Similarly, the Seventh Circuit gave the green light to North Western to go through with its long-planned sale of the Duck Creek South line to the Fox River Valley. The Duck Creek court said that it would be "absurd to make a railroad bargain over the sale of 99 percent of its lines, but not over the sale of 100 percent.[116] In the Duck Creek case, the North Western claimed that the decision to sell the line was a "minor dispute," and thus the status quo provisions of the RLA did not apply. Minor disputes are governed by the provisions for compulsory arbitration found in Section 3 of the act. If the courts hold that a decision to sell part of the line is a "minor" dispute (truly stretching the scope of that term, but that is apparently what the Seventh and Third Circuits have done), interpretations of the preexisting contract will go to adjustment by Public Law Boards, arbitrators, or the NRAB. However, the effects of the line sale on the remaining work force will be a mandatory bargaining subject and a major dispute, covered under Section 6 of the RLA. The ICC, faced with carriers gun-shy from the P&LE decision, who refused to apply for exemption from labor protection, ruled in the June 1990 Wilmington Terminal Case, that in nonexempt sales and leases to new carriers, the fledgling short line does not have to take on the old carrier's employees and collective bargaining agreements. At this writing, rail unions have appealed this ICC decision to the Court of Appeals.[117]

Meanwhile, the P&LE principles were extended beyond the line-sale situation and extended to the issue of labor protection following railroad mergers. In *Norfolk & Western Railway Co. v. American Train Dispatchers Association*, the Supreme Court of the United States held that once the ICC has approved a merger, such a consolidation is exempt from antitrust law "and all other law . . . as necessary to carry out the transaction."[118] By a seven to two decision, the Court indicated that this exemption included the Railway Labor Act and that law's duty to bargain over labor protection provisions. The Court held that the ICC was authorized to issue orders exempting parties from provisions of collective bargaining agreements.

The N&W case originated with the Norfolk Southern merger. In approving the merger, the ICC had imposed the standard *New York Dock* protection provisions[119] but had noted the possibility that future displacements of employees might arise as additional consolidations occur. In 1986 the merged Norfolk Southern decided to consolidate all locomotive dispatching in Atlanta, thus closing the N&W power distribution center in Roanoke. The unions had claimed that the moving of engine dispatchers would be a change in an existing collective bargaining agreement. The U.S. Supreme Court held that the ICC's decision allowing consolidation of the two railroads superseded collective bargaining obligations via the RLA.[120]

This may not be the end of the matter. The exemption from "all laws" includes only such exemptions as are necessary for the transaction. Section 11347 of the Interstate Commerce Act still requires the ICC to impose labor-protective conditions in mergers. Nonetheless, the N&W case broadens the ICC's authority in mergers at the expense of collective bargaining and the National Mediation Board.

As for the P&LE itself, that carrier ceased operations on September 11, 1992, after 113 years of service. The following day, the troubled railroad was sold to a new subsidiary of CSX, the Three Rivers Railway.[121]

The P&LE case did not declare the final word on labor protection in short line sales. Its effect on short line spin-offs was less than spectacular; railroads were making their own deals with a watchful eye to the courts.[122] But some form of labor protection is still requested for the mergers of mainline railroads.

NOTES

1. This chapter is adapted from William E. Thoms and Sonja Clapp, "Labor Protection in the Transportation Industry," *North Dakota Law Review* 64 (1988): 379–422. The authors wish to thank Sonja Clapp, Esq., for her assistance with this chapter and Chapter 8.

2. W. K. Ris, "Government Protection of Transport Employees: Sound Policy or Costly Precedent?" *Journal of Air Law and Commerce* 44 (1978): 509, 511. The

railroads were nationalized for a brief period during World War I and operated as a consolidated system. They were returned to private ownership in 1920.

    3. Transportation Act of 1920, Pub. L. No. 66–152, 41 Stat. 456, 481 (1921). *See* St. Paul Bridge & Terminal Ry. Control, 199 I.C.C. 588, 595–596 (1934). The tentative plan, calling for consolidation of the nation's railroads into nineteen lines, was never adopted. Consolidation of Railroads, 63 I.C.C. 455 (1921). A subsequent plan, calling for two systems in the East and three in the West, was adopted eight years later, but never came into force. *See* Consolidation of Railroads, 159 I.C.C. 522, 558, 567 (1929); see also Ris, "Government Protection," p. 513.

    4. St. Paul Bridge & Terminal Ry. Control, 199 I.C.C. 588, 595–596 (1934). The first statute dealing specifically with labor protection conditions was the Emergency Railroad Transportation Act of 1933, which froze rail employment at the May 1933 level for three years. Emergency Railroad Transportation Act of 1933, Pub. L. No. 73–68 Stat. 211, 214 (1934) (codified as amended at 45 U.S.C., sec. 661–669 [1982]). This was a different solution from the severance and displacement allowances found in today's labor protection provision, but the act had the effect of postponing large-scale layoffs during the worst years of the Depression.

    5. For the text of the Washington Job Protection Agreement, see 80 Cong. Rec. 7661–7662 (1936).

    6. Ris, "Government Protection," p. 516.

    7. 308 U.S. 225, 60 S.Ct. 248 (1939).

    8. United States v. Lowden, 308 U.S. at 238. In *Lowden*, the ICC had required labor protection provisions as a condition to a railroad merger. Opponents of labor protection stated that the ICC had no statutory authority to impose such conditions. The Supreme Court stated that "public interest" as used in the Interstate Commerce Act did not refer to matters generally of public concern, but rather public interest in the maintenance of a rail system. Therefore, since the conditions imposed promoted the public interest by facilitating the national policy of railroad consolidation, the Court concluded that the ICC had the authority to impose the protective provisions. Congress has since given the ICC specific statutory authority. Transportation Act of 1940, Pub. L. No. 76–785, 54 Stat. 898 (1941) (codified as amended at 49 U.S.C., sec. 10101-11914 [19821]).

    9. Transportation Act of 1940, Pub. L. No. 76–785, 54 Stat. 898 (1941) (codified as amended at 49 U.S.C., sec. 10101-11914 [1982]).

    10. *See* Ris, "Government Protection," pp. 519–520. Ris states "[a]ny discussion of the legislative history behind the 1940 Act cannot overemphasize the importance of the Depression in formulating Congressional policies. The worst economic crisis in the nation's history was superimposed upon a government policy promoting unification of railroads."

    11. Ibid., pp. 159–520.

    12. Interstate Commerce Act of 1940, ch. 722, sec. 5(2)(f), 54 Stat. 898, 906–907 (1941) (codified as amended at 49 U.S.C., sec. 11347 ([1982]).

    13. New Orleans Union Passenger Terminal Case, 282 I.C.C. 271 (1952). In *New Orleans Union Passenger Terminal*, construction of a consolidated rail terminal in New Orleans involved the abandonment of several older stations and a considerable amount of track. The ICC treated this as a merger case and imposed labor protection on the participating railroads.

    14. Ibid., p. 271.

15. Ibid., p. 281. The payments to the railroad employees were to begin from the date of the adverse effect (when the adverse economic effect was realized) and were to continue for a maximum of five years.

16. 80 Cong. Rec., pp. 7661-7662.

17. *New Orleans*, 282 I.C.C., p. 282.

18. Ibid., p. 275.

19. Norfolk & W. R.R.–New York, C. & S.L. R.R.—Merger, 331 I.C.C. 22, 41–42 (1967); Great N.P & B.L.–Great N. Ry—Merger, 331 I.C.C. 228, 276–279 (1967); Pennsylvania R.R.–New York C. R.R.—Merger, 327 I.C.C. 475, 543–546 (1967). Agreeing to reduce jobs only by attrition meant that the carriers agreed not to lay off large numbers of employees, although it would not replace retirees or those who quit the railroad. Paul S. Dempsey and William E. Thoms, *Law and Economic Regulation in Transportation* (Westport, CT: Quorum Books, 1986), p. 303. Usually, workers with more seniority bid into jobs, and so the senior trainman would then get the job of the departing railroader.

20. William E. Thoms, *Reprieve for the Iron Horse* (Baton Rouge, LA: Claitor's Pub. Division, 1973), p. 2.

21. *See* Rail Passenger Service Act of 1970, Pub. L. No. 91–518, 84 Stat. 1327 (1970) (codified as amended at 45 U.S.C., sec. 501–658 [1982]). Over one-fifth of passenger trains in 1970 were in discontinuance proceedings before the ICC.

22. Rail Passenger Service Act of 1970, Pub. L. No. 90–518, 84 Stat. 1327 (1970) (codified as amended at 45 U.S.C., sec. 501–658 [1982]).

23. Rail Passenger Service Act of 1970, 45 U.S.C., sec. 501 (1982).

24. 45 U.S.C., sec. 565(a) and (c) (1982) (railroad shall provide fair and equitable arrangements to protect interest of employees of terminal companies upon commencement of operation in the Amtrak System).

25. The railroads were directed to provide labor protection provisions no less favorable than those provided by the Interstate Commerce Act in connection with mergers. *See* Thoms, *Reprieve*, p. 43. Thus the Amtrak takeover was treated as a merger.

26. As the debt of Amtrak was ultimately to be absorbed by the government, the taxpayers were for the first time involved in guaranteeing labor protection costs. *See* Dempsey and Thoms, *Law and Economic Regulation*, p. 303.

27. *See* New York Dock Ry. v. United States, 609 F.2d 83 (2d Cir. 1979); New Orleans Union Passenger Terminal Case, 282 I.C.C. 271 (1952). In 1971, pursuant to the statutory authority of the Rail Passenger Service Act, the Secretary of Labor certified a labor protection agreement known as Appendix C-1, which shifts the burden from the employee to the employer to prove the factors of the employee's worsened position. *New York Dock,* 609 F.2d at 89.

28. *New York Dock,* 609 F.2d at 89.

29. Ibid.; Ris, "Government Protection," p. 521.

30. 45 U.S.C., sec. 565 (1982). Because Amtrak was responsible for labor protection for its own employees, critics of the Reagan administration's plan to close down Amtrak in 1985 pointed out that it would be more costly to pay these job protection benefits in fiscal year 1986 than to keep the railroad running.

31. *See,* e.g., Oregon S.L. R.R.–Goshen—Abandonment, 354 I.C.C. 584, 595–596 (1978) (protections afforded by 49 U.S.C., sec. 5(2)(f) (the New Orleans Conditions) and those required by the 4-R Act (which amended the Rail Passenger

Service Act) provided an increased level of protection in a railroad abandonment); New York Dock Ry. v. United States, 609 F.2d 83 (2d Cir. 1979) (New Orleans Conditions and Rail Passenger Service Act provisions applied to railyards merger).

32. New York Dock Ry. v. United States, 609 F.2d 83, 94–95 (2d Cir. 1979).

33. Ibid., p. 96.

34. Ibid., p. 91.

35. 45 U.S.C., sec. 771–780 (effective January 2, 1974, repealed August 13, 1981).

36. 45 U.S.C., sec. 741(b) (1982) (effective January 2, 1974).

37. Ibid.

38. *See* Thoms, *Reprieve*, pp. 47–48.

39. 45 U.S.C., sec. 779 (1976) (repealed 1981).

40. Penn Central Merger and N.&W. Inclusion Cases, 389 U.S. 486, 88 S.Ct. 602 (1967); Erie R.R. and Delaware, L.&W. R.R.—Merger, 312 I.C.C. 185 (1964) (mergers covered the territory of New England to Chicago, merging several eastern lines).

41. 45 U.S.C., sec. 775(c) (1976) (repealed 1981).

42. 45 U.S.C., sec. 775(b) (1976) (repealed 1981). Although this section of the Rail Passenger Service Act was repealed in 1981, benefits could still be received by railroad employees if they had accrued before October 1, 1981, and if the employee filed a claim within ninety days of the repeal. Act of August 13, 1981, Pub. L. No. 97–35, sec. 1144, 95 Stat. 669 (1981).

43, *See.* Staggers Rail Act of 1980, Pub. L. No. 96–448, sec. 509(a), 94 Stat. 1895, 1955 (1980). The House of Representatives increased the revised level of benefits reimbursed to Conrail by $235 million, bringing the authorized level to $480 million.

44. William E. Thoms, "Clear Track for Deregulation," *Transportation Law Journal* 12 (1982): 183, 205.

45. Most of the Rock Island was ultimately abandoned and what remained of the Milwaukee was merged into the Soo Line in 1985. *See* David J. Ingles, "The Plain-Vanilla Railroad Ingests Some Orange Sherbet," *Trains*, November 1986, p. 29.

46. Milwaukee Railroad Restructuring Act, Pub. L. No. 96–101, 93 Stat. 736 (1979) (codified at 45 U.S.C., sec. 901 [1982]).

47. 45 U.S.C., sec. 909 (1982).

48. Rock Island Railroad Transition and Employee Assistance Act of 1980, Pub. L. No. 96–254, 94 Stat. 399 (1980) (codified at 45 U.S.C., sec. 1001–1018 [1982]). RITA allowances were not to exceed sserverance $20,000. 45 U.S.C., sec. 1005(a) (1982).

49. Railway Labor Executives' Association v. Gibbons, 455 U.S. 457, 102 S.Ct. 1169 (1982).

50. Ibid., pp. 460–461.

51. Ibid., p. 463. Justice Marshall, in his concurring opinion, stated that a law such as RITA, which applies to only one debtor, does not have a uniform application and is unconstitutional.

52. *See* Thoms and Clapp, "Labor Protection."

53. Douglas Leslie, *Cases and Materials on Labor Law: Process and Policy*, 2d ed. (New York: Little, Brown, 1985), pp. 30–32.

54. Lawrence Tobey, "Costs, Benefits, and Future of Amtrak," *Transportation Law Journal* 15 (1987): 245, 265–269.

55. *See* 45 U.S.C., sec. 1111 (1982) (giving the ICC the power to determine compensation paid to Amtrak for the right-of-way commuter costs for the Northeast Corridor).

56. Northeast Rail Services Act of 1981, Pub. L. No. 97–35, 95 Stat. 643 (1981) (codified as amended at 45 U.S.C., sec. 1101–1116 [1982]).

57. *See* Omnibus Budget Reconciliation Act of 1981, Pub. L. No. 97–35, sec. 1131–1169, 95 Stat. 357, 643–687 (1981).

58. 45 U.S.C., sec. 1113 (1982).

59. 45 U.S.C., sec. 585(b) (1982) (Amtrak Commuter authorized to operate commuter service previously provided by Conrail).

60. Maryland and Massachusetts have contracted with Amtrak to operate their trains; New Jersey and Pennsylvania operate their trains directly; New York formed the Metro–North Commuter Railroad to run its suburban trains, with which Connecticut contracts for its service. Congress later directed that Conrail be sold directly to the public, rather than to another rail carrier. William E. Thoms, "Is the Clock Running Down for U.S. Rail Commuters?" *Trains*, October 1983, p. 30.

61. 45 U.S.C., sec. 1102(2), 1103 (1982). NERSA transferred some Conrail commuter service responsibilities to provide Conrail the opportunity to become profitable. It also provided for employee protection provisions different from those set forth in the Regional Reorganization Act.

62. 45 U.S.C., sec. 797(a) (1982).

63. 45 U.S.C., sec. 797a(a) and (d) (1982).

64. Omnibus Budget Reconciliation Act of 1981, Pub. L. No. 97–35, sec. 1131–1169, 95 Stat. 357, 583 (1981).

65. 45 U.S.C., sec, 797(c) (1982). Board shall maintain a register of pensions separated by railroad employment and place at the top of the list those employees entitled to priority.

66. 45 U.S.C., sec. 797(d) (1982). Any employee who accepts benefits under NERSA has waived employee protection benefits otherwise available.

67. Ris, "Labor Protection," p. 520.

68. *World Almanac and Book of Facts* (New York: Press Publishing Co., 1988).

69. William E. Thoms, "The Shortest Transcontinental," *Passenger Train Journal*, January 1981, p. 26.

70. 45 U.S.C., sec. 1201, 1203 (1982).

71. Alaska Railroad Transportation Act of 1982, Pub. L. No. 97–468, 96 Stat. 2556 (1982) (as codified at 45 U.S.C., sec. 1201–1214 [1982]). Employees subject to the civil service retirement law who transfer to the state-owned railroad shall continue to be subject to the civil service retirement law, unless the state-owned railroad elects to provide benefits in accordance with the Alaska Railroad Transportation Act. 45 U.S.C., sec. 1206(a) (1982).

72. 45 U.S.C., sec. 1206(a), (b), and (c) (1982).

73. 45 U.S.C., sec. 1206(d) (1982).

74. This section is adapted from William E. Thoms, Frank J. Dooley, and Denver D. Tolliver, "Railroad Spinoffs, Labor Standoffs, and the P&LE," *Transportation Law Journal* 18 (1989): 57–83.

75. *See Ex Parte No. 392* (Sub-No. 1), "Class Exemption for the Acquisition and Operation of Rail Lines Under 49 U.S.C., sec. 10901," 1 I.C.C. 2d 810 (1985), *aff'd mem.*, 817 F.2d 145 (D.C. Cir. 1987).

76. *See Ex Parte 392*, 1 I.C.C. 2d at 811. *See also* H.R. Rep. 1430, (1980).

77. *Ex Parte 392*, p. 811.

78. Ibid., p. 814. "It is our established policy that the imposition of labor protective conditions on acquisitions and operations under 10901 could seriously jeopardize the economics of continued rail operations and result in the abandonment of the property with the attendant loss of both service and jobs on the line." Ibid., p. 813.

79. 845 F.2d 420, 423 (3d Cir. 1988).

80. *See* Burlington N. R.R. v. United Transportation Union, 848 F.2d 856 (8th Cir. 1988).

81. *See* Railway Labor Executives' Association v. Chicago & N.W. Transp. Co., 855 F.2d 1277 (7th Cir. 1988).

82. Pittsburgh & Lake Erie R.R. v. Railway Labor Executives' Association, 491 U.S. 490, 109 S.Ct. 2584 (1989).

83. In the five years before the case, P&LE lost $60 million. *P&LE*, 491 U.S. at 494.

84. The RLEA is an organization made up of various labor unions representing railroad workers.

85. 45 U.S.C., sec. 156 (1988). Section 156 (Section 6 of the original act) requires that the party proposing to change rates of pay, rules, and working conditions post notices on the property proposing a bargaining session before such changes can be made.

86. *P&LE*, 491 U.S. at 496, 109 S.Ct. at 2589.

87. 49 U.S.C., sec. 10901 (1989). This requires noncarriers (Chicago & West Pullman's Railco subsidiary was not an operating railroad) to obtain ICC approval before buying existing railroad.

88. *P&LE*, 491 U.S. at 496, 109 S.Ct. at 2589.

89. Norris–LaGuardia Act, Pub. L. No. 72–65, 47 Stat. 70 (1932) (as codified at 29 U.S.C., sec. 101 [1982]). This law limits the power of the federal courts to grant injunctions in labor-management disputes, unless Congress has specifically prescribed injunctive relief.

90. *P&LE*, 491 U.S. at 498, 109 S.Ct. at 2590.

91. Ibid., 491 U.S. at 501, 109 S.Ct. at 2591.

92. Ibid. The District Court for the Western District of Pennsylvania entered an injunction against the strike.

93. Railway Labor Executives' Association v. Pittsburgh & Lake Erie R.R., 831 F.2d 1231 (3d Cir. 1987).

94. Ibid.

95. Railway Labor Executives' Association v. Pittsburgh & Lake Erie R.R., 677 F.Supp. 830 (W.D. Pa. 1987).

96. Ibid.

97. Railway Labor Executives' Association v. Pittsburgh & Lake Erie R.R., 845 F.2d 420 (3d Cir. 1988).

98. Pittsburgh & Lake Erie R.R. v. Railway Labor Executives' Association, 491 U.S. 490, 109 S.Ct. 2584 (1989).

99. Ibid., 491 U.S. at 494, 109 S.Ct. at 2588.

100. Ibid., 491 U.S. at 511, 109 S.Ct. at 2597.

101. Ibid., 491 U.S. at 503, 109 S.Ct. at 2592.

102. Ibid., 491 U.S. at 504, 109 S.Ct. at 2593–2594.

103. Ibid., 491 U.S. at 509, 109 S.Ct. at 2595–2596.

104. Ibid., 491 U.S. at 510–511, 109 S.Ct. at 2596.

105. Ibid., 491 U.S. at 513, 109 S.Ct. at 2597.

106. James Abbott, "Short Line Sales to Go on Despite P&LE, Say Class Is," *Traffic World*, July 31, 1989, p. 6.

107. *P&LE*, 491 U.S. at 507–509, 109 S.Ct. at 2594–2596.

108. Ibid., 491 U.S. at 508, 109 S.Ct. at 2595.

109. 362 U.S. 330, 80 S.Ct. 761 (1960).

110. *P&LE*, 491 U.S. at 508, 109 S.Ct. at 2595.

111. Ibid., 491 U.S. at 512, 109 S.Ct. at 2597.

112. Ibid., 491 U.S. at 512, 109 S.Ct. at 2597, n. 19.

113. *See* Abbott, "Short Line Sales," p. 6. Class I railroads, prospective short line buyers, and bankers feel that P&LE v. RLEA is irrelevant. Future sales may involve negotiations with unions, labor protection payments, or other legal challenges.

114. Railway Labor Executives' Association v. Chicago & N.W. Transportation Co., 890 F.2d 1024 (8th Cir. 1989).

115. Ibid., p. 1026.

116. Chicago & N.W. Transportation Co. v. Railway Labor Executives' Association, 908 F.2d 144, 152 (7th Cir. 1989).

117. Wilmington Terminal R.R. Co.—Purchase and Lease of CSX Transp. Co., 6 I.C.C. 2d 799 (1990). *See* Frank Wilner, "Income Protection Sets Carriers, Unions Apart," *Trains*, March 1991, pp. 23–24.

118. 499 U.S. 117, 111 S.Ct. 1156 (1991).

119. 366 I.C.C. 173 (1982).

120. Norfolk & Western Railway Co. v. American Train Dispatchers Association, 499 U.S. 117, 11 S.Ct. 1156 (1991).

121. "P&LE Gives It Up," *Trains*, December 1992, p. 6.

122. See Abbott, "Short Line Sales," p. 6.

6

Labor-Management Relations[1]

Our first national labor law, the Railway Labor Act (RLA)[2] has governed labor-management relations on the common-carrier railroads since 1926. Although significantly different in its approach from the National Labor Relations Act (NLRA),[3] the RLA is predominantly concerned with settlement of labor disputes through collective bargaining, an ongoing process involving unions and management. The RLA establishes clear statutory guidelines for bargaining between carriers and unions to establish new contracts. The Act compels labor and management to meet and confer about wages, hours, and terms and conditions of employment. There also is a duty to bargain in good faith.

REQUIREMENTS OF THE RAILWAY LABOR ACT

The duty to bargain is expressed by the Railway Labor Act, which views collective bargaining as essential to its statutory scheme. The RLA requires that carriers and employee representatives meet and confer about wages, hours, and terms and conditions of employment. Both sides have a duty to bargain and to reach agreement.[4] However, the law does not compel either side to reach a compromise or make a concession. At some point, impasse may be reached and the parties are then free to seek economic self-help.

The purposes of the RLA, as set forth in Section 2, are:

1. to avoid any interruption to commerce or to the operation of any carrier engaged therein;

2. to forbid any limitation upon freedom of association among employees or any denial as a condition of employment or otherwise, of the right of employees to join a labor organization;

3. to provide for the complete independence of carriers and of employees in the matter of self-organization to carry out the purposes of this Act;

4. to provide for the prompt and orderly settlement of all disputes concerning rates of pay, rules, or working conditions;

5. to provide for the prompt and orderly settlement of all disputes growing out of grievances or out of the interpretation of application of agreements covering rates of pay, rules, or working conditions.[5]

These terms of art have developed special meanings. The phrase "avoid any interruption to commerce" means a statutory basis has been established to reduce the threat of unannounced strikes that would disrupt passenger travel and freight shipments.[6] "Freedom of association of employees" means railroad employees are free to self-organize, to form, join, or assist labor organizations.[7] Alternatively, employees are free to refrain from bargaining collectively if a union is rejected. "A 'major dispute' is one which arises over the formation of collective agreements or where there is no such agreement. A 'minor dispute' contemplates the existence of a collective agreement [and] the dispute arises over the meaning of the agreement or the proper application of the agreement."[8]

In regard to the fourth and fifth purposes of the RLA, the Act requires certain procedures be followed in resolving major and minor disputes. The law does not itself settle major disputes or contract issues. Rather, "its underlying philosophy is almost total reliance upon collective bargaining or major dispute settlement."[9] Thus the parties are expected to resolve major contractual issues through collective bargaining and self-help (strikes and lockouts).

Further procedures of the Railway Labor Act are invoked only when the parties fail to reach an agreement. Minor disputes on the railroads are settled by the National Railroad Adjustment Board (NRAB).[10]

PROCEDURAL STEPS IN MAJOR DISPUTES

If a major dispute between management and labor arises, the RLA requires that the parties attempt to resolve their dispute through the collective bargaining process.[11] However, the RLA process as it appears through collective bargaining has been so formalized that it bears little resemblance to dynamic bargaining. Unlike labor contracts in other industries, railroad labor contracts usually have no expiration dates. They continue in effect until one of the parties is dissatisfied and wants to change them.

If the parties cannot negotiate a settlement, the party seeking to change the existing contract may post a "Section 6 notice."[12] The filing of a Section 6 notice invokes the collective bargaining procedures of the RLA. The filing must give the other party at least thirty days written notice of any intended changes in working conditions. Often times, the party who has been served the notice will file counterproposals for concurrent handling with the other party's notice, or, as an alternative, reserve the right to file counterproposals.[13]

A Section 6 notice filed by a carrier or its unions is the only recognized way for changing work rules and triggering the bargaining process. The process typically involves several steps before an agreement is reached between the carrier and labor. The parties must agree on a time and place to meet and confer within ten days of receipt of the notice. The conference must begin within the thirty days provided for in the notice. Neither party may change the existing rules nor pay during this period.[14]

There is no time limit as to how long the parties may negotiate. Either party may notify the National Mediation Board (NMB) that they are unable to settle the dispute.[15] In that case, the NMB will try to either mediate the dispute or recommend arbitration.

When a case goes to mediation, the NMB or a mediator works with the parties, trying to help them resolve their differences. The mediator will be present at negotiating sessions. The mediator may also meet privately with each side. No time limit exists for mediation.[16]

If the efforts of a mediator fail to produce an agreement, the final act of the NMB is to proffer arbitration.[17] The provisions for arbitration are found in Section 7 of the RLA.[18] If arbitration is accepted, the dispute is resolved. However, either side is free to reject the NMB's offer of arbitration. Usually, arbitration is not accepted. If arbitration is rejected, the NMB must notify the parties in writing. Neither party may change the work rules until thirty days after the NMB has concluded its efforts.[19]

Theoretically, the bargaining attempts would end there and the impasse could lead to a strike. However, the RLA provides that the NMB shall notify the President if it determines that a strike or lockout would "threaten substantially to interrupt interstate commerce to a degree such as to deprive any section of the country of essential transportation service."[20] Almost every strike of a major railroad will deny some part of the country some essential services.

The wording of the statute is so broad that the NMB usually does notify the president. This notice sets another moratorium ticking. When the emergency provisions (Section 10) of the RLA are invoked, the president is asked to create an emergency board to look into the dispute.[21] The president is not required to establish an emergency board. Generally speaking, emergency boards have been established in railroad disputes but not in airline strikes since deregulation.[22]

The emergency board consists of knowledgeable, neutral individuals. Neither arbitrators nor mediators, the emergency board is given the investigative powers of fact finders. Within thirty days, the emergency board is to report to the president on the potential effects of the threatened strike and the underlying issues. The parties must maintain the status quo during the thirty days that the emergency board has to make its report.

Obviously, the president could also read about the strike and its causes in the daily newspapers. Thus, it is a fair assumption that one of the purposes of this section is to extend the cooling-off period for another thirty days. During this time the parties may be able to resolve the issues themselves. Meanwhile, the emergency board is supposed to investigate and possibly come up with recommendations. If the emergency board's recommendations are ignored and no agreement is made, the parties are free to exercise "self-help."[23] This could include strikes, lockouts, or imposing new rules on the work force.

Until the 1980s rail unions and carriers bargained on a nationwide basis. That meant that a strike on one carrier could eventually be a strike against all, since the RLA does not prohibit secondary boycotts.[24] If circumstances such as these arise, an additional ad hoc stage may be introduced to the negotiating process. When faced with the possibility of such a nationwide shutdown, Congress has opted for three types of resolution. In some instances, Congress has appointed a board of arbitration to decide the dispute. In others, it has imposed a settlement that other unions had agreed to upon an uncompromising union and in still other cases, Congress has enacted a compromise package of its own.[25]

Inherent in these interventions by Congress is the expression of the very purposes for which government became present in the dispute in the first place. First, Congress aims to thwart interruption of the national transportation system by virtue of an emergency resolution. Second, it seeks to compel the parties to recommence a negotiated settlement of their dispute.

THE ROLE OF THE NATIONAL MEDIATION BOARD

The agency administering the Railway Labor Act is the National Mediation Board, an independent administrative agency.[26] The members of the NMB are appointed by the president, with the advice and the consent of the Senate.[27] The NMB has three members, no more than two of whom may belong to the same political party, who serve staggered terms. None of them may be affiliated with a railroad nor airline nor unions that represent rail or airline workers.[28] In addition, there are about twenty-five mediators throughout the country employed by the board. Mediators are not members of the NMB and are not subject to such political considerations as all being from the same political party.

The primary jurisdiction of the NMB is supervising the selection of a bargaining representative by a craft of airline or railroad employees and overseeing the bargaining process.[29] Unlike other national labor agencies, the NMB does not have a detailed list of unfair labor practices to control.

Rather, it is governed by general considerations of fair dealing and the duty to bargain toward an agreement.

Central to the NMBs' responsibilities is enforcing the duty to bargain in good faith.[30] The NMB has the responsibility of seeing that the union is truly the representative of its craft and that the employees it claims to represent are, in fact, employees of that carrier. The parties must maintain the status quo while the bargaining process goes on.[31] The NMB may be asked to participate by one of the parties, or the board may offer its services at any time during the bargaining process. The NMB has several other responsibilities. First, NMB may proffer its services to help the parties mediate major disputes.[32] Second, it appoints neutral arbitrators (also called referees or umpires) for tripartite arbitration as well as for the system boards of adjustment on airlines.[33] Third, the NMB controls the arbitration process stipulated in Section 7 of the Railway Labor Act.[34] Fourth, it interprets agreements that have been reached through mediation. Finally, the NMB notifies the president of the United States that an emergency exists, so the president might name an emergency board to handle the dispute.[35]

THE DUTY TO BARGAIN

Section 2, First, provides that parties "exert every reasonable effort to make and maintain agreements concerning rates of pay, rules, and working conditions."[36] It appears that, unless parties are to be required to bargain over every issue, the mandatory subjects under the RLA must be limited to those enumerated in the Act. Given the parties' duty to exert every reasonable effort to reach agreement on these mandatory subjects, a refusal to bargain over these issues until an agreement is reached on a non-mandatory subject would violate a party's duty to bargain under Section 2, First.[37]

The duty to bargain implies recognition and respect for the opponent's representatives. The union must deal with the management representative selected by the carrier.

Many railroad management personnel have come up through the ranks. A good number of this group hold on to their union membership, possibly to retain retirement benefits, or perhaps because of a feeling of solidarity and sentiment.[38] Retaining union membership also protects the individual if he or she should be bumped from a management position back to the rank and file. For the union to discipline a member because of its dissatisfaction with his or her activities as a negotiator or an adjuster for management would be coercion of the carrier in its selection of representatives.[39]

Similarly, the carrier must deal with the union as the sole representative of its employees. There should be no going around the union or attempting to interfere with its position as the exclusive bargaining representative. Neither side may use self-help until an impasse has been reached. Until that time, the duty to bargain over mandatory bargaining subjects remains.

No matter how weak a union is economically, the employer has a duty to bargain with it. No matter how much an employer is despised, the union has a duty to bargain with it. The RLA states, "it shall be the duty of all carriers, their officers, agents, and the employees to exert every reasonable effort to make and maintain agreements."[40]

SETTLEMENT OF DISPUTES

Major and Minor Disputes

The language of the RLA does not use the words "major" and "minor." However, labor lawyers and courts use these terms to differentiate the types of conflict (besides representation cases) that arise under the RLA.

Major disputes are those that arise in contract negotiations.[41] They are the subject matter for contracts, having to do with wages, hours, and work rules. The resolution of a major dispute is either an agreement or an impasse. The latter can lead to economic self-help such as strikes and lockouts.

Minor disputes, on the other hand, concern the interpretation or application of an existing contract.[42] A railroad labor agreement is often hammered out after weeks or months of tough negotiation. The parties often reduce their understanding to writing under last-minute pressures. In many cases, the final contract contains compromise words that may encompass different meanings.

Thus, a contract, reached to settle major disputes, may be so vague that it gives rise to minor disputes. The Railway Labor Act requires that minor disputes be "adjusted," that is, submitted to compulsory arbitration.[43] The RLA provides an automatic and decisive mechanism for its settlement of minor disputes. Strikes can occur only over major disputes; minor disputes are adjusted.[44] However, the distinction between "major" and "minor" disputes is not as clear as it might be. The facts of a case often do not indicate to which category a dispute might belong.

Depending on the facts of a particular case, one party may prefer presenting the case as a major or minor dispute. For example, since a Section 6 notice is required to initiate a major dispute, the parties are likely to serve such a notice in any dispute arising out of any ambiguous situation to make the controversy appear more like a major dispute. However, it has been pointed out that undue emphasis must not be placed on the maneuvers of the parties.[45] Furthermore, the parties cannot agree to specify the type of dispute. "[E]ven though the parties thought it was a major dispute, their designation is not controlling."[46]

Interest Arbitration of Major Disputes

The RLA is detailed as to the rules for voluntary arbitration of major disputes. Section 7 of the Act provides for tripartite arbitration of major disputes.[47] This means that each side names an arbitrator and the two arbitrators agree upon a neutral referee. If the two arbitrators cannot agree upon a third person to be the neutral party, the National Mediation Board will select the referee. Either a three or six person arbitration panel will be chosen by this method.

The agreement to arbitrate must be in writing and must refer to the RLA. The decision of the arbitrators is final, but is limited to the questions posed by the agreement to arbitrate. In addition, the "award," as the decision is called, may not be appealed. However, it can be "impeached."[48] Impeachment occurs if the court is convinced that the arbitrators acted ultra vires (beyond their powers granted by the agreement), or that the award was obtained by bias or fraud, or was not in conformity with the procedures of the RLA.[49]

Despite RLA provisions, voluntary arbitration for major disputes (interest arbitration) is rare in the railroad and airline industries. Carriers and unions want to retain control over the bargaining process. Both parties are reluctant to hand over their powers to an arbitrator who may act in an unforeseen manner.[50] There are special procedures for emergency boards to investigate labor-management disputes on commuter railroads with quasi-compulsory settlement procedures.[51]

National Railroad Adjustment Board

Minor disputes are subject to "adjustment" or compulsory arbitration by the National Railroad Adjustment Board.[52] This agency is unique in the fact that it is not composed of federal appointees or employees.

The NRAB meets in Chicago. It has thirty-four members, one-half of whom are chosen by the unions and the other seventeen by railroads. It has four separate divisions: the First Division has jurisdiction over operating employees; the Second over shop employees; the Third over nonoperating employees (except for shop, supervisory, and waterborne); and the Fourth over marine and supervisory employees. As the divisions are evenly split between labor and management, impasses are normal and expected. Usually the division will choose a neutral referee; if they cannot agree upon a referee, the National Mediation Board will select a neutral party.[53]

The NRAB seeks to "adjust" grievances, that is to interpret contracts upon the filing of a grievance by a nationwide union. Because the two sides are often deadlocked, the referee usually is responsible for the decision. If the NRAB has made a decision, the courts will enjoin a strike aimed at enforcing an award.[54] The 1966 amendments to the Railway Labor Act made appeals to the courts a right both of the losing and winning parties.[55] In addition, Public Law boards have been used to ease the NRAB's substantial backlog. As airlines have their own system boards of adjustment,[56] and industries under the NLRA have their own private grievance mechanisms, the railroad industry is the only one that has its grievance adjustment costs borne in part by the government.

The distinction between a "major" and "minor" dispute is important for the outcome of the controversy. A minor dispute will go to the NRAB and be conclusively settled; a major dispute will be subject to the provisions of Section 6, and self-help is a factor.

Compulsory Arbitration

The railroad industry is the only field to have had disputes settled by acts of Congress; not once, but a dozen times. This governmental intervention began in 1963, with a one-shot arbitration law[57] designed to end a nationwide dispute over the employment of firemen on diesel locomotives. Since then, Congress has used a variety of approaches, including imposing a settlement, giving more time for the parties to reach an agreement, making an issue nonstrikeable, or creating a special arbitration board to settle the dispute.[58]

The most recent example of such ad hoc legislation occurred on June 26, 1992. On that date, President Bush signed into law a bill passed in the early morning hours by Congress, ending a nationwide rail lockout of less than twenty-four hours' duration. The shutdown had begun with a strike called two days previously against CSX Transportation by members of the Machinists' union. Concurrently, a strike vote had been taken against Amtrak by several operating and shopcraft unions, and negotiations with Conrail had also reached impasse. Amtrak employees had postponed their strike against the passenger carrier (which was subsequently settled), but once the picket lines went up at CSX, all Class I freight railroads locked out their employees, shutting down freight operations and also locking Amtrak trains off their tracks. (The exception was the Boston-Washington corridor, where Amtrak owns the railroad.)

It appears that the railroads had locked out their employees in part to force congressional action ending the strike threat. Nonetheless, the law called for compulsory arbitration of the dispute. It required a cooling off period of thirty-five days; a requirement for the sides to resume collective bargaining; submission of the best final offer from each side within twenty-five days of the beginning of negotiations; and at the end of thirty-five days, the arbitrator was directed to pick and choose the best final offer, which was submitted to the president of the United States. When President Bush approved that, the decision went into effect as a contract term. If he had not so approved, the unions would have been free to strike and management to lock out.[59]

This was the twelfth time that Congress had legislated an end to a rail strike. Congress' constant interference with the bargaining process makes the right to strike and the duty to bargain collectively somewhat illusory.

SELF-HELP AFTER IMPASSE

Economic Self-Help

The state of impasse is reached when bargaining can go no farther, the parties are fixed in their positions, and mediation has failed. At this point, the union is free to strike.[60]

In NLRA cases the employer may shut down the operation and lock out the employees.[61] Rather than waiting for the union to strike, this is an attempt to get a settlement more favorable to the employer.

There is a complicating factor in railroad strikes. The carrier is under a duty to service the public, that is, to operate as is feasible under the circumstances.[62] This duty arises from the traditional definition of a common carrier. At the common law, a carrier was a corporation that had been given a license and protection from competition by the government. In return for this privilege, the carrier had the duty to maintain operations for shippers and passengers.[63]

A strike does not sever the relationship of carrier and employee.[64] However, the contractual relationship between them is suspended during the strike.[65] The carrier is free to permanently replace the strikers.[66] Returning strikers are, however, placed on a preferential hiring list.[67] Strikers cannot be fired for striking. That is a cold comfort to an employee who finds that his job has been given to a replacement.

Because a strike is so risky, unions have tried many devices short of strikes. These include job actions, refusal of overtime, informing prospective passengers about strike conditions, slowdowns, and misrouting of baggage.[68] Recently, unions have opened negotiations with "white knights" about to take over a carrier and free it from an anti-union management.[69] This might be a breach of the duty to bargain with the carrier's management.

Limits of Self-Help

The union may or may not have the right to engage in sympathy strikes. This is based upon the limitations of any no-strike clause in its agreement with the carriers. Even nonunion employees may engage in a sympathy strike, if it is "concerted activity."[70] Particularly since the deregulation movement began in 1978, there are actually few statutory or judge-made constraints against the right of either party to engage in self-help. Unless the parties limit themselves by contract or mediation, there is a great potential for a "law of the jungle" situation in rail and airline labor relations. The extent of this freedom from injunctions has yet to be determined. The Norris–LaGuardia Act,[71] barring the use of labor injunctions in federal courts, is broad in its application.

During the 1989 Eastern Airlines strike, striking machinists placed a picket line outside New York's Grand Central Terminal, used by rail carriers Amtrak and Metro–North Commuter Railroad, both subject to the Railway Labor Act. The picketing was enjoined by a U.S. District Court, but few limits have been placed on inter-airline or inter-railroad picketing.[72]

STRIKES, BOYCOTTS, AND INJUNCTIONS

Right to Strike

A strike is an all-or-nothing proposition in the United States.[73] The type of situation one sees in Europe, where railroad workers lay down tools for an hour or more in a day to select certain targets for strike action is unknown. In this country partial strikes or work interruptions are not allowed and may be enjoined.[74]

A strike is pure economic warfare. Historically, a strike was waged by the union in hope of attaining its economic goals. More recently, it appears that unions have become concerned with keeping their status intact rather than losing hard-won gains to management cost cutting.

When a carrier is on strike, its employees are the first to suffer. They receive no wages and must depend on whatever war chest a union has managed to amass for a strike fund.[75] Management also suffers from strikes. Idled cars and locomotives continue to require maintenance costs and interest payments. Railroad management also suffers diversion of freight to other carriers. This gives carriers an incentive to resume operations using either management or replacement personnel.[76]

When a legal strike is called, the membership is asked for a "strike vote" to authorize the action. Union members are advised to withdraw their services. A picket line is placed at areas where the carrier does business, including its corporate headquarters, downtown ticket offices, and stations served by the carrier. They not only communicate the union's message, but they act as a signal to would-be passengers. The messages say, "please don't patronize; join us in our struggle; or at least stay neutral." To union members it is a sign to stay away. There is an implied promise that if you honor our picket line, we may help you if you go on strike against your employer.

Right to Picket and Boycott

Because of the implicit tension and possibility of violence, courts have taken a strict look at picketing.[77] The right to march on public property with picket signs is not completely protected by the First Amendment.[78] Courts and agencies have upheld time, place, and manner restrictions on picketing, reasoning that picketing is free speech plus a signal. The National Labor Relations Board, for example, has outlined explicit restrictions on what can be placed on signs.[79] The Railway Labor Act, on the other hand, was conceived of as mediatory legislation.[80] As such it is ill equipped to referee disputes that have turned to self-help during strikes.

Because the railroad system is a unified skein of tracks 4' 8 1/2" wide, the framers of the Railway Labor Act realized that interconnectivity is a fact of life. In recognition of that reality, no restrictions on secondary boycotts were placed in the RLA.[81] Unions may and do engage in sympathy strikes in support of job actions on other carriers. Absent any contractual limits on secondary activity, air and rail employees generally have the right to do so.[82] The right to strike and picket, then, is only restrained by contract. There are few safeguards against the dispute spreading to other carriers.

REPRESENTATION DISPUTES

The National Mediation Board is responsible for oversight of the process of selecting a bargaining representative.[83] The Railway Labor Act requires that the bargaining representative be a "craft" or within a "class" of employees. Except for specifying that the principle of majority rule should govern, Congress left the procedure and definition of craft or class to the NMB.[84]

Before determining who would represent craft employees, the NMB excludes certain jobs. Trainees, managerial employees, and confidential employees are excluded from the craft. Every craft is entitled to its own representation election. Each union is considered the exclusive representative of its craft.[85] As a rule, the NMB will only certify a bargaining representative if a majority of the craft employees vote in the NMB-run election and if the union wins a majority of the votes cast. Unlike the National Labor Relations Act, the Railway Labor Act includes "subordinate officials" as employees. There is no requirement that guards, or railroad policemen, be designated a separate craft, although they are usually placed in a separate bargaining unit.[86] In an NMB election, both strikers and their replacements are eligible to vote as long as the strikers are willing to return to their job.

The NMB has ruled that it will find only carrier-wide units of a craft or class appropriate.[87] The purpose of this rule is to prevent a railroad from being shut down by the strike of a small local union. Following a railway merger, the NMB must make a decision as to whether one or more carriers remain in existence. The NMB has ruled that when one railroad takes over another, a new single carrier is presumed to exist, unless it can be shown that the merger partners continue to operate as separate railroads.

The NMB ballot does not have "no union" as a choice on its ballot. Thus, if you do not want to be represented by any union, you would merely refrain from voting. If less than 50 percent of a craft votes, the NMB will not certify the vote. The NMB may set aside an election if there was interference with a free vote.[88]

Unlike the NLRA, the RLA contains no formal decertification procedures. Thus, if employees wish to get rid of a union, they must either choose another union, or vote for an individual, say John Doe, to represent them. Once John Doe wins the election, he may advise the NMB that he will not perform the representative function.[89] Employers are not permitted to be parties to representation matters.[90] Judicial review is severely limited, permitted when constitutional questions exist, when the NMB acts ultra vires, or where the issue involves a question of "international urgency."[91]

THE FUTURE OF THE RAILWAY LABOR ACT

The Railway Labor Act was conceived in the post–World War I days when railroads were the preeminent carriers of passengers and freight.[92] It was extended to airlines in 1936, largely on the behest of the Airline Pilots Association, who wondered about the constitutionality of the newly passed Wagner Act, and wanted a tried and true system for adjudicating disputes.[93] During the first fifty years of the act, both railroads and airlines were heavily regulated by federal agencies, along the lines of public utilities.[94]

Since 1978 substantial structural change has occurred in both industries. Regulation has been relaxed and oligopoly has replaced competition in many markets. Several major railroads dominate the industry; airlines have been reduced to five or six viable carriers. There have been mergers within the rail and air unions as well. In view of the striking changes in the framework of the industries, many commentators have questioned whether or not the two separate streams of labor law should remain.[95]

However, few of these criticisms come from within the railway labor bar. Practitioners and the parties involved have long preferred working with a statute where the results are predictable, and where labor peace is given a high priority.[96] Commentators have insisted that agreements be made by the parties involved and that each change be heavily deliberated.[97] Nonetheless, with management pushing for structural changes in the workforce of the railroad industry, the status quo presumption arising from the operation of Section 6 in major disputes tends to favor labor. Management would favor making most changes appear to be minor disputes and set them for adjustment, rather than making them strikeable issues.[98] Therefore it is for the courts to finally resolve what is and what is not a major dispute and a subject of bargaining.

Although other industries have grown up with the National Labor Relations Board procedures, the railroads and their unions have adapted and have worked together with the Railway Labor Act and its processes. At this writing, there seems to be no push to merge the two administrative bodies and the laws that they carry out. Railroads and their unions are working toward a shared, though uncertain future in the twenty-first century.

The legal literature dealing with the future of the Railway Labor Act highlights its strengths and shortcomings, compared to those of the National Labor Relations Act. Professor Northrup criticizes the tendency of the act to frustrate dynamic bargaining by holding parties to the status quo. He claims Eastern Airlines to be the "most dramatic example of the power of the NMB to hold parties in limbo regardless of their desire for settlement; it is certainly not the only one."[99] He cites the frequency of emergency boards under the statute (177 on the railroads, 34 on the airlines, 18 on the commuter lines) and the propensity of Congress to settle disputes by ad hoc compulsory arbitration.

Northrup's criticism of the National Railroad Adjustment Board is that the parties do not pay the cost of the procedure. Northrup recommends that with minor disputes, a method be established for selecting referees independent of the NMB, and that the parties be required to pay for their dispute resolution, as is done on the airlines.[100]

The Northrup position calls for repeal of the act. As to whether or not that is politically feasible, Northrop asks: "The question undoubtedly arises as to why the Act has stood so long and been administered as it has been without public outcry and calls for reform. The answer seems to be that the Act is of such little concern and so unknown to a broad public that obvious inequities in the Act and its administration do not lead to pressures for change."[101] Northrup calls for a transfer of the National Mediation Board's functions to the Federal Mediation and Conciliation Service and the National Labor Relations Board. Apparently, he would then include railway and airline workers within the definition of "employee" found in the National Labor Relations Act.

If that is not politically feasible, his second choice would be for amendment of the act, ending the preclusion of the Mediation Board from judicial review, limiting the board's discretion to appoint mediators, and ending the status quo after sixty days of the commencement of mediation (or when a final offer is rejected). He calls for transfer of representation disputes to the NLRB and an end for funding for the NRAB and Public Law Boards, as well as an end to emergency boards in "disputes that clearly are not emergencies."[102] Although not mentioned, the Northrop approach would substantially increase the workload of the NLRB and require some changes in that statute in order to accommodate the additional transport workers.

Among the champions of the Railway Labor Act is Frank N. Wilner, a prolific author who serves as vice-president for the Association of American Railroads. Wilner praises the Act for its accommodation to the realities of collective bargaining on the railroads and for its prevention of time lost to strikes. He does, however, call for modification of the act to prohibit secondary picketing, which he claims to be a vital change necessitated by deregulation of transportation.[103] He also calls for longer terms for members of the National Mediation Board, less fragmentation in representation, and a greater restraint by the White House in declaring an emergency on the railroads, and with Congress, in trying a quick fix through compulsory arbitration. Despite these criticisms, Wilner believes the RLA to be a superior vehicle to the NLRA in rail labor relations. He acknowledges the abysmal rate of return on the railroads (you can do far better putting your money in a savings bank) and the glacial pace of work-rules, but suggests that these distortions are the product of government interference and not necessarily due to the Railway Labor Act.

In an article in the University of Miami Law Review's symposium on labor issues, Miami Professor of Law Dennis O. Lynch (now Dean of the College of Law at the University of Denver) deals mostly with the NLRA, but mentions the Railway Labor Act in passing, by way of comparison. Dean Lynch is concerned with the tendency of courts to find that rail disputes that arguably arise out of a collective bargaining agreement are minor and thus subject to arbitration. Meanwhile, the railroad can put into effect changes without bargaining with the union. With major disputes, the status quo would tend to favor labor, but courts are finding it easier to classify disputes as minor.

With respect to arbitration on the railroads and airlines, Dean Lynch concludes: "There is a marked shift from court adjudication for conflicts involving tensions in statutory policies under the RLA to arbitration of the disputes."[104] In these cases management tends to have a free hand to act pending arbitration, and the statutory policies of the RLA are often ignored by the arbitrators, whose scope of review is limited by the Railway Labor Act.[105] Dean Lynch does not address the question of which is the better statutory vehicle, but suggests that both statutes may become irrelevant as arbitration, rather than bargaining, takes the front stage.

In an article whose title asks the question "Is the Railway Labor Act or the National Labor Relations Acts the Better Statutory Vehicle?," Conrail lawyer Dennis Arouca and Villanova Professor Henry Perritt[106] end up concluding that neither is the preferred choice. Deregulation of transportation, they claim, means an "abstentionist mode" of government involvement in labor-management relations. But, they conclude, the RLA would be a better adaptive model. Change is easier to effect through the RLA, the authors conclude, and the virtual immunity of the National Mediation Board to judicial review can develop strike timing and bargaining unit policies compatible with today's facts, not yesterday's history.[107]

In a separate, more detailed article in the *Pepperdine Law Review*,[108] Perritt discusses the effect of the RLA on labor-management cooperation. Most cooperation, he believes, is illusory, but the fault cannot be traced to the Railway Labor Act. As to recent concessions by unions, he traces the new era of cooperation to the liquidation of the Milwaukee and Rock Island Railroads, thus disabusing labor of the idea that the government would never let a major railroad go under.[109] (Earlier railroads had been abandoned, but they were white elephants like the Colorado Midland and then the New York, Ontario and Western, which should have never been built in the first place.) Perritt concludes his discussion of the Railway Labor Act by saying:

It would be wrong to conclude that the RLA has prevented adaptation to change in railroad and airline industries. It may have slowed it down, but it did not prevent it. As Professor Rehmus pointed out, collective bargaining in the railroad industry has adapted to enormous employment declines and changes in technology. It may be that the degree of resistance and the degree of governmental intervention was necessary, given the magnitude of the changes and their adverse impact on legitimate employee and union institutional interests.[110]

And it is true; the Railway Labor Act has seen the disappearance of the prop plane and the steam engine, the privately operated passenger train and the caboose. Perritt does not fault the Railway Labor Act for slowing change, nor does he believe the National Labor Relations Act would be a better vehicle.

Professor Douglas McCabe of Georgetown's Business School gave a critique of the RLA's Procedures to the 1989 Transportation Research Forum. McCabe does not call for the supplanting of the RLA by the NLRA, but instead concentrates on the drawn-out processes for both major and minor disputes, in particular the workings of the NRAB, where the cost of processing grievances is picked up by the government. He has some specific recommendations, broad-based industrial-type unions, a permanent panel of arbitrators instead of an ad hoc emergency board, and a greater choice of strike-ending weapons available to the president. He also calls for a re-establishment of nationwide bargaining and for the good offices of the Department of Labor, now notably absent from the railroad collective-bargaining scene.[111] Congressional action is called for, but not by folding the specialized techniques of the Railway Labor Act into the NLRA.

Professor Katherine van Wezel Stone of Yeshiva University is an avowed enthusiast for the Railway Labor Act. In a recent article in the *Stanford Law Review*,[112] Professor Stone calls the act a force for economic democracy in the transportation industry. Although her article focuses on airlines, most of her comments apply to the rails as well.

To start out, the RLA contains the assumption that all agreements are the product of collective bargaining and represent the will of the parties. She finds the RLA, much more than the NLRA, to be a vehicle for participation by labor in management decisions. She criticizes recent Supreme Court and federal cases that expand the amount of management rights and control and bypass the Section 6 bargaining procedures, as in consistent with the spirit of the act. Is less union participation required by deregulation? Professor Stone writes:

The RLA thus gives unions more power to affect those decisions most important to their members' welfare and their own institutional survival than does the NLRA. The differences between the two statutes lie in the particular way each one blends regulation and private ordering. The RLA achieves its participatory result by permitting parties to enlist judicial power to ensure that issues of importance are determined by agreement rather than by fiat. In contrast, the NLRA establishes a system of labor relations that keeps judicial power out of the parties' relationship, thereby reinforcing preexisting disparities of power and permitted in the stronger party to compel the weaker to bargain away its bargaining rights.[113]

Professor Stone finds little to criticize about the RLA. She believes that bargaining and impasse procedures are intentionally lengthy in order to give the side that wants to make a change an incentive to compromise with the other. "Only on those issues about which both feel strongly and have opposite positions is compromise difficult to attain."[114] She points out rightly that no labor-management agreement exists in a vacuum, and were the RLA to disappear, either NLRA or common-law rules would come to take its place. "One cannot make law disappear. At most, one can decide between different possible ways that the law can organize the labor-management relationship."[115]

In a recent issue of the *Journal of Air Law & Commerce* (Summer 1990) based on his S.J.D. dissertation at the University of Pennsylvania, Athanassios Papaioannou deals with the duty to bargain in the airline industry. Dr. Papaioannou suggests that the recent trend toward recognizing "management rights" and regulation disputes to the minor (i.e., nonbargainable) category is destructive of the intent of the Railway Labor Act.[116] The P&LE case is credited by Papaioannou for introducing the concept of management rights into the RLA, and he faults the courts for stretching the concept of "arguably within the interpretation of a contract," to make very important disputes minor, and thus not subject of Section 6 bargaining. While admitting that delays are replete under the act, he suggests that was the importance that Congress gave to deliberations between railroads and their workers. Change should come from Congress, not the courts. With respect to minor disputes that result in large-scale layoffs: "Managerial decisions which result in massive layoffs are precisely the types of disputes that cause strikes. These types of disputes certainly are not of 'comparatively minor character' unlikely to cause 'interruption of peaceful relations.' . . . When the contract has expired, the solution should be obvious: the dispute is always major. The author adds a caveat: 'The RLA itself, however, was not examined to determine if amendment is needed to provide more efficient solutions.' "[117] Analysts familiar with the air and rail industry generally favor keeping the Railway Labor Act in some form, often noting certain changes that should be made, such as eliminating secondary boycotts (seldom used on the railroads), changing representation procedures and, most importantly, speeding up the bargaining process.

Compared to the experience of European railways, our railroad unions are not strike-happy, and labor peace has ensured throughout most of the postwar era. However, there have been declines in the fortunes of the railroads and their employees. The economic history of the railroads, following World War II, and the airlines, following deregulation, is not a pleasant one. However, it is difficult to determine how much of the economic malaise of transport can be laid at the door of the RLA. The airlines, in particular, seem to have achieved productivity gains and labor peace without the dissension and confrontation that plagued the rail industry, while operating under the same statute. (Air labor troubles and financial woes, including bankruptcy, seem to have resulted from the after-effects of the Airline Deregulation Act rather than from labor hostility or the procedures of the RLA.)

The literature contains one clear message: there is trouble on the rails and labor contracts are part of it. All authors agree that the Railway Labor Act has fulfilled the task it was originally set out to do; the problem is adapting this system to the twenty-first century and an age of deregulation. Can we replace the historic RLA with something else or will the cure be worse than the disease?

NOTES

1. This chapter is adapted, in part, from William E. Thoms and Frank J. Dooley, "Collective Bargaining Under the Railway Labor Act," *Transportation Law Journal* 20 (1992): 275.

2. 45 U.S.C., sec. 151 (1990).

3. 29 U.S.C., sec. 151 (1986).

4. 45 U.S.C., sec. 152 (1990).

5. 45 U.S.C., sec. 151(a) (1990).

6. Detroit & Toledo Shore Line R.R. v. United Transportation Union, 396 U.S. 142, 148 (1969).

7. 45 U.S.C., sec. 152 (1982).

8. Piedmont Aviation, Inc. v. Air Line Pilots Association, Int'l, 347 F.Supp. 363, 365 (M.D.N.C. 1972).

9. Frank N. Wilner, "The Railway Labor Act: Why, What and for How Much Longer, Part I," *Transportation Practitioners Journal* 55 (1988): 242, 281.

10. 45 U.S.C., sec. 184 (1982).

11. 45 U.S.C., sec. 152 (1982).

12. 45 U.S.C., sec. 156 (1982).

13. John W. Gohmann, *The Railway Labor Act—A Judicial History* (Chicago: Lake Shore Litho, Inc., 1976), p. 323.

14. Railway Labor Act, sec. 6, 45 U.S.C., sec. 156 (1990).

15. 45 U.S.C., sec. 183 (1982).

16. Railway Labor Act, sec. 5, 45 U.S.C., sec. 155 (1990).

17. 45 U.S.C., sec. 155 (1982).

18. 45 U.S.C., sec. 157 (1982).

19. Railway Labor Act, sec. 5, 45 U.S.C., sec. 155 (1990).

20. 45 U.S.C., sec. 160 (1982).

21. Railway Labor Act, sec. 10, 45 U.S.C., sec. 160 (1990).

22. *See* Herbert R. Northrup, "The Railway Labor Act—Time for Repeal?" *Harvard Journal of Law and Public Policy* 13 (1990): 441, 466.

23. Ibid.

24. Chicago & N.W. Ry v. United Transportation Union, 402 U.S. 570, 91 S.Ct. 1731 (1971).

25. *See* Paul S. Dempsey and William E. Thoms, *Law and Economic Regulation in Transportation* (Westport, CT: Quorum Books, 1986), pp. 299–301.

26. 45 U.S.C., sec. 154 (1982).

27. Railway Labor Act, sec. 4, 45 U.S.C., sec. 154 (1990).

28. Ibid.

29. 45 U.S.C., sec. 155 (1982).

30. Railway Labor Act, sec. 2, 45 U.S.C., sec. 152 (1990).

31. Railway Labor Act, sec. 6, 45 U.S.C., sec. 156 (1990).

32. Railway Labor Act, sec. 2, 45 U.S.C., sec. 152 (1990).

33. Railway Labor Act, sec. 5, 45 U.S.C., sec. 155 (1990).

34. Railway Labor Act, sec. 7, 45 U.S.C., sec. 157 (1990).

35. 45 U.S.C., sec. 160 (1982).

36. Railway Labor Act, sec. 2, 45 U.S.C., sec. 152 (1990).

37. Airline Pilots Association v. United Air Lines, 802 F.2d 886 (7th Cir. 1986).

38. Unlike the NLRA, the Railway Labor Act includes "subordinate officials" as employees. *See* Northrup, "Railway Labor Act," p. 481.

39. Railway Labor Act, sec. 2, 45 U.S.C., sec. 152 (1990).

40. 45 U.S.C., sec. 152 (1982).

41. Railway Labor Act, sec. 6, 45 U.S.C., sec. 156 (1990).

42. Railway Labor Act, sec. 3, 45 U.S.C., sec. 153 (1990).

43. 45 U.S.C., sec. 153, 184 (1982).

44. *See* Northrup, "Railway Labor Act," p. 445.

45. Airline Flight Attendants v. Texas International Airlines, 411 F.Supp. 954, 961 (S.D. Tex. 1976).

46. Piedmont Aviation v. Airline Pilots Association, 347 F.Supp. 954, 961 (M.D.N.C. 1972).

47. 45 U.S.C. sec. 157 (1982).

48. Railway Labor Act, sec. 9, 45 U.S.C., sec. 159 (1990).

49. Ibid.

50. Northrup, "Railway Labor Act," p. 462.

51. Railway Labor Act, sec. 9A, 45 U.S.C., sec. 159a (1990). *See also* Northrup, "Railway Labor Act," pp. 449–451.

52. 45 U.S.C., sec. 153 (First)(i) (1982).

53. Robert E. Garrison, "The National Railroad Adjustment Board: A Unique Administrative Agency," *Yale Law Journal* 46 (1937): 567.

54. Northrup, "Railway Labor Act," p. 468.

55. Ibid.

56. Ibid., pp. 477–478.

57. Pub. L. 88–108 (1963). *See* William E. Thoms, "The Vanishing Fireman," *Loyola Law Review* 14 (1967): 125.

58. Northrup, "Railway Labor Act," p. 468.

59. *Denver Post*, June 26, 1992, p. 18A, c.1. Arbitrators gave their award on July 31, 1992, which President Bush allowed to stand. *Trains*, October 1992, p. 20.

60. Northrup, "Railway Labor Act," p. 468.

61. Dennis A. Arouca and Henry H. Perritt, Jr., "Transportation Labor Regulation: Is the Railway Labor Act or the National Labor Relations Act the Better Statutory Vehicle?" *Labor Law Journal* 36 (1985): 145, 154–55.

62. Brotherhood of Railway & Steamship Clerks v. Florida East Coast Ry., 384 U.S. 238, 86 S.Ct. 1420 (1966).

63. The first purpose of the Railway Labor Act is stated "to avoid any interruption to commerce or to the operation of any carrier engaged therein," 45 U.S.C., sec. 151a (1990).

64. Douglas M. McCabe, "The Railway Labor Act: A Procedural Reappraisal," *Journal of the Transportation Research Forum* 30 (1989): 210, 211–212.

65. Northrup, "Railway Labor Act," pp. 451–461.

66. Michael H. Campbell and William N. Hiers, Jr., "Management Decisions to Close or Sell Part or All of the Enterprise Under the Railway Labor Act—The Air Carrier's Dilemma," *Employee Relations Law Journal* 14 (1989): 327.

67. Ibid.

68. The Northwest-Republic merger of 1986 resulted in an number of slow-downs, including tearing off baggage tags from passengers' luggage. Virtually all these activities were enjoined.

69. In cases involving Frank Lorenzo, carrier employees negotiated with any outsider in an attempt to deliver them from Lorenzo—even the dreaded Carl Icahn! Similarly, railway unions were instrumental in the rescuing of Delaware and Hudson from antiunion Guilford Transportation and its eventual inclusion in Canadian Pacific's system.

70. 29 U.S.C., sec. 101 (1990). *See* Wilner, "Railway Labor Act," p. 285.

71. 29 U.S.C., sec. 101 (1982).

72. Long Island R.R. v. International Association of Machinists, 874 F.2d 901 (2d Cir. 1989). Court noted that the parties' agreement did not contain specific no-strike clause, but implied an obligation not to engage in sympathy strike from other terms of the Long Island R.R. contract.

73. Campbell and Hiers, "Management Decisions," p. 327.

74. "Concerted activity" is protected, but shutting down a railroad for an hour a day (during the commuter rush) has not been considered protected activity.

Strikes are only protected if Section 6 procedures are used and bargaining has proceeded to impasse. There is no right to strike over grievances. *See generally*, Dennis O. Lynch, "Deferral, Waiver, and Arbitration Under the NLRA: From Status to Contract and Back Again," *University of Miami Law Review* 44 (1989): 237.

75. Railroad strikers can be eligible for unemployment benefits after the strike lasts over four weeks.

76. Katherine van Wezel Stone, "Labor Relations on the Airlines: The Railway Labor Act in the Era of Deregulation," *Stanford Law Review* 42 (1990): 1485, 1543–1545.

77. Wilner, "Railway Labor Act," p. 242.

78. Ibid., pp. 246–255.

79. 29 U.S.C., sec. 158(b)(4) (1990).

80. *See* Northrup, "Railway Labor Act," pp. 442–446.

81. Ibid., pp. 507–509.

82. Ibid.

83. Ibid., p. 496.

84. Ibid., pp. 483–485.

85. Ibid., p. 483.

86. Ibid., p. 481.

87. Ibid., p. 483.

88. Ibid., p. 496.

89. Ibid., p. 501. *See* Russell v. National Mediation Board, 714 F.2d 1332 (5th Cir. 1983).

90. Ibid., p. 500.

91. United States v. Feaster, 410 F.2d 1354 (5th Cir. 1969).

92. Wilner, "Railway Labor Act," p. 243.

93. Northrup, "Railway Labor Act," p. 500.

94. Stone, "Labor Relations," pp. 1486–1493.

95. Elizabeth L. Cocanougher, "Merging the RLA and the NLRA for Eastern Air Lines: Can it Fly?" *Univeristy of Miami Law Review* 44 (1989): 539.

96. *See* Wilner, "Railway Labor Act," p. 281.

97. Frank N. Wilner, "The Railway Labor Act: Why, What and for How Much Longer, Part II," *Transportation Practitioners Journal* 57 (1990): 129.

98. Dennis O. Lynch, "Statutory Rights and Arbitral Values: Some Conclusions," *University of Miami Law Review* 44 (1989): 617, 620–625..

99. Northrup, "Railway Labor Act," p. 460.

100. Ibid., p. 476.

101. Ibid.

102. Ibid., p. 515.

103. Wilner, "Railway Labor Act, Part II," p. 155.

104. Lynch, "Statutory Rights," p. 625.

105. Ibid.

106. Arouca and Perritt, "Transportation Labor Regulation," p. 145.

107. Ibid., p. 171.

108. Henry H. Perritt, Jr., "Aspects of Labor Law Affecting Labor-Management Cooperation in the Railroad and Airline Industries," *Pepperdine Law Review* 16 (1989): 501.

109. Ibid., p. 524.

110. Ibid., p. 569.

111. McCabe, "Critique," p. 215.

112. Stone, "Labor Relations," p. 1485.

113. Ibid., p. 1537.

114. Ibid., p. 1545.

115. Ibid., p. 1547.

116. Athanassios Papaioannou, "The Duty to Bargain and Rejection of Collective Agreements under Section 1113 by a Bankrupt Airlines: Trying to Reconcile R.L.A.with Bankruptcy Code," *Transportation Law Journal* 18 (1990): 219.

117. Ibid.

7

Railroad Passenger Service

DERAILING THE PASSENGER

With the exception of the heavily traveled Boston-Washington corridor, service levels on American passenger trains are the most infrequent of any industrial nation. Much of this decline has been the result of government emphasis on highways and private automobiles for movement of people between cities. Other modes of transit have filled the gap previously met by passenger trains; airlines have developed an internal system much more rapidly in the United States than elsewhere, and the intercity bus system developed on a relatively untrammeled private basis.

Passenger trains are labor-intensive, due to the necessity for on-train services, fare collection, and because of agreements between the railroads and the operating brotherhoods. The railroads, which devote most of their interest to freight traffic, found it more profitable to discontinue the trains rather than to renegotiate the labor agreements. The pricing of rail travel was between bus and air fares, but on a fully allocated basis, the rail fare would have to have been higher than that of air travel. If that were done however, virtually no one would ride the trains.

For this and other reasons (obsolescence of equipment and need for replacement, freight train interference, wish to be free of bad public relations, etc.) the major railroads moved to discontinue passenger service on a piecemeal basis during the 1950s and 1960s. Sometimes this was done through downgrading of service on trains so as to reduce patronage. The train would show a greater loss and impress regulators with the urgent need for relief.[1]

The ICC had supplanted the state regulatory agencies in permitting exit from the passenger train business in 1958. Less influenced by hometown considerations, the ICC was more lenient about allowing exit than the states had ever been. During this time, most of the major passenger routes were down to one train a day, and even these were being posted for discontinuance. The commission attempted a sort of moratorium while Congress was deliberating what type of bill to pass.

Assuming the political necessity of passenger trains, and seeing that traditional regulation could not preserve the last trains on many routes, Congress wrestled with the need for government intervention. Proposals took two forms: subsidies or nationalization. Subsidies proved to be politically unpopular, since the beneficiaries would be the same railroads that had done their best to discourage the few remaining passengers, and nationalization sounded much too left-leaning for the Nixon administration.[2] The result was that Congress rejected both alternatives in favor of an ostensibly private National Railroad Passenger Corporation, first known as Railpax, but which soon emerged as Amtrak.[3]

THE AMTRAK APPROACH

On paper, the National Railroad Passenger Corporation is a for-profit private entity and not a part of the U.S. government.[4] Even though Amtrak is considered private (and obligated to pay property tax to the local communities through which it runs), over one-quarter of its budget comes from government subsidy.

How, then, was Amtrak, as a private concern, supposed to succeed where other private lines had failed? The theory was that a streamlined system could reduce deficits by consolidating traffic on the stronger lines and consolidating terminals and other duplicative facilities. By ordering equipment on a nationwide scale and operating on a countrywide basis, economies of scale could be attained in marketing, purchases, and operations.

Perhaps the Amtrak scheme was never expected to be a money-maker. Congress may only have intended an effort to get the passenger monkey off the railroads' backs. In this way, the Rail Passenger Service Act was a prorailroad rather than a propassenger statute. Amtrak's first president, Roger Lewis, with his initial cautious moves, seemed to betray the fact that Amtrak was meant to be a passenger euthanasia scheme.[5] Every secretary of transportation since Volpe has come up with some variant of the slow withering-away of passenger service as his department's philosophy for Amtrak. However, Congress has come to the rescue of Amtrak again and again.[6]

Amtrak, outside the Northeast Corridor (which it owns), functions through the mechanism of contracts with operating railroads. The railroads supply trackage rights and are reimbursed their costs plus a small profit and incentive costs for on-time performance. With any cost-plus arrangement there is room for a great deal of manipulation of apportionment of costs between passenger and freight service. There is room for excess padding of costs to Amtrak, which are thus folded into the cost base for Amtrak. The result is an Amtrak deficit; this, of course, is picked up by the general taxpayer.

AMTRAK AND REGULATION

Since Amtrak is thought of as a proprietary program, it is a bit unusual to think of the Rail Passenger Service Act as a deregulation law. But inasmuch as it took passenger trains out from under ICC regulation, it can be seen as the first of the transportation deregulatory bills of the 1970s.

Upon passage, the Rail Passenger Service Act established a moratorium on abandonments, along with a delegation to the secretary of transportation to draw up a system for long-haul passenger trains.[7] From October 1970 to May 1971, no passenger train could be discontinued.

Upon a railroad's contracting with Amtrak to provide service, the carrier was relieved of the responsibility for operating its own passenger trains.[8] But if a railroad did not contract with Amtrak at its inception, it could not discontinue service until 1975.[9] Most lines were quick to take advantage of this provision, although some hung on as independent carriers for quite a while.[10] Even Amtrak was originally subject to the ICC if it wanted to eliminate trains in the "basic system," but that provision was later removed by amendment of the Amtrak law. Presently, the ICC has no role in Amtrak, and the passenger corporation is limited only by its own internal criteria (and whims of Congress) in discontinuing service.[11] As far as entry to and exit from market is concerned, Amtrak is a deregulator's dream. The route structure of the system is unregulated, and Amtrak can (theoretically) spend its resources as it sees fit.

Actually, Congress has not been content to let Amtrak pick and choose routes. Several times it has intervened to protect or institute certain politically sensitive routes. Congressmen are reluctant to let a service that benefits their district disappear. The only substantial cuts to date have been those that were implemented by congressional directive in 1979 and 1981. In 1979 the secretary of transportation was mandated to draw up a revised system, which is the basis for the slimmed-down Amtrak network that is operating today.[12] Even then, Congress set some standards to ensure "regional balance" into the criteria for discontinuance.

The ICC has never had any jurisdiction over Amtrak's fares, and the passenger corporation has tried all sorts of promotional schemes, excursion fares, and even one year giving children rides in exchange for Kellogg's box tops![13] This presents a problem because Amtrak is heavily subsidized and competes for traffic with carriers receiving no direct subsidy. As a result in 1978 Congress enacted a section giving some rudimentary control to the ICC if it discovers that Amtrak's rate-cutting is destructive or predatory as to its effect on a more independent carrier.[14] The ICC has not yet seen fit to exercise these powers. Amtrak, however, is directed to recover more of its costs from passenger fares. Currently, over 70 percent of Amtrak's revenues come from ticket sales.

The ICC had some oversight functions over Amtrak at the beginning. Section 801 of the original act gave the ICC the power to require certain standards (sleeping cars on overnight runs, dining cars at mealtime, stations open for service before the train arrives, etc.) that the commission had denied it possessed in the *Sunset Limited Adequacies* case.[15] These functions were not desired by either the ICC or Amtrak, and as part of general deregulation fervor, they were removed with the Amtrak Improvement Act of 1978.[16]

Amtrak's achievements include replacing and upgrading the passenger train equipment in the United States, improving and coordinating service, and reversing the secular decline in railroad passengers. Although there is less service today, what remains is of higher quality than was operated in the 1960s under private management.

AMTRAK AS A HARBINGER OF DEREGULATION

Rail passenger service—in 1970 handling less than 5 percent of intercity traffic—was considered a small, discrete area where one could determine if deregulation worked. It was an experiment for the liberalization of control of railroads, inasmuch as one segment of the industry operated without ICC supervision.

Amtrak is not a classic example of deregulation because there is only one provider of service, the service is heavily subsidized, and politics have played a big part in operations of the system. During the last twenty years, Amtrak supervision has shifted from the Interstate Commerce Commission to the Department of Transportation to Congress.

The Amtrak experience emphasizes one factor in deregulation: If Congress does not like the results, it can always recapture the power and attempt to regulate transportation itself. Since Amtrak is such a large recipient of federal funds, it seems natural that congressmen would want to direct what service is offered their constituents.

Amtrak represents an attempt to aid a regulated industry by unloading an unwanted and unrenumerative service on the general public. The same has occurred with commuter rail transportation, and the establishment of Conrail to isolate money-losing Eastern lines from the nationwide rail system. Conrail became profitable enough to be moved into the private sector; it now operates as an ordinary freight railroad. Amtrak, although still subsidized, receives more of its funds from the fare box than any other passenger railway in the world. Amtrak's projections are to not require any government subsidy for operations after the year 2000. However, capital funding would still be needed for equipment, trackwork, signaling, electrification, and other improvements to those rails that it, rather than freight railroads, owns.

AMTRAK AT TWENTY

The National Railroad Passenger Corporation enters its third decade as a fixture on the railroad scene. (For example, Amtrak is the largest customer of the Central Vermont Railway and an important contribution to the profit and loss picture of many freight railroads.) The Clinton administration has abandoned the Reagan-Bush rhetoric of zero funding for Amtrak and has placed the passenger system in its annual budget. Twenty-one years of rail operation have given the NRPC legitimacy in the political world.

What It Does and Where It Goes

Amtrak operates rail passenger service in forty-five states.[17] Virtually all service is intercity traffic, linking metropolitan areas of one million or more. The passenger corporation is restricted to intercity rail passenger traffic,[18] but it is also a contractor, providing commuter rail service for public transit authorities in Massachusetts, Maryland, Virginia, Connecticut, and California.[19] Since 1971, the number of annual intercity Amtrak passengers has grown from seventeen to twenty-two million (Figure 7.1). In 1991, there were almost as many contract commuter passengers as intercity passengers (Figure 7.1).

In addition to the operation of intercity passenger trains, Amtrak does repairs, overhauls, and rebuilds rail equipment for other carriers at its Beech Grove, Indiana, shops, operates a fiber-optic system along its Northeast Corridor lines, leases space in its stations to concessionaires, and conducts a package express service. A large amount of U.S. mail is carried in Amtrak long-distance trains.

Amtrak owns the railroad between Boston and Washington and branches to Harrisburg, Pennsylvania, and Springfield, Massachusetts. In addition, the corporation owns a considerable amount of trackage in Michigan. Service is operated out of the hubs of New York,[20] Philadelphia, Chicago, and Los Angeles. Most long-distance routes have one train daily; the most intensive service is found in the Northeast Corridor (Boston-Washington), between New York City and upstate New York, and between Los Angeles and San Diego.

Outside of Amtrak-owned trackage, passenger trains are operated under trackage rights agreements with the cooperating railroads. Railways are required to provide their tracks to Amtrak at reasonable rates for operation of passenger services. The current policy of Amtrak is to confine its routes to the main lines of the freight railroads. Not only are these lines better maintained, but potentially such a policy can reduce costs resulting from

Figure 7.1
Amtrak Intercity and Commuter Passengers

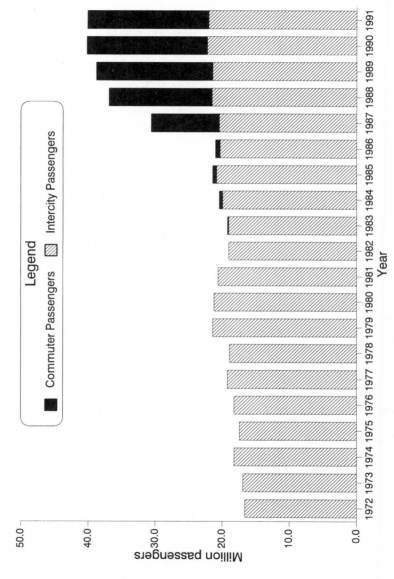

Source: Railroad Facts (Washington, D.C.: Association of American Railroads, various years)

avoiding secondary lines or passenger-only lines where Amtrak could be stuck with the bill of maintenance costs that are ascribed mostly to passenger operation. This means that when a freight railroad downgrades a main line, Amtrak will usually cooperate in finding a reroute.[21] As railroads have merged, there have been changes in the designation of mainline track and a certain amount of consolidation and rationalization of routes.

Amtrak's Trains: A Geographical Perspective[22]

Amtrak has been a dynamic passenger rail system its first two decades of existence. A quick analysis of Amtrak timetables for the past twenty years reveals a system network that has averaged more than four major route changes per year with some years seeing massive additions and deletions to the route structure. Through it all, however, Amtrak has settled down and is now maintaining a fairly stable network, although new routes are continuing to be evaluated for their feasibility and contribution to the national system. The national system peaked in 1979 with 27,000 route miles, but since that time has stabilized at 25,000 route miles (Figure 7.2).

The Northeast Corridor

Jean Gottman called the dense population corridor stretching between Washington, D.C., and Boston, Massachusetts, the Megalopolis.[23] The northeast corridor between Washington, D.C., and Boston has always been the bread and butter of the Amtrak system. The number of passengers traveling by train along the Amtrak system has always been dominated by the trains speeding along the corridor. Without this backbone of busy service, Amtrak would probably not exist today. The northeast corridor is essentially comprised of two segments: New York to Boston; and, New York to Washington. Between New York and Boston, nine through trains were included in the initial Amtrak system. The train names between Bean Town and the Big Apple included the Bostonian, the Bay State, the Colonial, the Yankee Clipper, the Senator, the Merchants Limited, the Patriot, the New Yorker, the Murray Hill, and Turboservice. The overnight Federal (the oldest named train in the country) between Boston and Washington was, however, discontinued between New York and Washington, and no changes were made to the predecessor Penn Central service, except that the overnight Federal and the connecting train to the Palmland/Gulf Coast Special were retired.

Twenty years later, the Amtrak system timetable shows through trains from Boston to Washington like the Night Owl, the Connecticut Yankee, the Mayflower, the Virginian, the Yankee Clipper, the Patriot, the Benjamin Franklin, the New England Express, the Bay State, the Senator, and the Merchants Limited. New names like Executive Sleeper and Night Owl

Figure 7.2
Amtrak System Miles

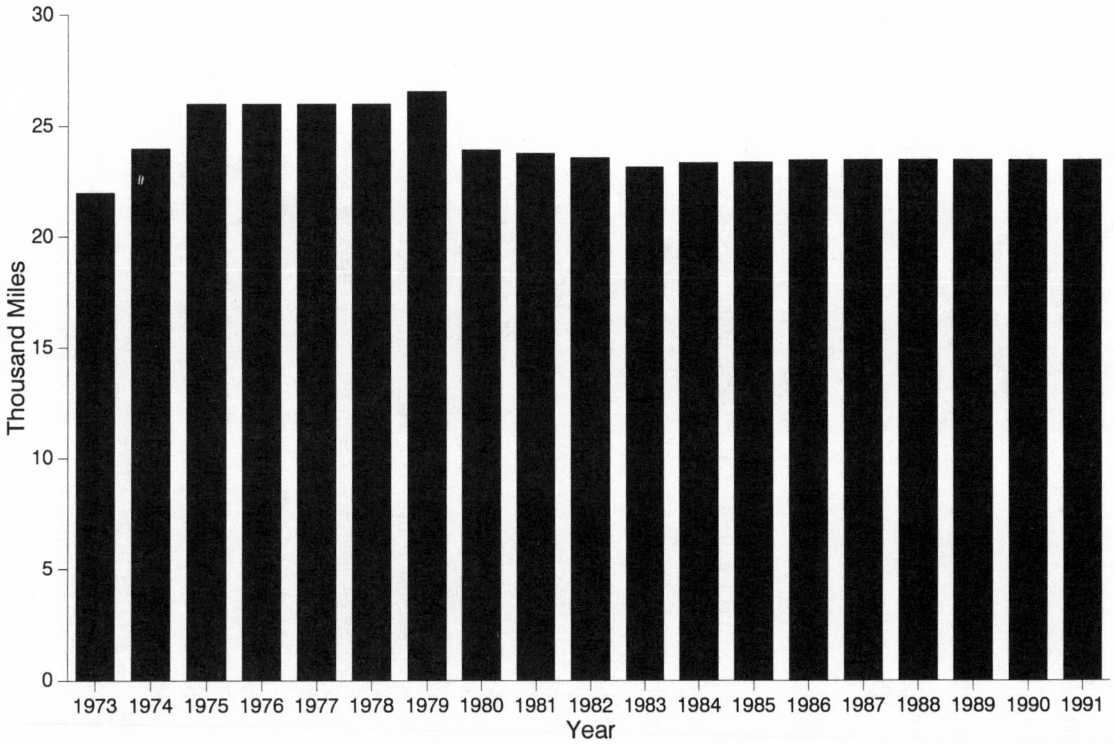

Source: *Railroad Facts* (Washington, D.C.: Association of American Railroads, various years)

reveal that Amtrak is running train service outside of normal business hours catering to overnight business travel in the northeast corridor.

The greatest single boost for Amtrak service in the northeast corridor came on April 1, 1976, when Amtrak became a "real" railroad and acquired its own trackage. Amtrak acquired 621 miles of right-of-way along the northeast corridor from the Penn Central, as well as another Penn Central line between Porter, Indiana, and Kalamazoo, Michigan. The ability of Amtrak to acquire property was possible because of the passage of the Regional Rail Reorganization (Three-R) Act of 1973 and the Railroad Revitalization and Regulatory Reform (Four-R) Act of 1976. However, none of the property acquisitions would have been meaningful without the resources to make massive improvements to the corridor, enabling Amtrak to improve corridor service and eventually compete with the regional airlines' shuttles. On March 31, 1977, the Northeast Corridor Improvement Project (NECIP) took off, allowing Amtrak to spend $2.5 billion to upgrade the railroading infrastructure along the corridor between Washington and New York to allow trains to run at 125 miles per hour. In 1994, work is now now underway to erect electric catenary on the remaining 150 miles between New Haven and Boston.

Empire Service

Penn Central's restructured Empire Service was cut from five to three round trips daily between New York and Buffalo. Four additional runs were retained between New York and Albany. This line was the first of Amtrak's routes to see substantial reduction in frequency of service.

Two decades later, Amtrak service between New York and Albany has grown to fourteen trains a day with several continuing on further beyond the New York State capital. Seven of the fourteen trains terminate in Albany-Rensselaer, while the other seven go on to reach terminals in Schenectady, Syracuse, Buffalo, Niagara Falls, Toronto, and Montreal.

The Empire Seaboard

Amtrak service along the east coast, that is, passenger train service south of Washington, D.C., and the northeast corridor, is characterized by service from New York to Florida. Frequency of through Amtrak service consisted of three trains in 1971. The Silver Meteor, the Silver Star, and the Champion, remnants of the Penn Central, the Richmond, Fredericksburg & Potomac, and the Seaboard Coast Line provided service three times per day to points in Florida, terminating in Miami and St. Petersburg.

Twenty years later, the Silver Star and Silver Meteor continue to provide daily service to Florida, although now Amtrak travels over the rails of the CSX Corporation south of Alexandria, Virginia. The Champion was lost in massive service cuts in 1979. Figure 7.1 above shows the drop in Amtrak route miles after 1979, and the Champion was one of those losses. However, the Palmetto was added to provide service between New York and Savannah. This train was later extended to serve Jacksonville.

The Southeast

The southeast quadrant of the United States benefited from passenger train service provided by roads like the Illinois Central, the Gulf, Mobile & Ohio, the Louisville & Nashville, the Atlantic Coast Line, the Seaboard Air Line, the Georgia Railroad, and most notably, the Southern Railway. Passenger routes crossed the South linking the Midwest with the South and the Atlantic Ocean with the Gulf of Mexico. In 1971, the only passenger service remaining was that provided by the Southern Railway between Washington, D.C., and New Orleans via Atlanta and Birmingham. The Southern Railway continued to provide passenger service from the northeast cities of New York and Washington to the southeast cities of Atlanta, Birmingham, and New Orleans until 1978. At that time the Southern turned over service to Amtrak and the service has continued through the second decade of Amtrak.

A second Amtrak route to the Southeast originated in the Midwest out of Chicago. The South Wind was upgraded to provide daily service when Amtrak began serving Louisville, Nashville, Birmingham, Montgomery, and Jacksonville. From Jacksonville, the train turned south down the Florida coast with coaches, sleepers, and a diner going to Miami, and coaches and sleepers splitting off south of Orlando for Tampa and St. Petersburg. This route later became the route of the Floridian, which, after several attempts at Auto-Train service, was discontinued in 1979 during massive Amtrak cuts.

The path across the Southeast from Chicago to Florida is a noticeable gap in the Amtrak national system map. However, with the Olympic games in Atlanta in 1996, that condition may change. As of this writing, Amtrak is actively studying route alternates south from Chicago via Louisville and Nashville or Cincinnati and Chattanooga.

Trunk Lines to the Midwest

The geography of passenger train transportation has changed much between the east coast and the Midwest through the years of Amtrak-provided service. As originally planned, Amtrak provided service between the east coast and Chicago via two routes: the Broadway Limited between New York and Chicago; and the National Limited between New York and Kansas City via St. Louis.

In the most controversial decision made by Amtrak, on May 1, 1971, the two largest cities in the nation at the time were limited to one train a day in each direction. The fact that, prior to that date, the two metropolises enjoyed seven trains per day over three different routes of the Penn Central, made this service cut proportionally the most severe cut in service within the basic system. The NRPC chose the Broadway Limited, the train with the highest ridership, and combined it with the Kansas City train east of Harrisburg and with the Washington train west of Harrisburg. In addition, a day train, the Dusquesne, was slated to run between New York and Pittsburgh. No service at all was provided initially to Cleveland and Toledo. The omission of Cleveland seemed inexplicable. The city, America's twelfth largest at the time, has a long tradition of local and intercity rail travel with a sizable terminal in the heart of the city. However, the Pittsburgh route was a bit shorter and faster, carried more traffic, and did not encounter the huge terminal costs of Toledo and Cleveland.

It was not long before the "Water Level" route omission was rectified. The Lake Shore was instituted May 10, 1971, as 403b service, nine days after the birth of Amtrak, but perhaps the original Amtrak planners knew better; for the Lake Shore was also the first Amtrak discontinuance, bowing out of service on January 5, 1972. This route still represented a significant corridor with substantial population density and a long tradition of train ridership. By 1975, the demand was back and the New York Central's famous Lake Shore Limited was reincarnated by Amtrak on October 31, 1975; this time for good.

Two decades into Amtrak service three major routes are available to the train passenger traveling between the east coast and Chicago. In addition to the Lake Shore Limited, the Broadway Limited continues to provide service between New York/Washington, and Chicago via Pittsburgh, and the Capitol Limited provides daily service between Chicago and Washington with connecting service north to New York and south to Miami. The Broadway Limited was an original Amtrak route and the Capitol Limited was created in 1981.

One of the losses during the large service cuts in 1979 was the National Limited, which provided service between New York and Kansas City via St. Louis. This former Penn Central route (New York to St. Louis and named the Spirit of St. Louis) was eliminated during the Carter years when the national system was evaluated with the goal of eliminating routes with patronage below the standards set.[24]

Service between Washington and Cincinnati was provided through the Appalachian hills on the George Washington via Alexandria, Charlottesville, and White Sulphur Springs. Assuming that the incoming train to Cincinnati was on time, passengers could then connect to the James Whitcomb Riley providing service to Chicago from Cincinnati via Indianapolis, Indiana. Unfortunately, passengers traveling east over this route were faced with a seven hour and thirty-five minute wait overnight in Cincinnati to make the James Whitcomb Riley to the George Washington connection. The James Whitcomb Riley and the George Washington were later combined to provide a through service from Chicago to Newport News and Washington. On January 8, 1982, Amtrak introduced the Cardinal with triweekly through service between Washington and Chicago via Cincinnati and Indianapolis. This train is still in operation with discussion ongoing about making the Cardinal a daily service.

Chicago Gateway

Chicago has always been a railroad city, marking the western terminus of most eastern railroads and the eastern terminus of most western railroads. In addition to being the major railroad crossroads of the country, Chicago also serves as one of two Amtrak gateways to points west. Short distance Amtrak trains radiate out of Chicago in several directions along well-traveled corridors. When Amtrak began in 1971, corridor routes from Chicago were established to Cincinnati, Carbondale, St. Louis, Milwaukee, and Detroit. These corridor routes have essentially stayed the same for the past two decades, but the noticeable change has been in the level of service provided. What began as one or two trains per day and four in the case of Chicago to Milwaukee, has expanded into even greater traffic.

Twice daily service to Detroit has grown to four trains a day with one, the International, going on to cross the Canadian border to Toronto and one, the Lake Cities, continuing on to Toledo Detroit service was extended to Pontiac in 1994. Amtrak service to Carbondale has stayed the same, but the name Illini has been given to the train that terminates in Carbondale. Hiawatha Service between Chicago and Milwaukee has increased from four round trips each way to seven round-trip trains. Passengers between Chicago and St. Louis now have three trains each way instead of the two originally included in the Amtrak system.

The only losses in Amtrak service out of the Chicago gateway have been the 1991 loss of the Calumet, which had provided service to Valparaiso; the Prairie Marksman to Peoria in 1981; the Illini to Decatur; and the Black Hawk to Dubuque in 1981. Other Amtrak trains have come and gone in the Midwest that were linked with Chicago, but Valparaiso, Decatur, Peoria, and Dubuque are cities where there were no other Amtrak passenger trains passing through, resulting in a loss of passenger train service altogether.

Still other cities have seen the addition of dedicated Amtrak service to their community out of Chicago. Indianapolis has been served by the Hoosier State every day since October 1, 1980, and Grand Rapids, Michigan, has been served daily by the Pere Marquette since August 4, 1984.

There is one additional train that radiates from Chicago, providing long distance service. The City of New Orleans, made famous in song by Arlo Guthrie and others, has remained relatively unchanged—except for flipping the schedule around to be a predominantly overnight train, rather than a daylight run.

Southwest

Amtrak service to the Southwest goes in two directions: south to the Lone Star State, and west to the Pacific coast. Prior to Amtrak's formation, the only through service to Texas was the Santa Fe Texas Chief via Kansas City, Oklahoma City, and Fort Worth. This train was continued by Amtrak with eventual rerouting through Dallas and then on to Houston. Later, a leg was also extended to San Antonio. In 1974 the Inter-American was moved to include Dallas and the route was extended to St. Louis. The intent from the beginning of Amtrak was to operate the Inter-American over the Dallas to St. Louis route, but contract negotiations with Union Station in Dallas involved four railroads and were not complete when Amtrak was ready to publish their first timetable. By 1976 the Inter-American was extended to Chicago with daily service provided during the summer season.

While the Inter-American was providing service within Texas, the Texas Chief was providing service to Texas from the Midwest. The Texas Chief operated from Chicago to Houston via Kansas City, Oklahoma City, Fort Worth, and Temple until October 1979, when all Chicago to Texas service was consolidated into the Inter-American. The Texas Chief had also changed names prior to this consolidation.

In April 1978 Amtrak signed contracts with the Missouri Pacific Railroad allowing it to operate from Chicago to Texas over Missouri Pacific tracks with two hours shaved off the schedule. However, the Inter-American was cut back from Laredo to San Antonio, and the Temple to Houston leg was eliminated. The Inter-American ceased to exist on September 30, 1981, and on October 1, 1981, the route was christened the Eagle, once the proud name of the crack Missouri Pacific trains operating south and west out of St. Louis. Through cars are handled via the Southern Pacific route to Los Angeles.

When Amtrak began operations, the former Santa Fe Super Chief was continued by Amtrak from Chicago to Los Angeles, but the Milwaukee Road/Union Pacific City of Los Angeles was discontinued, thereby ending, for a time, service to Las Vegas. Amtrak has continued to operate the Chief, although it has undergone a name change. Complaints by the Santa Fe Railroad about Amtrak's failure to maintain the onboard service standards of the Santa Fe prompted Amtrak to change the name of the Super Chief to the Southwest Limited. Currently it is called the Southwest Chief, a nice compromise.

Sunset Limited service from Miami to Los Angeles also traverses the southwest portion of the United States. The triweekly service adopted by Amtrak from the Southern Pacific Railroad has remained unchanged over the past two decades, but as of this writing big things are happening. When Amtrak began service, the Southern Railway was still providing passenger rail service between New York, Washington, and New Orleans. The Southern Railway's Crescent provided a convenient coast to coast connection, but did not provide a "true" transcontinental train. When the Southern turned over passenger operation to Amtrak, the connection continued as it has always been. In April 1993, the Sunset Limited became a true transcontinental train by extending its route eastward to Jacksonville, Florida, and then south to Miami.

Service to Las Vegas was restored on October 28, 1979, when the Desert Wind began service between Salt Lake City, Utah, and Los Angeles over Santa Fe tracks west of Las Vegas and Union Pacific tracks east of Las Vegas. The Desert Wind joins up with the famous California Zephyr in Salt Lake City on its eastward trek and is split from the CZ in the opposite direction.

Across the West

Except for the Sunset Limited, Chicago is the origin of all Amtrak trains to the West. When Amtrak began, there were only three major western routes: southwest via the Super Chief/El Capitan (as previously described); west to Denver and beyond on the Denver Zephyr and California Zephyr. respectively; and, northwest to Seattle on the Empire Builder. The great western routes offer some of the most spectacular train viewing in the world as they pass through the prairies, mountains, and deserts towards the Pacific coast. Amtrak aimed at preserving a scenic ride through the Rockies and Sierras and decided to combine the overnight Denver Zephyr of the Burlington Northern with a triweekly extension to San Francisco over the Rio Grande to Salt Lake City, the Western Pacific to Wells, Nevada, and the Southern Pacific beyond. The final route selection, however, showed apparent railroad influence.

Having discontinued its last passenger train after a bitter fight in 1970, the Western Pacific had no intention of getting back into the passenger business and refused to allow the NRPC to use its tracks, or even to allow its employees to talk with Amtrak officials.[25] The position of management was that, having divested itself of its passenger burden, there was no financial incentive for it to clutter its line with high-priority passenger trains. Thereupon, Amtrak entered into an agreement with the Union Pacific, whereby the Union Pacific would haul the train thirty-six miles between Salt Lake City and Ogden, forming a connection between the Southern Pacific and Rio Grande lines.

When the Rio Grande refused to join the NRPC, Amtrak had to work out a revised eleventh-hour agreement with Union Pacific to operate the train between Denver and Ogden. This route has neither the scenic selling points nor the year-round resort traffic offered by Colorado, and it did not serve Salt Lake City.[26] It did, however, preserve passenger service in Wyoming. Amtrak had the right under Section 402 of the Act to apply to the ICC to require the Rio Grande or Western Pacific to make their tracks available for the original route, but it did not take such action.[27] The Rio Grande was compelled to operate its triweekly Denver to Ogden Rio Grande Zephyr at least through 1973, which management inscrutably operated on the same days that the Amtrak train operated. In June 1971 the Rio Grande substituted a limousine for the Salt Lake City to Ogden portion of the run.

Finally, in the spring of 1983, the Rio Grande turned over service of the Rio Grande Zephyr to Amtrak, thereby allowing Amtrak to provide the cross-Colorado service it so desperately wanted. The California Zephyr was rerouted and then provided service from Chicago to Oakland. That negative impact resulting from the move to Rio Grande tracks was the loss of passenger train service across Wyoming. This situation was rectified in June 1991, when the Pioneer was extended eastbound from Ogden, Utah, to Cheyenne (Borie) and south to Denver.

On June 7, 1977, The Pioneer began service to the Northwest from Ogden to Portland, Oregon, and Seattle, Washington. This scenic route, however, was hindered by a less than rider-friendly schedule that had patrons leaving the West early in the morning and spending long hours waiting for connecting trains in Utah. This schedule was much improved in 1991, when the Pioneer was extended over Union Pacific tracks across southern Wyoming, a faster route, thereby allowing a later departure hour for eastbound passengers departing Seattle. Perhaps the greatest benefit was to the six Wyoming communities that saw passenger train service return to their towns after an eight-year absence. This service was reduced to tri-weekly in 1993.

One of the most famous routes west by passenger train has been the legendary route of the Empire Builder that traverses the upper Midwest out of Chicago to the Twin Cities and then across the plains to the Rocky Mountains and Glacier National Park. From the Continental Divide, the Empire Builder crosses the inter mountain basin of eastern Washington and then up and over the Cascades before arriving in Seattle. The Empire Builder has been in existence since the beginning of Amtrak, and this route was the first to see double-decked Superliner equipment in 1979. Until the rebirth of the Grand Canyon Railway, the Empire Builder was the only passenger train in the United States to provide direct service to a national park.[28] The Empire Builder now operates with a Portland section.

In Amtrak's first summer another western route was added to the Amtrak system map. The North Coast Hiawatha was initiated to provide passenger train service between Chicago and Seattle across the southern half of the state of Montana. This route gave access to people living in Butte, Montana, and other towns, but it also provided closer access to Yellowstone National Park. During the system cuts of 1979, the North Coast Hiawatha suffered the same fate as other famous named trains—the Floridian, the National Limited, and the Champion.

When Amtrak began in 1971, west coast service consisted of one train operating triweekly along the Pacific coast. In addition to the through service, two trains operated daily between Portland and Seattle; three operated daily between Los Angeles and San Diego; and the Los Angeles to Oakland service operated daily. Through service between Seattle and San Diego lasted a short time, but after a while, passengers were forced to change trains in Los Angeles for the short Surf Line run to San Diego. Triweekly service along the west coast was soon expanded to daily service during peak summer months, and has since evolved into the Coast Starlight daily service that has proven to be one of Amtrak's most popular trains in the West.

Increases in passenger train service in California are fast approaching the intensity of passenger trains in the northeast corridor. The second busiest Amtrak corridor is the route of the San Diegans operating between Los Angeles and San Diego. What started as three trains per day has grown to nine trains each way, with many passengers utilizing the service for commuting purposes in car-clogged southern California. Another route, the Capitol, has linked San Jose and Sacramento since 1991, and frequent service is also offered between Oakland and Bakersfield via the San Joaquin Valley.

Labor Agreements

As a privately owned railroad (albeit one with government subsidy and encouragement), Amtrak is considered a carrier under Part I of the Railway Labor Act. Its employees are not government workers; they are free to strike.

At Amtrak's inception, it contracted with freight railroads to provide crews and station personnel. Now, Amtrak is a railroad in its own right. It owns its busiest lines and operates under trackage rights agreement with host railroads elsewhere.

In 1982 after passage of the Northeast Rail Services Act, Amtrak-Northeast corridor employees had the option of remaining with Conrail in freight service, going with the newly constituted commuter rail operations, or becoming full-time Amtrak employees. Within the last ten years, Amtrak has become its own employer of all on-train crews (engineers included), and all station personnel.

One of the results of this takeover has been that Amtrak has the first straight-time contract of any railroad. Employees are paid on the basis of an eight-hour day, rather than any mileage formula. This change made it possible for Amtrak to reduce its operating losses and hence its need for subsidy. Amtrak has a far more favorable situation than the private railroads had in operating their passenger service and is in better shape to compete with airlines and buses for the travel dollar.

Because of its control of the work force, Amtrak is able to establish its own crew bases and seniority districts. At present, there are no definite plans for a universal roster, and not all Amtrak trainmen can bump less senior railroaders to any job in the country. In particular, the Northeast corridor maintains a separate seniority roster.

Because of its separate status, Amtrak continued operating over its own lines during the nationwide railroad strike of 1992. However, train operations ceased on those lines operated over freight railroads.

The fact that there has been no strike yet against Amtrak does not mean complete employee satisfaction. However, the political reality is if there was a strike, the passenger corporation would just cease running and not receive the congressional subsidies it still requires.

Since the Railway Labor Act does not outlaw secondary boycotts, Amtrak is vulnerable to having its facilities picketed by other railroads or even airlines. If this were to happen, its unionized employees might be expected to honor those picket lines, as happened during the 1992 railroad strike.

Eminent Domain and Trackage Rights

Passenger trains may provide operating headaches for freight railroads, in that these trains require speed and priority. Passengers complain if they are sidetracked for freights. They require a degree of track maintenance that freight trains might not need. While some railroads welcome the cash flow which Amtrak rental payments give them, other railroads just wish that Amtrak would keep its trains off their lines for good.

The law requires that the railroads make their tracks available to Amtrak for operation of its regular services, as well as for special trains and detour moves.[29] The Amtrak act also provided for a twenty-five-year period during which a host railroad must keep its tracks in at least as good operating condition as they were when Amtrak commenced operation.

In practice, Amtrak operations staff works closely with private railroads in choosing lines and designating preferred and alternate routes. This makes good business sense for Amtrak, as the passenger corporation wishes to avoid a situation where a line is primarily operated for passenger service and Amtrak would then have to pay most of the maintenance. A railroad must come to terms with Amtrak over operations, or an arbitrator is named to set terms for Amtrak's use of the line. (With detours, ad hoc decisions are made, and the route chosen depends upon reasonable alternatives. For example, Amtrak was prevented from using Rio Grande's Royal Gorge route through Tennessee Pass when the Grande's Moffat Tunnel route was blocked. However, an alternative route on the Union Pacific through Wyoming has been available to Amtrak.)

If a route is necessary, and the railroad refuses to make its track available, Amtrak does have the right to condemn the line through eminent domain powers.[30] This has only been used on one occasion to date.

Since 1972 Amtrak has operated the Montrealer between Washington, D.C., and Montreal, Canada, on a circuitous route through New Hampshire and Vermont. North of Springfield, Massachusetts, the train followed the Boston & Maine Railroad to White River Junction, Vermont, where a Central

Vermont crew took over the run into Canada. Track became worn out and, in places, a 10 mph speed limit was imposed. Amtrak suspended the popular train in 1987 and initiated proceedings to condemn Boston & Maine's track. Upon meeting a condemnation price set by the ICC, Amtrak immediately turned over the line to the Central Vermont Railway, which like Amtrak, had been a tenant of Boston & Maine's. (Amtrak, after the line was repaired, switched to an all-Central Vermont routing via New London, Connecticut.)

Although the ICC had approved the $2.3 million condemnation,[31] Guilford Transportation, the corporate parent of Boston & Maine, appealed the decision to the courts. The United States Court of Appeals for the District of Columbia Circuit held that the condemnation was not for Amtrak's purposes, but for the maintenance of a competing railroad. The court held that the Act does not permit Amtrak "to take property by eminent domain for which it concededly has no need itself merely because there is another private party that would like to have it and will pay Amtrak for the privilege of having it condemned."[32] Congress later passed legislation allowing such transfers.[33] The D.C. Circuit Court of Appeals stated that the new legislation must still call for a valid exercise of condemnation powers.[34]

The power of eminent domain remains intact, but Amtrak must use it for its corporate purposes, that is, rail passenger service, and must not be a cat's paw for a covetous freight railroad. Amtrak, of course, would prefer not to have to maintain its own lines for a one-train-a-day schedule, and generally works in cooperation with freight railroads, using their best lines. Avoiding the cost of using its own railroad, Amtrak usually functions under a contractual trackage-right arrangement with its host mainline. Still, the amicable agreements worked out have the underlying threat that that passenger corporation can use its statutory powers to compel the lines to reach an agreement.

The Future of Amtrak

After twenty years of operation, Amtrak is a definite steady component of America's transportation system. However, it provides frequent and speedy transportation only in the Northeast and in California. Otherwise, the system is of limited utility to business travelers. (Overnight services that attract a sleeping-car trade are Washington-Chicago; New York–Atlanta: Chicago-Denver, and Boston-Washington. Otherwise, the routes are too lengthy and time-consuming for business travel.)

W. Graham Claytor was president of Amtrak from 1982 until 1993. Formerly chief executive of the Southern Railway and more recently, secretary of the navy, Claytor was responsible for the nationwide labor agreements, for the continued reequipping of equipment, and for the purchase of stations and rail lines. Most impressive has been the reduction of subsidy requirements. In March 1991, the passenger railroad's revenue-to-cost ratio was 83 percent.[35] As a result, President Claytor forecast "no need for Federal subsidy beyond 2000." (However, he did count on appropriations for capital improvements, including rolling stock.) In 1993, Thomas Downs was appointed Amtrak president.

Service was restored to Wyoming in 1991, with intercity Denver-Seattle service via the Union Pacific line. This route was actually part of the original Amtrak system; transcontinental service was routed via the Union Pacific when Amtrak started twenty years ago. The train was transferred to the more scenic Rio Grande in 1983. The Wyoming train splits off from the California Zephyr in Denver, giving the traveling public an additional transcontinental route. Of the remaining states not served by the Amtrak system, Maine is currently served by Canada's VIA's Rail, but service between Boston and Portland seems a reasonable possibility in the near future.[36] A difficulty in the establishment of service to the Pine Tree State is a lack of a convenient connection between North and South Stations in Boston. Service to Oklahoma and South Dakota is more difficult to establish. In Alaska, the state-owned Alaska Railroad provides service between Anchorage and Fairbanks, and Hawaii merely has one private line, the 3-foot-gauge Lahaina, Kaanapaali and Pacific, which is operated for tourists on Maui.

The first priority of Amtrak management is to upgrade two long-distance trains that run triweekly, the New York–Chicago Cardinal and the Los Angeles–New Orleans Sunset, to daily status. New equipment will enable these services to be improved. (The utility of a train that operates less than daily, particularly for the carriage of mail and express, is limited. For one thing, people have trouble remembering what day the train runs.) Nonetheless, the triweekly Sunset was extended to run through to Miami in April 1993.[37] In 1996 contracts signed with the original railroad members in 1971 will expire. Amtrak will have to negotiate new trackage rights agreements, and some massive route changes may then occur.[38]

Since its rate structure is unregulated, Amtrak has been using sophisticated yield management to find the rate that will maximize revenues. President Claytor said, "We now charge the fare, on every route, that will produce the greatest possible revenue. If we have done this right, if we raised our fares we'd get less money. If we lowered our fares, we'd get less money."[39] A joint-ticketing arrangement with Midway Airlines at Philadelphia flopped when the airline, facing bankruptcy, contracted and closed its hub.[40] "Amtrak is currently engaged in massive track improvements and electrification of its 150–miles New Haven-Boston line. As part of the Northeast Corridor Improvement Project (NECIP), Amtrak tested the Swedish X-2000 tilting train to improve travel time and reliability on its northeastern routes."[41]

At 24,000 miles, Amtrak is second only to Burlington Northern as America's longest railroad, although 97 percent of this system is over trackage rights on freight railroads. It caters to business travelers on the northeast corridor and on routes in California, Pennsylvania, and New York, but otherwise caters to the discretionary market, with its emphasis on long-haul, once-a-day trains. On its twentieth anniversary, longtime rail editor J. David Ingles wrote:

Amtrak is parallel to other forms of transportation in the U.S., something lost on many people not involved in the field. We all pay taxes to support the highways on which (truckers) drive their rigs. Ditto for the publicly owned airports, which support the commercial airlines, passenger and freight. . . . Amtrak, certainly, is but a small part of the transportation picture. But it's a relatively visible part, and perhaps the most visible of all railroads. As cities come to perceive the need for a return to some degree of reliance on urban rail transportation. . . . Amtrak is bound to receive some trickle-down recognition and support. If nothing else, Amtrak is now a grown-up member of America's railroad family in the transportation community . . . a family and community whose lives are unalterably intertwined with both our personal lives and our nation's economic life.[42]

Amtrak is one of the few areas where the voter/taxpayer comes in contact with the railroad industry. And, for better or for worse, the railroads are still judged by the public for the way they treat the railroad passenger.

The Rail Passenger Service Act has experienced remarkably few changes in its twenty years. Originally conceived as a way to bail out Penn Central, it now stands as a relatively good example of public-private cooperation in providing a continuous and convenient public service, reaching most areas of the United States. At least in the areas of 100 to 500 miles (too far to drive, too short for a plane), Amtrak can be a viable transportation option, particularly when combined with other modes to provide a thoroughly intermodal transportation service.

COMMUTER RAIL SERVICES

Origin of Rail Suburban Passenger Service

Commuter service on the railways is provided to several metropolitan areas through the jurisdiction of state transportation authorities. The term "commutation fares" originated in the late nineteenth century. To encourage multiple riding from suburbs to major cities, railroads would "commute" or reduce the fare for regular customers. In time, the verb "commute" was taken to apply to the travel of the regular passenger, or "commuter," between the suburbs and cities.

As a result of traffic trends and the popularity of local rail travel, commuter trains were operated strictly within suburban areas and mostly for the benefit of monthly commutation ticket-holders. Because huge fleets

of equipment were required for what was essentially a twice-a-day movement (into the city in the morning, back to the suburbs at night), commuter
service became unprofitable and one by one, railroads moved discontinue it.

What commuter service remains today is provided by governmental
assistance. In the Northeast, state governments are often the rail operator
as well. The Northeast Rail Service Act of 1981 provided for an Amtrak
Commuter Services Corporation to contract with the states to operate
passenger trains formerly run by Conrail.[43]

Conrail was required to run trains until 1982, but the authorities in each
state had to decide whether to run the commuter trains on their own or have
Amtrak Commuter do it. However, Amtrak Commuter wound up with no
customers and was thus stillborn (although Amtrak does operate some
commuter service under contract for state authorities).

Since 1983 commuter rail authorities have acquired former Conrail
facilities to operate trains in the northeast corridor. This change resulted in
a large number of Conrail trainmen being transferred to commuter operating authorities, where their wages were lowered to a level closer to that of
subway and trolley motormen.

Commuter Service Provided to U.S. Cities

California
Authorities:	Caltrain (San Francisco), Metrolink (Los Angeles), San Diego County
Operator:	Amtrak

Connecticut
Authority:	Connecticut Department of Transportation
Operators:	Metro-North Commuter Railroad (to New York), Amtrak (Shore Line East)

Florida
Authority:	Tri-Rail
Operator:	CSX Transportation

Illinois
Authority:	Regional Transportation Authority (Metra)
Operators:	Chicago & North Western, Burlington Northern, Norfolk Southern, Metra, SouthShore

Indiana
Authority:	Northern Indiana Commuter Transportation Dist.
Operators:	SouthShore

Maryland
Authority:	Maryland Department of Transportation (and District of Columbia) (MARC)
Operators:	CSX, Amtrak

Massachusetts
Authority:	Massachusetts Bay Transportation Authority

        Operators: Amtrak

New Jersey
        Authority and Operator: New Jersey Transit

New York
        Authority: Metropolitan Transit Authority
        Operators: Metro-North Railroad, Long Island Rail Road

Pennsylvania
        Authority and Operator: Southeastern Pennsylvania Transportation
                                      Authority

Virginia
        Authority: Virginia Railway Express
        Operator: Amtrak

Amtrak is forbidden to engage in the commuter business directly, being exclusively an intercity operator. However, many services operated by Amtrak have been politically inspired short-range trains (Philadelphia-Harrisburg; Washington-Martinsburg, W.Va.; New Haven–Springfield, Mass.; Chicago-Valparaiso, Ind.) with commuter-like operations. Amtrak presently operates as a contract or for many commuter authorities and hauls almost as many commuters as intercity passengers.[44] Over 14 percent of Amtrak's revenues come from the contract operation of commuter trains.[45]

Regulation of Commuter Trains

Technically, the ICC retains jurisdiction over any passenger train in interstate commerce.[46] The commission's permission was required for the discontinuance of any passenger train. But the Amtrak law obviated the need for discontinuance proceedings for trains in the Amtrak system, and the ICC has power to exempt a rail operation from regulation if it has only a negligent effect on interstate commerce.[47] Thus, few passenger trains are subject to ICC regulation today.

With specific regard to surburban service, the ICC is authorized to exempt commuter trains from its regulations. The exemption is only available to rail mass transportation provided by a local public body, or a railroad contracting to provide mass transportation provided by a local public body, or a railroad contracting to provide mass transportation on a regular and continuing basis.[48] Charter and sightseeing services are expressly excluded.The fares charged must be subject to the approval of the governor of the state in which the commuter trains operate.[49]

Because of the necessity for local approval of fares and schedule changes, and because most of the travelers are local commuters, Congress allows these exceptions, reasoning that the effect on interstate commerce is minimal. Currently, Amtrak shares some stations with commuter trains but does not issue interline tickets or check baggage. This lack of interface causes some problems for through travelers, for example, from northeast corridor points to cities and towns on Long Island.

Most passenger trains in the United States are commuter trains. The Long Island Rail Road alone carries more daily passengers than does Amtrak. Huge urban terminals such as Grand Central in New York, North Western in Chicago, and Townsend Street in San Francisco are devoted completely to commuter traffic. In Philadelphia, the Center City Tunnel project united the formerly separate Pennsylvania and Reading terminals and commuter systems with a two-mile tunnel. This is, to date, the only U.S. rail commuter system running through a city from suburb to suburb. (Most commuter trains end at dead-end terminals within the central city.)

Since 1965 funding has been available through the Urban Mass Transit Administration (UMTA) for commuter service. Through UMTA assistance, the nation's commuter fleets have been replaced and revitalized, and new terminals and other fixed facilities have been constructed. The agency has now been renamed Federal Transit Administration.

AMTRAK RUNS FOR THE BORDER[50]

Train travel across international borders is not an uncommon phenomenon as can be witnessed around the world. The North American continent, however, does not offer much in the way of potential international connections by rail. When the U.S. Congress mandated Amtrak to initiate international service in 1972, it was not difficult to select a few key crossing points and provide international rail service to the United States' two international neighbors: Canada to the north and Mexico to the South. In addition, one Canadian Pacific train, the Atlantic, has served northern Maine for over a hundred years. This service between Montreal and the Maritimes continues under VIA Rail Canada at this writing.

North of the Border: Trains to Canada

The Pacific International was the first Amtrak entry into the international market linking Seattle with Vancouver, British Columbia, with service commencing on July 17, 1972. The train started as a small consist of two coaches and one dome-lounge-buffet-coach car, but eventually grew into a four coach consist. The Pacific International was not known for its speed over its 156-mile route. It took approximately four and one-half hours to cover the distance that an express bus could cover in only three hours. Several reasons contributed to the slow schedule, including freight congestion along the route, a twenty-minute customs inspection stop, and six intermediate stops: two in British Columbia and four in the state of Washington.[51]

For awhile during the fall and winter of 1979 and 1980, the Pacific International was extended south to Portland, Oregon, replacing the already existing Mount Rainier. This was done because the Pacific International's schedule had been moved back to a midday Vancouver departure to accommodate connections with VIA Rail trains. In order for passengers to connect with the Coast Starlight in Seattle, a bus connection was initiated linking the Vancouver VIA Rail station with Seattle. This bus connection was a foreshadowing of things to come.

In 1980 the Amtrak Board of Directors approved a 9.5 percent cut in Amtrak train miles to take effect with the beginning of the 1982 fiscal year. Several Amtrak routes were discontinued, and unfortunately, what had been Amtrak's first international train was discontinued. The brighter side of the issue was that the Pacific International was the only Amtrak route loss in the west. A dedicated bus now runs from Vancouver to Amtrak connections in Seattle.

The second international route for Amtrak was into Montreal, Quebec, Canada's largest city. Amtrak's biggest decision prior to initiating service to Montreal was selecting a route. Four options were presented, with the final decision being to route the train through Vermont through White River Junction, a service that had not operated since 1966. This route was much to the liking of Vermont, but slow operating conditions over Boston & Maine trackage made for an overnight Amtrak schedule that was twice as slow as an express bus route. The service was initiated on September 29, 1972, and operated until April 6, 1987, when it was suspended because of deteriorating track conditions. After suspension of the Montrealer, Amtrak provided connecting bus service between Burlington, Vermont, and Springfield, Massachusetts.[52] The route of the Montrealer has proved to be an interesting story in the legal history of Amtrak. In 1992 the U.S. Supreme Court ruled that Amtrak could condemn a portion of the Montrealer route that was owned by Guilford Industries. July 18, 1989, saw the return of the Montrealer, only this time the route was via New London, Connecticut.

Additional service was provided to Montreal on August 6, 1974, when Amtrak began operating the Adirondack between New York City and Montreal via Albany. This route was the brainchild of the New York Department of Transportation and the Delaware & Hudson Railroad.[53] The Delaware & Hudson provided the locomotive power, two diner/lounges, and eight coaches for the service, the state of New York provided the subsidy, and Amtrak provided the operations. The Adirondack continued to operate daily service from New York's Penn Station 381 miles to Montreal, although the tracks used are maintained by Amtrak, Metro-North, Conrail, Delaware & Hudson, Canadian Pacific Railways, and Canadian National Railways.

The third Canadian destination for Amtrak service was Toronto, Ontario. The Amtrak timetable effective April 26, 1981, included the Maple Leaf with daytime service between New York City and Toronto through the Empire

Corridor. This route represents an extension of previously existing international train service provided by the Toronto, Hamilton & Buffalo Railway (TH&B). The TH&B provided passenger service and connections to Amtrak and VIA trains throughout the 1970s by operating between Buffalo and Toronto. The current route of the Maple Leaf follows Conrail to Niagara Falls, and then operates as a VIA Rail train over Canadian National to the Ontario capital. In 1994, the overnight Niagara Rainbow was added to this route, operating westbound on Friday nights and eastbound on Sunday nights.

Toronto was connected to the American Midwest in 1980 when the International began operations between Chicago and Toronto. This train is operated by VIA Rail between Sarnia, Ontario, and Toronto, and by Amtrak over GrandTrunk Western and Conrail tracks in the United States. VIA Rail also runs trains between Toronto and Windsor, where limousine service is available into Detroit.

The Amtrak timetables effective for the period between October 29, 1989, and October 27, 1990, included connecting bus service between the Amtrak station in Grand Forks, North Dakota, and the VIA Rail station in Winnipeg, Manitoba, 150 miles away. This connecting bus service provided a connection between Amtrak's Empire Builder and the VIA Rail transcontinental trains. The dedicated bus service was eliminated in late 1990, although an incidentally connecting schedule operated by Triangle Transportation bridges the 150–mile gap between the two rail systems.

South of the Border: Trains to Mexico

Less than a year after Amtrak service was initiated to Canada, a route was established by congressional directive to privide service to Mexico with connections to the National Railways of Mexico. On January 27, 1973, the Inter-American began triweekly service between Fort Worth and Laredo, Texas. The name Inter-American proved to be a bit of a misnomer as the train did not travel between the Americas, but was really an "Intra-Texan" train, never crossing any borders.[54] The Inter-American was moved to include Dallas, and the route was extended to St. Louis. The intent from the beginning of Amtrak was to operate the Inter-American over the Dallas–St. Louis route, but contract negotiations with Union Station in Dallas involved four railroads and were not complete when Amtrak was ready to publish its 1973 timetable. By 1976 the Inter-American was extended to Chicago with daily service provided during the summer season.

Service south of San Antonia Was discontinued on September 30, 1981, and on October 1, 1981, the route was rechristened the Eagle, once the proud name of the crack Missouri Pacific trains operating south and west out of St. Louis. The Inter-American, which really never did provide true international service, was now merely another intercity train. Mexican National

Railways trains run from cities opposite the Rio Grande from the United States, and a connection of sorts is available to and from the Sunset in El Paso and Ciudad Juarez.

PRIVATE TRAIN OPERATIONS

Although Amtrak operates as a monopoly over most routes in its system, there is some room for competition. Within the northeast corridor, for example, you can ride Amtrak trains or commuter trains between most of the major cities. Auto-Train operated a private service between Florida and Virginia throughout the 1970s; that service is presently being operated by Amtrak. VIA Rail Canada, Inc., the Canadian intercity passenger system, operates its Atlantic Limited daily through the Maine North Woods. And the state-owned Alaska Railroad provides daily service between Anchorage and Fairbanks, as well as on several branch lines.

Private operators can and do enter the railroad passenger excursion business. Such private train services are handled by contract with the freight railroads and are exempt from ICC regulation.[55]

One of the longest-running private operations is the Rio Grande Ski Train between Denver and Winter Park, Colorado. This seasonal train is now operated by ANSCO Investment Corp.—over the tracks of the Southern Pacific—every winter weekend. This service originated in 1940 under the auspices of the Denver & Salt Lake Rail road and has been connecting Denver with ski country ever since. The train was extensively reequipped and renovated in 1987 and is available for charter anywhere on the Southern Pacific rail system.

More common are tourist railroads that operate passenger service, often with historic steam locomotives, for sightseeing and vacation purposes, rather than for point-to-point transportation. The oldest of these lines, the Strasburg Rail Road in Pennsylvania, is a common carrier of freight and passengers, operating under ICC regulations. Only the Baltimore & Ohio is older. The Tourist Railroad Association (TRAIN) lists over 100 tourist railroads. One of the most historic and popular is the Durango & Silverton Narrow Gauge Railroad in Colorado. A former Denver & Rio Grande (D & RG) branch, it was transferred to short line operation by order of the Interstate Commerce Commission.[56] Another D & RG narrow gauge line, the Cumbres & Toltec Scenic Railroad, is a joint effort of the states of Colorado and New Mexico.

In addition to the private trains and tourist railroads, excursion trains are found on mainline railroads under special contracts with the host line. By virtue of its statutory monopoly, Amtrak has the right of first refusal over these lines, and a railroad must come to an agreement with the passenger corporation for these special moves, or have the movement submitted to arbitration by a special panel. If Amtrak does not want to perform the transportation, a private railroad or private car operator (many of whom are railroad historical societies) can contract for such one-day service. Many tour operators have encountered difficulty in obtaining liability insurance, so such operations are limited.

GOVERNMENT ASSISTANCE AND REGULATION OF PASSENGER TRAINS

The federal government, through the Federal Railroad Administration, still provides up to one-third of Amtrak's operating budget. This makes Amtrak the largest recipient of funds through the FRA, but it still makes the passenger system the most cost-effective of any national railroad. Amtrak, of course, is still considered a private, not a nationalized carrier; President Claytor cited this as one of its strengths: "If it weren't for that, a lot of us wouldn't be here, because I don't think it is possible to run a railroad as a government agency and not have it be a disaster."[57]

State governments, with some assistance from UMTA, are the funding factors behind commuter service. Most commuter services cross state lines (SEPTA goes into Delaware and New Jersey; Metro-North services Connecticut; MARC serves Washington, D.C., and West Virginia), and those states incidentally served generally pay the operating state for the stations served by those trains.

Some passenger service is operated by state-owned railways. Alaska took over its operation of the Alaska Railroad from the federal government in 1985, and New York operates a 115 mile passenger route on the Long Island Rail Road. States also support additional Amtrak service under the Section 403(b) "put up or shut up" program—California is the leader in such services.

Economic regulation of passenger trains is a thing of the past; but Amtrak and commuter operators are subject to the FRA's safety regulations, including the possibility of drug testing and licensing for railroad employees. The FRA classifies track speeds for passenger trains and makes sure that rolling stock meets its standards. In that respect, many aging private car fleets are now sitting on sidings because they no longer comply with FRA and Amtrak standards.

Passenger service is but a small part of railroad operations, but its visibility and utility serve to heighten public awareness of the need for rail service and for maintaining safe and speedy mainline railroads.

New passenger cars, such as those ordered by Amtrak in 1991 (140 Superliner double-deck cars from Bombardier Inc. and 50 single-level Viewliner cars from competitive bidders), must meet requirements mandated by Congress in the American with Disabilities Act. Enacted in July 1990, the law requires all new rail passenger cars to be accessible to individuals with disabilities. Currently, much of the fleet consists of high-platform cars that require a negotiation of stairs—although the Superliners have wheelchair-accessible lower levels. Another congressional requirement is that the new fleet have waste-retention toilet systems. Apparently Amtrak had been dumping waste along rights of way, and Congress had to step in after the passenger corporation threatened to stop service to Florida if state authorities were to clamp down.[58]

The new law requires commuter equipment as well to be handicapped accessible and environmentally sound. The twentieth-first century will see new railroad passenger equipment that will be a lot easier to use than the basic 1950s design which underlies most intercity rail equipment today. (However, our nation's rail passenger fleet is newer, on the average, than the age of U.S. commercial airliners in service today.)

NOTES

1. *See* William. E Thoms, "Regulation" of Passenger Train Discontinuances," *Journal of Public Law* 11 (1973): 103, 119–124.

2. *See* Robert Harbeson, "The Rail Passenger Service Act of 1970," *I.C.C. Practitioners Journal* 38 (1971): 330.

3. Amtrak, standing for "American track" was coined by image-maker Lippincott & Margulies in 1971 for what had tentatively been known as "Railpax" since the passage of the Rail Passenger Service Act of 1970. In 1979 amendments to the Rail Passenger Service Act made the definition official. 45 U.S.C., sec. 502(1) (1979).

4. 45 U.S.C., sec. 541 (1976).

5. Southern Pacific president B. F. Biaggini predicted at the time that Amtrak's mission should be to "preside over the orderly dissolution of railroad passenger service," while Burlington Northern's president Lou Menk (also a director of Amtrak) urged the corporation to allow the long-distance train to follow the stagecoach into oblivion. On the long-term hostility of rail presidents to rail passenger, *see generally* Peter Lyon, *To Hell in a Day Coach: An Exasperated Look at American Railroads* (Philadelphia: Lippincott, 1968).

6. Act of Oct. 30, 1971, Pub. L. No. 91–518; Act of Oct. 28, 1974, Pub. L. No. 93–496; Act of May 26, 1975, Pub. L. No. 94–25; Act of Oct. 19, 1976, Pub. L. No. 94–555; Act of Sept. 29, 1979, Pub. L. No. 96–73.

7. 45 U.S.C., sec. 521 (1976).

8. 45 U.S.C., sec. 561 (1976).

9. 45 U.S.C., sec. 564(a) (1976).

10. The Rock Island lasted until 1978, the Southern until 1979, and the Rio Grande until 1983. These railroads, when they did discontinue service, were subject to ICC jurisdiction.

11. 45 U.S.C., sec. 564(b) and (c) (1990).

12. 45 U.S.C., sec 564(c)(1–3) (1980).

13. Interview with Paul Reistrup, former president, Amtrak, *Trains*, February 1981.

14. 45 U.S.C., sec. 546(a) (1980).

15. Act of Nov. 30 1980, Pub. L. No. 91–518, title VIII, sec. 801, 84 Stat. 1339 (1980); Act of Nov. 3, 1973, Pub. L. No. 93–146, sec. 14, 87 Stat. 554 (1973).

16. Act of Sept. 29, 1979, Pub. L. No. 96–73 title I, sec. 111(b), 93 Stat. 541 (1979).

17. Service to Wyoming was restored in June 1991. States still excluded are Maine, South Dakota, Oklahoma, Hawaii, and Alaska.

18. 45 U.S.C. 502(5) (1990). *See generally,* William E. Thoms, *Reprieve for the Iron Horse* (Baton Rouge, LA: Claitor's Pub. Division, 1973), pp. 38–39.

19. Such commuter services are not operated as part of the Amtrak system, but are strictly the responsibility of the suburban rail authorities. William E. Thoms, "When Amtrak Runs the 5:45," *Trains,* April 1993, p. 24.

20. All Amtrak service in New York was consolidated at Pennsylvania Station in April 1991. Amtrak then vacated historic Grand Central Terminal.

21. Interview with James Larson, Amtrak vice-president, operations and planing, *Passenger Train Journal,* May 1991, p. 49. A principal reroute was encountered in 1990 when the New York/Washington-Chicago trains were rerouted off the old Pennsylvania main line and on to the mainlines of Conrail (ex– New York Central) and CSX (ex-Baltimore and Ohio).

22. This section was compiled by Steven Hick, a geographer specializing in remote sensing and aerial mapping. Mr. Hick completed this project as part of his work for the Ph.D. degree in geography at the University of Denver.

23. Jean Gottman, *Megalopolis: The Urbanized Northeastern Seaboard of the United States* (New York: Twentieth Century Fund, 1961).

24. Other discontinuances included the Champion, the Hilltopper, the Floridian, the North Coast Hiawatha, the Lone Star, and the Southwest Limited.

25. "At the request of Mr. A. E. Perlman, President, all employees must refrain from offering any information in regard to operations in the event they are approached by representatives of the National Rail Passenger Corporation (Railpax). Please be governed accordingly." Western Pacific Railroad directive issued April 14, 1971.

26. *Passenger Train Journal,* Spring 1971, p. 15.

27. Pub. L. No. 91–518, 84 Stat. 1335, sec. 402 (1970).

28. Alfred Runte, *Trains of Discovery: Western Railroads and the National Parks* (Flagstaff, AZ: Northland Press, 1984).

29. 45 U.S.C., sec. 562(a) (1982).

30. 45 U.S.C., sec. 562(d)(1) (1982).

31. National Railroad Passenger Corp.—Conveyance of B&M Corp. Interests in Connecticut River Line in Vermont and New Hampshire, 4 I.C.C. 761 (1988).

32. Boston and Maine Corp. v. I.C.C., 911 F.2d 743, 749 (D.C. Cir. 1990).

33. Independent Safety Board Act Amendments, Pub. L. No. 101–641, sec. 9(a), 104 Stat. 4658, amending 45 U.S.C., sec. 562(d)(1) (1990).

34. Boston and Maine Corp. v. I.C.C., 925 F.2d 427 (D.C. Cir. 1991).

35. *Railpace,* June 1991, p. 18.

36. *Passenger Train Journal,* May 1991, p. 49.

37. Bob Johnston, "Getting Ready for the Sunset," *Trains,* March 1993, p. 63.

38. Mike Schafer, "Amtrak's Atlas," *Trains,* June 1991, p. 49.

39. Quoted in *Trains,* June 1991, p. 24.

40. *Passenger Train Journal,* May 1991, p. 24.

41. *Trains,* March 1993, p. 26; April 1993, p. 6.

42. David Ingles, "All Grown Up?" *Trains*, June 1991, pp. 5–6.

43. Pub. L. No. 97–35, 95 Stat. 828, Title E, 45 U.S.C., sec. 581 (1990).

44. Thoms, "When Amtrak Runs," p. 24.

45. Kathy Keeney, "Amtrak Hits Big 20," *Modern Railroads*, May 1991, p. 39.

46. 49 U.S.C., sec. 10908 (1992).

47. 49 U.S.C., sec. 10505 (1992).

48. 49 U.S.C., sec. 10504 (1992).

49. *See* Southeast Pennsylvania Transp. Auth.—Exemption from 49 U.S.C. Subtitle IV, I.C.C. Finance Docket 30145 (1983).

50. This section was contributed by Steven Hick of the University of Denver.

51. *Passenger Train Journal*, Summer 1972, p. 29.

52. *Trains*, June 1992, p. 8.

53. *Passenger Train Journal*, Fall 1974, p. 31.

54. Bruce Goldberg, *Amtrak: The First Decade* (Silver Springs, CO: Alan Books, 1981), p. 60.

55. 49 U.S.C., sec. 10505 (1992).

56. Durango & S.N.G. R. Co.—Acquisition & Operation, 363 I.C.C. 292 (1979). This railroad is now under the jurisdiction of the Colorado Public Service Commission.

57. *Trains*, June 1991, p. 25.

58. Keeney, "Amtrak Hits," p. 39.

8

The New Rail Regime in Canada[1]

DEREGULATION COMES TO CANADIAN RAILWAYS

Railroads in Canada have operated on a different basis from those south of the forty-ninth parallel. The United States still has no true transcontinental railway (Robert R. Young used to argue that a hog could cross Chicago without changing trains—but *you* can't), while Canada has two—the Canadian National (CN) and the Canadian Pacific (CP).

Moreover, these two railroads are essentially the only important railways in Canada.[2] Canadian National Railways is a Crown Corporation—owned by the government, as was Air Canada and as is the Canadian Broadcasting Corporation. CN and CP at one time also competed in hotels, telecommunications, and air carrier services.

Thus, deregulation would seem to have less appeal in a country where the market is already dominated by a duopoly. Nonetheless, the same National Transportation Act that brought deregulation to the skies and highways applies to Canada's two transcontinentals and a few provincial railways as well.[3]

Both Canada and the United States developed their framework of railroads under regulation by their federal governments. The Constitution Act of 1867 gave the federal parliament the right to legislate for a "work for the general good of Canada,"[4] and development of the railroads has taken place under federal regulation. The intent of regulation was to promote competition between the privately owned CP and the publicly owned CN.

The railway system in Canada operates in nine of the ten provinces, having exited Prince Edward Island in 1988. Canada is also one of the few countries in the world still adding to its railway network, building extensions to serve economic activity in the hinterland.[5] Although the narrow-gauge Newfoundland Railway was abandoned in 1989, the Quebec, North Shore and Labrador Railway still serves the mainland of that province.

Both the United States and Canada have maintained continent-wide railroad systems with an extensive private component. In the United States private ownership is the rule, while in Canada the privately owned Canadian Pacific is one of the largest railroads in the world.[6] Both U.S. and Canadian railroads face competition from motor carriers, although long-distance trucking is less significant in Canada than in the United States. Both countries' railroads have lost the bulk of their passenger business to airways and, to a lesser extent, to buses.[7] Both nations find that their rail systems are overbuilt for today's traffic needs.

Between 1970 and 1980 the United States substantially demolished the statutory system of economic regulation of trucking, buses, airlines, and railroads.[8] Within the United States rail passenger service was spun off to Amtrak in 1971;[9] and commuter rail service was turned over to the states a decade later.[10] Unprofitable eastern railways were lumped together and turned over to Conrail, a federal entity, in 1976. Conrail was later returned to the private sector.

The key point of rail deregulation in the United States was the Staggers Rail Act of 1980.[11] The Staggers Act was based upon a finding by Congress that modernization of regulation was essential,[12] and an intention to rely upon competition to the greatest extent possible.[13]

Under Staggers, entry in to the rail industry was relaxed, which facilitated the start-up of short line railroads.[14] Similarly, abandonment of rail lines was accelerated and made much easier for railroads to accomplish.[15] The Staggers Act provided for less supervision of ratemaking, with no maximum rates unless the carrier had market dominance, and a great deal of ratemaking freedom.[16] Rates themselves may be virtually irrelevant, as the Staggers Act also allowed railroads and large shippers to contract for the shipment of goods without any recourse to regulatory approval.[17]

Reliance on competition in the United States meant turning to intermodal competition, as few new railroads were coming onto the scene. In fact railroads have now become even more of an oligopoly under deregulation, with seven major railroad systems dominating the U.S. industry ten years after the passage of Staggers—four west of the Mississippi and three to the east.[18] Canada, with two major railroad systems, nevertheless saw the need to meet the competition of the Yankee railroads, which were competing for coast-to-coast traffic with the CN and the CP. As with airlines, the Canadian government chose to follow the U.S. example and substantially deregulate the rails.

Passenger service had already been spun off from CN and CP by the establishment of VIA Rail Canada, Inc., a Crown Corporation, to take over intercity passenger service in a similar fashion to Amtrak in the United States.[19] Commuter service in the Toronto and Montreal areas had been lifted from the railways and placed under the operating authorities of Ontario and Quebec, respectively.[20] The repeal of the Crow's Nest Pass rates, which mandated uneconomical rates for movement of western grain, brought on a more realistic rate base for agricultural products and ended a cross-subsidization of freight traffic.[21] Now it was Parliament's turn to examine the regulation of the freight railroad industry in Canada.

THE NATIONAL TRANSPORTATION ACT

The National Transportation Act of 1987 contains the most far-reaching changes in the regulation of railways since Confederation. Its aim is to strengthen the railway system by allowing it to better compete with other modes, and to allow the railways to modernize, even though such modernization might deprive many communities and shippers of freight service. In many ways the partial deregulation experience in the United States through the implementation of the Staggers Act is replicated north of the border.

Many of the Canadian deregulation features in the National Transportation Act were originally found in the Staggers Rail Act in the United States. For example, it is now easier for Canadian and United States railroads to enter and leave markets. True, few new railroads are being built either in the U.S. or Canada, but the new law makes it easier for a Canadian short line to obtain Letters Patent to take over and operate an existing line that a major railroad no longer wants. (The Staggers Act makes this process easier for U.S. railroads.) With abandonments, the burden of proof has been shifted to shippers and passengers to prove that the line is still required for the needs of the public.[22]

The agency that has replaced the Canadian Transport Commission (CTC), the Natural Transportation Agency (NTA), is directed by the statute that states traditional regulation of railroads is to be used as a last resort.[23] Such time-honored practices as collective ratemaking are no longer allowed, and railroads are allowed to enter into contracts with their shippers. Currently in the United States most freight moves by contract rather than tariff rates, and a shift to "confidential contracts" (as they are called in Canada) is occurring in Canada as well.[24]

The philosophy of the National Transportation Act is found in the government's White Paper, "Freedom to Move." Following a study by the Canadian Transport Commission on railway problems, it endorsed the need of Canadian shippers to have confidential contracts, but moved away from the then-current policy of allowing the two railroads to exchange information on costs and to file joint and common rates.[25] In an informative article published in the *Transportation Law Journal*, Canadian economist Anthony P. Ellison writes: "By removing the exchange of cost information and the setting of common rates, the . . . National Transportation Act withdraws the legislative protection afforded the fifty year old rail cartel. The (National Transportation) Agency, with its proposed direction over running rights, joint-track usage and joint rates, is empowered to facilitate rather than limit intramodal competition."[26]

The act's section 3 clarifies Canada's National Transportation Policy, which includes safety as a key objective, but then relies upon competition and market forces as the prime agents in providing a transportation system. Competition is regarded as desirable both between modes and within each mode. Carriers are to set rates that do not discourage movement of commodities nor the development of primary and secondary industry nor export trade.[27]

The act creates a National Transportation Agency, of not more than nine permanent members plus up to six temporary members, appointed by the Prime Minister and the Cabinet. The Governor in Council may revise annual decisions of the agency. The NTA requires a complaint an application to trigger its jurisdiction except for matters relating to safety or licensing.[28] In its independence from Cabinet, the NTA has some features of the Interstate Commerce Commission in the United States.

BRANCH LINE ABANDONMENTS

Abandonment proceedings have been streamlined: if a railroad applies to abandon a branch line and nobody objects, the railway is automatically permitted to close the line. If a party protests the application, then the NTA must determine if the line is profitable or has some prospect of becoming so. The NTA also has power to establish short lines or to subsidize operations over the branch for years. There is a cap on abandonments, as no railroad may abandon more than 4 percent of its system during reach of the first five years of the act. This 4 percent limit was at first objected to by the railways, but proposals for abandonment have in no instance come close to 4 percent of the total of either of the two transcontinental systems, nor of the smaller railways.[29]

The rail abandonment process before the NTA works like this:

A railway company must give the National Transportation Agency (the Agency) and the public in areas served by the rail line a Notice of Intent to apply for abandonment.

Ninety days after the Notice of Intent the railway may apply to the Agency for abandonment authority.

Within sixty days of the application, any party may oppose abandonment in writing to the Agency.

If the application is not opposed within the sixty days, the Agency *must* order abandonment.

If the application is opposed, the Agency investigates the present and future economics (costs and revenues) of the line.

The Agency must decide *within six months* of the application whether or not to allow abandonment of the line, according to the following provisions in the National Transportation Act:

(a)   if the line is deemed to be uneconomic, with no reasonable probability of becoming economic, the Agency must order abandonment;

(b)   if the line is deemed to be economic (now or in the future), *but* is not required in the public interest, the Agency *must* order abandonment;

(c)   if the line is found to be uneconomic, but is deemed to have a reasonable probability of becoming economic and is required in the public interest, the Agency must order the line retained and reconsider the application within three years;

(d)   if the line is found to be economic (now and in the future) and required in the public interest, the Agency must dismiss the application for abandonment.

Public interest considerations are examined only if the line will be or has a reasonable probability of becoming economic in the future.

The agency may hold public hearings if there is opposition to the application and it considers hearings necessary.

There is no opportunity for Ministerial intervention in the abandonment process once an application has been received.[30]

There are several limitations to the rail abandonment process:

A railway company cannot abandon more than 4 percent of its total route mileage in any of the five years including 1992.

The existence of passenger service on a line does not prevent the line from being ordered abandoned (for freight traffic).

The effective date of an abandonment order would be set so that VIA Rail would have six months to decide if it wants the rail line for its passenger services and another six months to negotiate the terms of the line's transfer.

VIA Rail may abandon the rail line if subsequently it is no longer needed for passenger rail service.

The Agency can order a line retained for as long a period of time as a province, municipality, or other interested person pays the actual losses of the line.[31]

Once the agency has announced its decision, there are three mechanisms for appeal including rehearing by the Agency ,appeal to the Federal Court of Canada, or appeal to the Governor in Council for a delay of up to five years if there are inadequate alternate facilities in the area.[32]

The largest abandonment of 1988 was concluded outside of the NTA's abandonment processes. The narrow-gauge Newfoundland Railway had been transferred to the central government of Canada when that province entered the Confederation in 1949. Under a deal worked out in June 1988 between the Newfoundland and federal governments, the Canadian

National (the line's operator) was allowed to abandon the entire railway. Included in the agreement was over $800 million in federal funding to improve highway and other transport facilities in the province, plus labor protection provisions for displaced railway employees, who will not be required to leave Newfoundland to obtain railway work elsewhere. (Most were engaged in the demolition of the railway.)[33] Under new legislation, once a railroad line is abandoned, disposition of reinstatement becomes a provincial responsibility. As the wreckers were tearing up the 42–inch gauge track, the province stepped in to save a few segments for tourist and historical purposes. Because an isolated railway is now a provincial, and not a federal responsibility, Newfoundland is now in the railroad business, and is responsible for the upkeep of the remaining segments.

During 1989 the Canadian National also abandoned what little trackage remained on Prince Edward Island under the provisions of the National Transportation Act. The same year Canadian Pacific reorganized its entire system in the Maritimes (which also passes through the state of Maine) as the Canadian Atlantic Railway. Some observers suggested that such a move was made to isolate the costs involved in operating in the Atlantic provinces as a separate profit centre, which could be abandoned if losses prove to be too onerous. This is apparently why Canadian National had set up its Newfoundland operations as Terra Transport in the years preceding abandonment.[34] Canadian Pacific announced in early 1993 that it planned to abandon its Canadian Atlantic stepchild. The NTA gave preliminary approval, but the ICC has, in 1994, not yet given approval for the discontinuance of CP's line through Maine.

COMPETITIVE ACCESS

Most substantive changes under the Transportation Act of 1987 parallel the changes in the Staggers Act for U.S. railroads. The uniquely Canadian difference is competitive access for captive shippers. We have seen that in most cases there are only two Canadian railroads and not much opportunity for intramodal competition. To remedy this defect, the new law establishes an "interswitching limit" of 30 kilometers. That means that if a factory is located on a CN siding and there is an interchange with the CP some 25 kilometers away, the shipper can choose CP service; the CN must then allow the CP switcher to use its tracks and haul the car away.[35]

A shipper that is served by only one railway at either origin or destination may request that railway establish a competitive line rate to or from the nearest interchange with a competing railroad. The shipper may designate the route for the competitive line rate (for example, a Manitoba shipper might request a rate to Emerson from the CN and via the Soo Line or Burlington Northern beyond). If a cost-effective continuous route from origin to destination is available entirely in Canada, the shipper is precluded from selecting a route involving a U.S. carrier. If a carrier fails to establish a competitive line rate upon request, then the National Transportation Agency will do so. Competitive line rates are not available for containers or trailers on flat cars, unless the intermodal shipment is export or import traffic moving to or from a port. The percentage of the distance to or from the interchange point cannot be more than 40 percent of the total rail mileage or 750 miles, whichever is greater. Unless agreed upon otherwise between the carrier or shipper, a competitive line rate will remain in force for one year.[36]

One interesting feature of this competitive access provision is that it is not limited to CN, CP, or the local Canadian railways (British Columbia, Algoma Central, Ontario Northland, Quebec, North Shore & Labrador). Four U.S. railroads (Burlington Northern, Norfolk Southern, CSX, and Conrail) also operate into Canada. If they come within the interswitching limit, Canadian shippers can take advantage of U.S. competitors as well. It is also easier for a U.S. railroad to obtain trackage rights over Canadian lines and possibly abandon their own Canadian track.[37] CN and CP are both vulnerable to competition by Burlington Northern, Conrail, and other northern U.S. lines.

PROSPECTS FOR RAIL FREIGHT DEREGULATION

Both national railways have made it clear that they would like to slim down their systems In 1994, CP and CN annouced plans to consolidate their operations and abandon redundant lines east of Winnipeg.. The 4 percent cap may limit the size and scope of the abandonments. But a quick look at the rail map of Canada will show a pre-auto-age map crisscrossing the country without the consolidation and rationalization of lines that characterizes American railways.

In 1988, the National Transportation Agency issued twenty decisions relating to the abandonment of 645 rail lines as shown in Table 8.1.

In 1989 the railways submitted sixty-five applications for abandonment of 1,306 miles. As one result, all lines on Prince Edward Island were abandoned. In addition, the agency had twenty-three applications for 1,008 miles carried over from 1988, including reconsideration of previous decisions on lines that were ordered retained and were due for review in 1989. Short of amending the National Transportation Act, there is no mechanism for the Minister or Governor in Council to override the abandonment process currently set out in the NTA.[38]

During the last decade large U.S. railroads have been turning over tremendous segments of routes to short lines or regional railroads. Locally operated with lower labor costs and a friendly connection to the parent railroad, they are providing service to communities that might otherwise be bypassed. But such an easy turnover has not been possible in Canada.

Table 8.1
Canadian Railroad Abandonment

Province	Miles Abandoned	Miles Retained	Total Miles
British Columbia	27	100	127
Alberta	15	0	15
Saskatchewan	48	0	48
Manitoba	71	0	71
Ontario	267	0	267
Quebec	38	69	107
New Brunswick	10	0	10
Prince Edward Island	0	0	0
Nova Scotia	0	0	0
Newfoundland	0	0	0
Total Miles	476	169	645
Percent	73.8	26.2	100.0

Source: Paul S. Dempsey, William E. Thoms, and Sonja Clapp, "Canadian Transport Liberalization," *Transportation Law Journal* 19(1990):113, 150.

The Canada Labor Code provides that a successor employee inherits not only the same union, but the same collective bargaining agreement as its predecessor. This means that the same work rules that hampered economical operation of the major railroad will still prevail. It may also mean that there might be no takers for these castoff lines.[39]

One important role for the NTA is the mediation of disputes between a shipper and a carrier or between two railways. A dispute may be referred to the NTA for mediation, which must be completed within thirty days. The mediation process is nonbinding and confidential, unless the parties agree to disclosure, and is available for all traffic except for grain movements and rail-water intermodal traffic.[40]

A shipper may apply to the agency for final offer arbitration when dissatisfied with a railroad rate. Unlike traditional arbitration, the NTA is obliged merely to select from the final offer of the shipper and the final offer of the railroad. The agency may pick the arbitrator if the parties cannot select one, and both parties share in the cost of arbitration, which must be completed with ninety days.[41]

Not only shippers, but the public in general, may request the NTA to investigate any rate, act, or omission of a carrier believed to be prejudicial to the public interest. The proceedings are informal, with no requirement for the appellant to prove a prima facie case, but in any case they must be completed within 120 days.[42] In all matters affecting rail transportation, these procedural provisions may be suspended by the NTA if they have an unfavorable impact on the viability of Canadian railways.

Liberalization of railway regulation has not meant an end to rate regulation. The statute still requires that rates be compensatory (cover the variable cost of the particular movement of traffic).[43] A noncompensatory rate must be disallowed unless it is proved by the carrier that the rate was not designed to be anticompetitive and does not, in fact, lessen competition.[44] But a railroad need only publish tariffs on a request of a shipper.[45] There are four types of rates allowed: agreed charges, published tariffs, confidential contracts, and statutory rates.[46] Published tariffs must not contain secret rebates, discounts, or allowances. Even though confidential contracts are expected to move most bulk traffic in Canada by the end of the century, even these may be appealable if they are not compensatory.[47]

The traditional common carrier obligations in Canada have been reiterated by the National Transportation Act: a railway must provide cars, deliver traffic offered to it, and maintain facilities for receiving freight. It must interchange with connecting railroads and handle their cars. The NTA will police violation of common carrier obligations, but shippers and railways may agree to modify these obligations.[48]

The NTA also may approve running rights and joint track usage, and determine whether railroads should build connections between the two of them. The agency can also order one railroad to operate over the tracks of another. The aim of these new powers is to produce a more streamlined and efficient railway system for Canada.[49]

Canadian railroads have extensive operations in the United States. The Canadian National operates three railroads south of the border: the Duluth, Winnipeg & Pacific; the Grand Trunk Western; and the Central Vermont Railway. The DW&P links up with CN lines at Fort Frances, Ontario, and runs to the Twin Ports of Duluth-Superior, Wisconsin. From here, CN has an agreement with Burlington Northern for the forwarding of its cars to Chicago, where the Grand Trunk runs to border points at Detroit and Port Huron, Michigan. Grand Trunk Western hosts the Amtrak-VIA International, while the New England carrier Central Vermont carries the Amtrak Montrealer over its entire length. CN markets its services as "CN North America," giving its customers a choice of routes, north and south of the border. It has placed the Central Vermont up for Sale.

Even more ambitious has been the system of U.S. railroads controlled by Canadian Pacific, marketed under the name "CP Rail." The Soo Line has now been purchased by longtime shareholder Canadian Pacific. The Soo, which includes what remains of the old Chicago, Milwaukee, St. Paul & Pacific (but which has spun off many of its original lines to the Wisconsin Central) runs from Montana through the Midwest to Chicago. There, Soo has arranged for trackage rights over CSX to connect its lines with CP proper at Detroit/Windsor. At Niagara Falls and Montreal, CP interchanges with Delaware & Hudson, an ancient American carrier purchased by CP at its most recent bankruptcy sale. The D&H, operating over trackage rights awarded with the 3–R Act in 1976, takes CP Rail service to Philadelphia, Baltimore, and Washington, D.C.

RAIL PASSENGER SERVICE

Until recently Canada relied upon passenger trains connecting its large cities with virtually every hamlet of the Dominion. For the last dozen years, Canada has followed a regime similar to that of the United States: long-haul passenger service was made a responsibility of the central government (Amtrak in the United States; VIA Rail in Canada), while commuter service is the responsibility of state or provincial governments. (In Canada, extensive commuter operations in both Montreal and Toronto are supported by the Quebec and Ontario governments.) There is also a modicum of passenger service by the provincially owned railways (British Columbia and Ontario Northland), and some privately-owned trains hang on as long as the Algoma Central and Quebec North Shore and Labrador keep going.

VIA Rail is a relatively new Canadian institution, limited to providing intercity passenger rail service. In the mid-1970s, the Canadian rail transport system was an anomaly. Other nations had converted their rail networks to public ownership. The U.S. Congress had passed the Rail Passenger Service Act of 1970, which established the National Railroad Passenger Corporation—Amtrak. Amtrak is not a public entity; technically it is a private corporation owned by four participating railroads—but it has continued to exist by virtue of congressional funding and government support. In contrast to this, Canada persisted in its competition between the public and private sector. The privately owned Canadian Pacific was decidedly unhappy about continuing to foot the passenger burden, and took steps to reduce its passenger deficit by replacing conventional trains with rail diesel cars, and discontinuing secondary and branch line runs, as well as some intercity service. Even the publicly owned Canadian National was chafing under its mandate to provide essential passenger services. Its experiments with innovative fare pricing policies had not stemmed the rising tide of red ink, and by 1975 the CN was in the process of studying the best way to use its passenger fleet effectively.

In October 1976 the first VIA joint timetable was issued by Canadian Pacific and Canadian National. The latter railroad also announced it was adopting the VIA logo for its equipment, with an eye to coordinating service, a necessary first step before a government-sponsored revitalization of that service could occur. Via Rail Canada, Inc., was incorporated in January 1977, under the Business Corporation Act and approved by the Parliament of Canada in March of that year.[50] Originally VIA was a subsidiary of the Canadian National and was charged only with the planning and marketing of services. Equipment, stations, and employees would continue to be provided by CN and CP. VIA was to collect all the revenues and would pay the carriers 100 percent of the costs incurred in providing the service, as opposed to 80 percent under the 1967 National Transportation Act.

VIA found it difficult, however, to conduct negotiations with a railroad of which it was a subsidiary. In order to maximize the efficiency of VIA and make it more even-handed in its dealings with both the CN and CP, it was made a Crown Corporation on April 1, 1978.[51] It operates basically as a private corporation, but is subsidized by the federal government and must submit an annual report and request for funding to the Canadian government. The new corporation now has the powers of a railway company and is regulated by the NTA. The company at first was not to be responsible for any rail service until the old CTC completed its rationalization process for that particular service. Then the government would enter into a contract with VIA for that particular route. VIA would contract with CN or CP to provide locomotives and crews. VIA acquired CN and CP intercity equipment, after selecting the best of the aged fleet for its purposes. It has since ordered rail equipment of its own.

Like Amtrak, VIA is set up as an independent, ostensibly "for-profit" corporation dedicated to providing improved intercity passenger service by rail. Neither country is yet ready to declare outright nationalization of their railroads, or even of their passenger function. However, VIA is owned, as is Canadian National, by the Crown, whereas Amtrak was legally the property of four cooperating railroads. Also similar to Amtrak's legislation is the limiting of VIA's service to intercity passenger trains. VIA does not run commuter or suburban routes.

The main thrust of VIA was to reduce the deficit of rail passenger operations in Canada. While VIA is labeled a "for-profit" corporation, it was never expected to be a money-making venture. It has, however, slowed down the increase in losses.

The rationalization and emergence of VIA was the end product of a CTC study on the implications of Amtrak for Canada. One of the implications was that by 1978, the United States would have a better rail passenger system than Canada.

Furthermore, if Amtrak's estimate of its FY 1978 deficit is at all accurate and, if Canada's passenger train subsidies continue to increase at about the same rate as they have in the past, it is likely that Canada will pay more for its 80% subsidy program than the United States will be paying for Amtrak. Another implication has to do with the roadbed problem. Are passenger and freight systems just as incompatible in Canada as they apparently are in the United States? Not enough is known to provide a definitive answer to the questions. A great deal of additional research needs to be done to reveal the system-wide effects of "efficient" 250 car freight trains.

Finally, the findings and conclusions of this study do not seem to indicate that Amtrak, in its present form, is an appropriate model for Canada. Amtrak was, and is, a pragmatic compromise developed within the larger United States context of bankrupt railroads owned by successful holding companies. Canada, with a program of 80% subsidy and a Crown Corporation in railroading, has an institutional context quite different from the United States—and perhaps even more complex. Certainly, further study of institutional arrangements for providing future rail passenger service in Canada is required.[52]

All Fool's Day, 1978, brought VIA into the rail business directly. Until that date, the corporation had been proceeding on a step-by-step, route-by-route basis. But observers felt that route was too complicated and inefficient. Thus, April 1, 1978, was set for VIA's takeover of every CN or CP train not rationalized out of existence by that time.[53]

VIA is organized into four regions: Atlantic, Quebec, Ontario, and West. At its inception, it acquired approximately 2,800 unionized employees and 500 nonscheduled management and professional employees. Approximately 2,300 additional employees were later transferred from CN and another 500 from CP.

Labor negotiations between the parties were governed from the outset by federal government legislation enacted in October 1977. The parties were unable to agree, and a special mediator was called in to help the parties reach a settlement, with one issue—separation from service—submitted to binding arbitration. As a result, the unionized employees did not come under the VIA plan until July of 1978.

Since April 1, 1978, CN and CP have sent the bills for their passenger service to VIA—100 percent of the avoidable costs. Ministry of Transport officials were expected to keep a close check on the fledgling carrier's finances since the ministry is VIA's banker. The relationship of the ministry to its creature, VIA, is very much like that between the government and Air Canada, until 1989 a Crown corporation. The government does not run the corporation; it arranges that the corporation is well run. A ministry spokesman described the role of the government as giving the general direction, providing management, and verifying that management is working in the direction outlined. The corporation should handle the specifics. The first combined tariff was filed for VIA trains, effective June 15, 1978.[54] (Unlike Amtrak, the corporation must have regulatory approval of rates and fares.)

From the start, VIA Rail's costs relative to the size of the population to be served proved to be a problem. In 1978 David P. Morgan, the respected rail journalist and editor of *Trains*, wrote:

Those inexorable economics show no respect for national boundaries. Or to quote Canadian National President Robert A. Bandeen, "Passenger services cannot be provided on a profit-making basis under North American conditions." To which, we think, VIA's (Garth) Campbell would add, any passenger service: rail, road, or air. The trains' losses are visible, he argues, while the deficits of the competition are hidden in publicly provided airways and roadways.

Be that as it may, the VIA system is going to cost 23 million Canadians more than the Amtrak network costs 216 million Americans:

	VIA	AMTRAK
Route-Miles	14,000	26,000
Passengers (millions)	7	19.2
Revenues (millions)	$120	$311.2
Loss (millions)	$300	$536.6

The assumption is that Parliament will be more benign about these statistics than is Congress. However, thinly populated, Canada's land mass is larger than that of the U.S., thus eight times as many passenger route-miles per capita may be justified. Item: There's no U.S. equivalent for CN's line up to Hudson Bay, with a terminus at Longitude 94 and Latitude 59 (on a parallel with Juneau, Alas.), and in consequence no Amtrak counterpart for the triweekly passenger train that goes there.[55]

There are many similarities between Amtrak and VIA that show a basic affinity in the statutory schemes. Both are independent corporations with government guidance. Both are nationwide in scope and intend to effect savings by combining formerly separate systems. Both involve marketing schemes to increase patronage and reduce deficits, and both replace railroad-operated passenger services that the railroads involved wanted to dump. Both are concerned only with intercity, long-distance passenger services. VIA and Amtrak do not operate commuter trains, which are a local responsibility.

In the last decade, VIA Rail has compiled a slower track record than Amtrak. It was too late in refurbishing its equipment as a tenant of the railroads and has had trouble keeping a handle on costs or scheduling reliability. Part of the problem is that the VIA Rail system, almost the length of Amtrak's with a similar deficit ($600 million a year), is being supported by one-tenth the population. Whereas Amtrak's deficits cost every American $3, the equivalent deficit costs each Canadian $30 to support VIA. It is like trying to run the Trans-Siberian Railway with the population of New York State.

VIA was left out of much of the planning that resulted in the Transportation Act. Furthermore, the government planned a VIA Rail Act to complement the other transport legislation, but none was forthcoming. The Mulroney government viewed rail passenger and freight services as discrete problems. In contrast to the plans for other Canadian transport modes, VIA is deregulated but publicly owned. The main issue concerning VIA is cost limitations and government subsidies.

In 1990 there were severe cutbacks in the VIA Rail system, ordered as a cost-saving measure by the Mulroney government.[56] As a result, VIA Rail today operates daily service only in Quebec and Ontario, where most of the country's population lives. The corridor between Quebec City and Windsor, Ontario, which includes the Montreal-Toronto main line, receives fairly extensive service.

Outside of the corridor, services operate on a triweekly basis at best. VIA operates a transcontinental train, the Canadian, over the CN route between Toronto and Vancouver, via Winnipeg, Saskatoon, and Edmonton. To the Maritimes, VIA runs the triweekly Ocean over the CN route through Levis and Matapedia, linking Montreal and Halifax. On a different three days, VIA's Atlantic Limited covers the CP route via Sherbrooke and Saint John. This route, the only passenger service currently serving the state of Maine, is jeopardized by CP's threatened abandonment of the Canadian Atlantic line east of Sherbrooke.

Other trains operated by VIA are so-called "remote services," which the passenger corporation is ordered to serve for lack of surface transportation alternatives.[57] They include the Skeena between Prince Rupert and Jasper; the Hudson Bay between Winnipeg and Churchill (with two connecting mixed trains serving Manitoba's north woods); the Chaleur linking Montreal and the Gaspe peninsula; and certain other remote services in Quebec and Ontario. These trains also operate on a triweekly basis.

A 1992 Royal Commission on passenger transportation, commissioned in 1990, came out in favor of ending VIA subsidies, as well as subventions of air and bus service. The report was quietly tabled, as the future of rail passenger service in Canada awaited the results of the 1993 Parliamentary elections. The new Chétien government, although sympathetic to VIA, has budgetary constraints that prevent any expansion of the passenger system.

VIA Rail only operates intercity and remote services. There are two extensive commuter operations in Canada; the GO Transit network operating out of Toronto, operated by the Government of Ontario, and the STCUM commuter rail net operated by the Société des Transports de la Communauté Urbaine de Montréal. These services each operate more trains than VIA and carry more passengers.

In addition local passenger service is operated by the British Columbia Railway, the Ontario Northland Railway, the Quebec, North Shore and Labrador Railway, and the Algoma Central Railway in Ontario. The latter service has been ordered to continue for an additional five years by the National Transportation Agency, which cited the necessity of service to remote northern Ontario communities. The decision entitles the Algoma Central to government compensation for losses.[58]

The concept of railroad deregulation, which originated in the United States with many private carriers, has now been exported to Canada. The world's second largest country has long relied on rail duopoly—the Crown corporation (CN) to keep the private sector honest; the private (CP) corporation to keep the Crown efficient. In a leap of faith, Canadians have embraced free enterprise and competition to keep their vast country running efficiently. One unfoer seen development in 1994 has been the proposal by CN and CP to merge their freight systems east of Winnipeg. There would be one main line to compete with U.S. railroad for transcontinental traffic.

NOTES

1. This chapter is adapted from Paul S. Dempsey, William E. Thoms, and Sonja Clapp, "Canadian Transport Liberalization," *Transportation Law Journal* 19 (1990): 113, 143–163.

2. Anthony Ellison, "The Formation and Dissolution of the Canadian Rail Cartel," *Transportation Law Journal* 15 (1987): 175, 186.

3. National Transportation Act of 1987, 35–36 Eliz. II, ch. 34 (1987).

4. British North America Act of 1867, retitled Constitution Act of 1867, by the Canada Act of 1982.

5. C. Phillips, *Railways in Canada* (Ottawa: Transport Canada Surface Administration, Railway and Grain Transportation Report, March 1986), p. 2. The report mentions that B.C. Rail has just completed the first modern electrified line in Canada, the sixty-nine mile Tumbler Ridge branch, and that CP is engaged in a $600 million project for tunneling and the line relocation in the Rockies.

6. Ibid. *See also* Ellison, "Formation," p. 176.

7. *Rail Passenger Services in Canada: A Framework for the Future* (Ottawa: Transport Canada, Report of Transport Minister Mazankowski, 1985), p. 1.

8. *See* Paul S. Dempsey and William E. Thoms, *Law and Economic Regulation in Transportation* (Westport, CT: Quorum Books, 1986), pp. 3–34.

9. Amtrak began operation of America's intercity passenger trains, with some exceptions, on May 1, 1971. William E. Thoms, *Reprieve for the Iron Horse* (Baton Rouge, LA: Claitor's Pub. Division, 1973), pp. 55–61.

10. The Northeast Rail Services Act provided for state operation of commuter services formerly operated by Conrail. Northeast Rail Service Act of 1981, Pub. L. No. 97–35, 95 Stat. 643 (1981) (codified as amended at 45 U.S.C., sec. 1101–1116 [1982]).

11. Staggers Rail Act of 1980, Pub. L. No. 96–448, 94 Stat. 1895 (1980).

12. William E. Thoms, "Clear Track for Deregulation," *Transportation Law Journal* 12 (1982): 183.

13. Ibid.

14. The public convenience and necessity need only permit (not require) construction or acquisition and operation of a rail line. 49 U.S.C., sec. 10901(d) and (e) (1980).

15. Abandonment is now limited to a 330-day process. 49 U.S.C., sec. 10904 (1980).

16. Staggers Rail Act, Pub. L. No. 96–448, sec. 207, 94 Stat. 1895, 1907 (1980).

17. Staggers Rail Act, Pub. L. No. 96–448, sec. 208, 94 Stat. 1895, 1908 (1980).

18. The seven are: Santa Fe, Southern Pacific, Union Pacific, Conrail, Norfolk Southern, CSX, and Burlington Northern.

19. *See* William E. Thoms, "VIA Rail: A Canadian Amtrak?" *North Dakota Law Review* 55 (1979): 61.

20. *See* William E. Thoms, "Commuting in the Great White North," *Trains*, December 1986, p. 18.

21. Ellison, "Formation," pp. 197–201.

22. National Transportation Act, sec. 157–177 (1987).

23. National Transportation Act, sec. 3 (1987).

24. Confidential contracts are allowed by Section 120 of the NTA. The parties may agree to a contract concerning rates, level of services, equipment, and other conditions. Neither party may apply for final offer arbitration nor public interest appeal of that contract unless the other party concurs.

25. *Freedom to Move*, Cat. 722-69/1985 (Ottawa: Transport Canada White Paper, July 1985).

26. Ellison, "Formation," p. 216.

27. National Transportation Act, sec. 3 (1987).

28. National Transportation Act, sec. 44 (1987).

29. Interview with rail planners Peter Hoisak and Ralph Jones, Ministry of Transport, Ottawa, Sept. 15, 1989. The 4 percent limit is found in the National Transportation Act, sec. 157–160 (1987).

30. This outline is adapted from "Railway Branch Lines," Railway and Grain Transportation Act of 1989 (Ottawa: Transport Canada, Surface Administration, 1989). (Memorandum). The pertinent parts of the statute can be found in National Railway and Grain Transportation Act of 1989, sec. 157–177.

31. Ibid., p. 2.

32. Ibid. The relevant sections are National Transportation Act, sec. 45, and sec. 165(2) (1987).

33. Bill Crawford, "Newfoundland Railway Farewell," *Trains*, January 1989, p. 26.

34. David Nett, "Canadian Pacific's Maine, Line," *Railfan & Railroad*, July 1989, pp. 34–39; National Transportation Act, sec. 152 (1987).

35. National Transportation Act, sec. 134–142 (1987).

36. National Transportation Act, sec. 148–149 (1987). In addition to the freight railroads, Amtrak has running rights over CN and CP into Montreal and operates joint services with VIA Rail into Toronto.

37. Data from Rail Planner Hoisak, Transport Canada, and included "Railroad Branch Lines," p. 5.

38. Ibid.

39. *See* William E. Thoms, "How Long is a Short Line?" *Trains*, October 1986, p. 37; William E. Thoms, "Dereg Comes to Canada," *Trains*, December 1988, p. 26. The first spin-off railway in Canada was the Central Western Railway in Alberta. In April 1992, Rail Tex Corp. took over two short lines in Ontario. *Trains*, March 1993, p. 30.

40. National Transportation Act, sec. 46 (1987).

41. National Transportation Act, sec. 47–57 (1987).

42. National Transportation Act, sec. 58–63 (1987).

43. National Transportation Act, sec. 110–119 (1987).

44. Ibid.

45. Ibid.

46. National Transportation Act, sec. 129–133 (1987).

47. National Transportation Act, sec. 120 (1987).

48. National Transportation Act, sec. 144–147 (1987).

49. National Transportation Act, sec. 148–152 (1987).

50. Section 52d of Appropriations Act No. 1, 1977, Can. Stat. 1976–77, Ch 7. *See* Thoms, "VIA Rail," p. 61.

51. Ibid. A Crown corporation is established for some public or quasi-public purpose. VIA Rail's sole responsibility is the carriage of intercity passengers. *See* Tom Nelligan, VIA Rail Canada: The First Five Years (Park Forest, IL: PTJ Publishing, 1982).

52. Peter. Dawes and Edward Johnson, *A Study of Amtrak's Effectiveness* (Ottawa: Queens Printer, 1974), pp. 168–169.

53. *Passenger Train Journal*, October 1977, p. 28.

54. *Passenger Train Journal*, June 1978, p. 35.

55. David P. Morgan, "On the Verge of VIA," *Trains*, August 1978, pp. 28–29.

56. Glen Allen, "Derailing VIA," *Maclean's* August 21, 1989, pp. 20–22. *See* William E. Thoms, "VIA Gets the Axe," *Trains*, January 1990, p. 22. (The cuts included abandonment of the entire Canadian Pacific passenger line between Montreal and Vancouver.)

57. Greg W. Taylor, "There is No Other Access," *Maclean's*, August 21, 1989, p. 25.

58. *Trains*, March 1993, p. 18.

9

Clear Track Ahead: U.S. Railroading in the Twenty-First Century

HIGH-SPEED RAIL TRANSPORTATION

Trainwatchers gathered at the tracks of the northeast corridor throughout 1993 to watch two foreign visitors swoop by on the electrified tracks. The Swedish X2000 was the first of the experimental consists to operate in Amtrak service. The point of the high speed trains was to demonstrate that existing roadbeds can be used for rapid passenger transportation, despite the curves of the nineteenth-century rights-of-way developed by the Pennsylvania and New Haven railroads. The electrified train was towed outside of electric territory by Amtrak's gas-turbine power cars. It was limited in its demonstration capacity by the requirement that it meet the schedule of an ordinary Metroliner and for the need to share the tracks with slower-moving trains.[1]

Later that same year, the German ICE arrived to take its place on Amtrak rails (and for a short time on the Canadian Pacific as well). The acronym stands for the English words "Inter-City Express;" apparently "Zwischen-stadtliche Schnellzug" does not come trippingly even to the Teuton tongue. The ICE was also placed into northeast corridor service after touring nonelectric parts of the system behind Amtrak's F69 diesels, repainted to match the German livery.[2]

The point of these public excursions was to compete for money authorized by Congress for Amtrak to acquire new equipment that would reduce travel time on its busiest routes and possibly reduce the need for new airports in our most congested regions. President Clinton's secretary of transportation, Federico Peña, fresh from the debacle of cost overruns and access problems at the Denver International Airport, held forth that the day of new airports was over and that high-speed rail was a cost-effective alternative. The visits of the foreign trains were sponsored by their European manufacturers, ABB of Sweden and Siemens of Germany. Both companies had licensing arrangements with American manufacturers, and, if their model were selected, the trains would be built in the United States. The Spanish Talgo train began running between Portland and Seattle in 1994. The French TGV is expected to enter trial service in 1995.

Despite the initial enthusiasm of the Clinton administration toward high-speed rail, it appears that progress will be incremental at best, given the U.S. deficit. Few funds are available for track improvement. Some high-speed corridors have been identified out of Chicago and on the Seattle-Portland line, but work will be straightening a curve here, elevating track there, taking out a grade crossing or two, nothing elaborate. New railroads that have been built in France, Germany, and Japan are not in the cards, and at this writing, the future of electrification east of New Haven is in doubt. High-speed rail is a noble cause, but it takes quite a bit of money to even clip a quarter hour from existing schedules, and money is one thing that Uncle Sam can no longer throw around.[3] Worse, Amtrak is hard-pressed to live on its operating budget (and a disastrous accident involving the Sunset Limited at Mobile, Alabama, decimated its self-insurance fund), and some minor cutbacks occurred in the fall of 1993. They included the elimination of the Kansas City–New Orleans River Cities (to be replaced by a chartered bus linking connecting trains at St. Louis and Carbondale), and the reduction of the Chicago-Texas Eagle and the Denver-Seattle Pioneer to thrice-weekly operation. Some Harrisburg-Philadelphia shuttle trains were also eliminated.[4]

High-speed rail is still the policy of the Clinton administration, and some form of fixed-guideway operation will no doubt emerge to connect cities with distant airports (like Denver International) and to link cities with recreational areas. But institutional arrangements may doom any large-scale developments. The freight railroads, upon whose roadbeds any high-speed system would have to develop, are insisting that the passenger operator assume all liability, even if an accident is the fault of the host railroads. Railway and construction unions, cut out from the labor market during the long famine of railway-building, are insistent on full employment of their members and labor protection provisions for any high-speed operation. Further development in high-speed technology is constrained by the need to share tracks with freight trains, which may have incompatible needs with those of the high-speed operator.[5]

The Liberal government elected in Canada in October 1993 has a similar bias toward public works and infrastructure, but the overwhelming deficits of the Mulroney years may leave Prime Minister Jean Chétien with the same financial constraints as those of President Clinton. It is unlikely that high-speed service, or any significant expansion of VIA Rail, will occur in Canada until these budgetary problems are worked out.

INTERMODAL TRANSPORTATION

On main lines devoid of Amtrak trains, the hottest things on rails are the intermodal trains, which carry containerized cargo at passenger-train speeds from one coast to the other, or carry an entire shipload to inland cities. Formerly known as "piggyback" trains, intermodal trailers can be hauled in regularly scheduled freights, but are more often handled in exclusive intermodal consists. No dispatcher worth his salt would dare delay one of these mainliners.

Intermodal service takes three forms: trailer on flat cars (TOFC), where a semitrailer is detached from the over-the-road tractor and loaded onto a specially fitted flat car, container on flat cars (COFC), where a box without wheels and running gear is taken from a ship or chassis and loaded on a flat car, to be unloaded on a waiting trailer frame elsewhere, and the RoadRailer system, where a trailer is fitted with rail wheels and operated as an exclusive RoadRailer train, or is added behind a passenger consist. Currently, the principal operator of the RoadRailer is Triple Crown Service, a service of the Norfolk Southern Railroad, operated in connection with Conrail in the east and CP Rail in Canada. On western routes, COFC trains are operated with double-stack cars, and clearances in the east are being raised so these Leviathans of the rails can operate all the way to Philadelphia, Boston, Baltimore, or the New York area.[6]

The intermodal train is symbolic of a shift in railroad consciousness. Since the ICC relaxed its restrictions on intermodal ownership, railroads have become seamless intermodal transportation companies, offering door-to-door service. But in many cases the railroad is a silent partner, handling the over-the-rail haul in place of highway transportation by a motor carrier. In this respect, it is interesting to note that the country's largest intermodal shipper, UPS, handles all its own billing and marketing, commandeering entire trains for its specially designed trailers. J.B. Hunt, the upstart trucking company of the 1980s, has become a fully integrated transportation company using rails for a substantial part of its long-haul business. And major shipping companies use intermodal rail as a land bridge or minibridge connection, saving valuable days over shipments through the Panama Canal.

SUPER-RAILROADS AND REGIONAL RAILROADS

The United States still has no true transcontinental railway. The Burlington Northern, with mainlines running from Seattle to Mobile and Pensacola, comes the closest. What mergers have occurred in the 1990s have so far been mopping-up operations; the Kansas City Southern's taking over of Mid-South's regional railway, and the Union Pacific's moving to finally gain access to Chicago by taking control of longtime friendly connection

Chicago & North Western. Chicago and the Mississippi River remain barriers to true transcontinental railroads, such as the Canadians have. In 1994, Burlington Northern and Santa Fe announced merger plans.

Currently there are no plans for merging the operations of eastern and western railroads, although cooperation among the big carriers is substantial. The status quo seems to hold; but if there is to be one transcontinental, there will be three, as each eastern railroad will scramble to find a western partner.

Side by side with the Big Seven megarailroads are medium-sized regional railways. Now approaching the size of Class I railroads thirty years ago, these lines include carriers like the Guilford system in New England, the Wisconsin Central in the Great Lakes area (which acquired short lines Green Bay & Western and Fox River in 1993), the Kansas City Southern (augmented by its purchase of Mid-South in 1993) serving the Gulf Coast, and such Northern Pacific reincarnations as the Red River Valley & Western and the Montana Rail Link in the Northwest. Chicago & North Western is also a midsized railroad, but it may be totally integrated into Union Pacific by the turn of the century; its western extensions have either been abandoned or folded into such short lines as the Dakota, Minnesota and Eastern. Illinois Central has jettisoned its east-west lines and now concentrates its activity on the spine line between Chicago and New Orleans, much as it did when Casey Jones worked there. The midsize category may also include the American subsidiaries of Canadian National and Canadian Pacific, but CN and CP are both integrating their operations into continental systems with little regard for such niceties as the forty-ninth parallel. At the smaller end of the medium-sized railways are New England's Providence & Worcester (which has taken over most of the freight operations of the old New Haven), the Susquehanna, operating in the middle Atlantic states, and the Florida East Coast, a north-south fast freight line that is still the bane of organized labor. Illinois Central and Kansas City Southern plan to consolidate their rail lines in 1995.

Whatever the rail system looks like in the twenty-first century, it will be privately owned. Uncle Sam will have enough trouble raising the modest sums for high-speed passenger trackage plus the amounts earmarked for infrastructure upgrading under the Intermodal Surface Transportation Efficiency Act (ISTEA) without setting aside massive sums for the purchase of roadbeds that the private sector is maintaining quite nicely, thank you. Although many rail systems, like CSX, have limited freight train speeds to 40 or 50 mph to reduce wear and tear on the rails, the rail network is in better shape than in any time since the dawn of the diesel age. But there are fewer miles of track every year, and that trend is expected to continue. Although there are obvious inequities with private freight railroads expected to pay taxes on their roadbeds while truckers and Greyhound operate over taxpayer-supplied highways, the efficiency of private ownership of the rails seem apparent in this postsocialist era. Such countries as Japan have privatized their railroads, and the Canadian government is looking toward privatizing Canadian National as they did with Air Canada.

Rail freight's future still depends on competitive equity with other modes. Although the threat of coal slurry pipelines has disappeared for the moment, state laws that allow two- and three-trailer rigs to operate on the interstate highways cast a pall on the ability of intermodal trains to compete, making the break-even point a longer and longer haul, until the railroad runs out of continent. Currently air freight and rail freight are two discrete markets, although intermodal shippers such as UPS have it within their power to decide by which mode traffic will move.

While federal ownership of rail lines will be limited to those required for Amtrak or high-speed operation, state ownership for limited purposes may be growing. Predominant among these uses will be acquisition of lines for commuter rail operations, ownership of locally vital branch lines about to be stranded by rail abandonment, and rail banking for future goals. Some of these projects are ambitious: Southern Pacific has given an option to Los Angeles to acquire its entire San Jose–L.A. Coast Line, onetime home of the Lar and Dayligh and the shortest route between California's largest cities.

The summer of 1993 brought floods rivaling Noah's to the upper Midwest. For a time, the Chicago and North Western's Overland Route was the only mainline open across the Upper Mississippi. Chicago's Metra commuter system supplied a pair of ex-North Western's E8 streamliners to gingerly lead Amtrak's California Zephyr across the rising waters.[7] Meanwhile, other railroads adopted innovative and bizarre detours to get their freights across the continent. Santa Fe adopted both a "North Pole " route via North Dakota and a "South Pole" route through Louisiana, both over lines of nominally competing railroads. Most railroads operated by the National Detour Agreement, by which carriers have agreed in advance to cooperate in rerouting trains, and which provides for a fixed fee for the handling of "foreign" trains by the "home" carrier. (Amtrak, by statute, has the right to operate over other lines at cost, without regard to the standard detour agreement.)[8]

The floods of 1993 pointed out the ability of private railroads to adapt and cooperate. The deluge also exemplified the growing divergence between ownership of trackage and operating rights. At this writing, Southern Pacific trains cross the thousand miles of Great Plains between Pueblo and Chicago over a patched-together extension of its Rio Grande route, mostly on other people's rails.[9] For the last two decades, the former Erie mainline through New York and Pennsylvania has hosted trains of Conrail, Susquehanna, and Delaware & Hudson (now CP Rail). In Canada, CP and CN are considering consolidating their operations east of Winnipeg, using only one transcontinental mainline through Ontario. More consolidation of mainlines can be expected in the United States, as the economies of reduced track maintenance and lower property taxes become apparent.[10]

The railroads of the twenty-first century will be more oriented to north-south than east-west transportation. Now that the North American Free Trade Agreement has become law, railroads are looking toward becoming the prime carriers of the new continental market. The push by Canadian railroads to operate in the United States is matched by American carriers opening routes to interchange at the Mexican border.

THE RAILROADER AND HIS JOB

One of the authors financed his law school education with a night job on the New York, New Haven, and Hartford Railroad. Thirty years ago, the New Haven was already in bankruptcy, and rumors of its liquidation circulated in the Connecticut press each day. By mid-1994, facing retirement from teaching law, he was bemused to find that many of his colleagues at the New Haven still had the equivalent of tenure from the NYNH&H's successors. Had your scribe continued with the railway, he might, too, have retained his position. Meanwhile, the jet-propelled go-getters who worked for Eastern Air Lines have been on the unemployment rolls for two years. Only Southwest Airlines is making a profit on the hauling of passengers in the midnineties; Greyhound Bus merged with Trailways after surviving bankruptcy and a bitter strike; the latter has been settled, but the drivers are working for considerably lower salaries and benefits than they had anticipated a decade ago.

The fate of the New Haven railroaders is, of course, an anomaly. Of the passenger routes operated by the railroad in 1964, only two short branches: Danbury-Pittsfield and New London–Worcester are freight-only three decades later. Amtrak and various commuter authorities keep the Camelot era of passenger service alive in New England, even to the extent of painting the locomotives in New Haven's psychedelic vermilion color scheme. On the other hand, carload freight in southern New England has all but disappeared, with Conrail having exited the region in favor of short line operators like the Housatonic, Guilford, or Providence & Worcester. And, of course, this longevity was not matched elsewhere. No combination of politics and legislation was enough to save the jobs of employees of the Rock Island or the Milwaukee. The New Haven had the benefit of passing through five states and having ten U.S. senators from the region interested in the idea of putting together a northeast corridor to relieve the pressure on New England's highways and airways. Other regions were just not that lucky.

Aside from job preservation through government-supported passenger service and severance benefits from labor protection, employment is down every year on Class I railroads—to the extent that railroaders and legislators alike worry about there being more retirees than active railroaders. Such a situation creates unfunded liability problems for the Railroad Retirement System. Stalemate between railroads and the plaintiff's bar has stalled any meaningful reform of the Federal Employers' Liability Act, with its lottery characteristics. No real workers' compensation alternative has emerged to the FELA.

The Railway Labor Act continues, as it has endured for the last seven decades. With a Democratic president and Congress more attuned to labor's wants than their predecessors, it does not appear as if any scheme to repeal or modify the act (such as merging it into the NLRA) will get very far. Furthermore, despite some failings in connection with airline bankruptcies, the Act has a pretty good reputation for avoiding strikes or lockouts, although negotiations are protracted. (In November 1993, President Clinton short-circuited the Emergency Provisions of Section 10 of the RLA in favor of urging arbitration on the parties to the American Airlines flight attendants' strike. But no government intervention could prevent the six-week Soo Line strike of 1994.))

The RLA was designed for an era when Class I railroads ran on military discipline, and an adversarial culture prevailed on the rails. More than in most industries, this corporate ethos still prevails in railroading, but there are some exceptions. The RLA model does not fit well to a loose and flexible organization like Southwest Airlines. Nor does it adapt itself well to many short line railroads, with their emphasis on shared responsibility and breaking down craft lines. A 1993 study by Tolliver, Thoms, and Casavant for the Mountain–Plains Consortium illustrated how our federal laws applicable to railroads are often ill-suited for locally based short line operations, and the Railway Labor Act may be one of those anomalies.[11]

The prevalent styles of management advocated by industrial psychologists and taught in schools of organization and administration emphasize labor-management cooperation and teambuilding. With its emphasis on grievance adjustment and the confrontation of Section 6 notices, the RLA is ill-suited for accommodating current approaches to organizational behavior. Nor is it at all clear whether such cooperation might be in violation of the RLA's proscription of company unions, by blurring the lines between labor and management. Productivity and competitiveness teams might well violate the spirit, if not the letter, of the 1926 act. As often happens in industries with declining employment, unions tend to favor the interest of members with long seniority; thus decisions are made that may help the old-timers but are disadvantageous to the entry-level worker and much of the membership.

Railroading is still a hazardous business. In 1992, it followed mining and agriculture as the most accident-prone occupation. But in the midnineties, more attention is being paid to the stressful nature of rail employment. Management and labor are attempting to make changes in the uncertainty of work hours and the problem of crew fatigue. But currently, a middle-aged conductor with a decade or two of service still cannot count on a regular job, with predictable hours, that is considered a given in most middle-class occupations.

A LOOK BACK AT DEREGULATION

Unlike the dismal tales of air carrier decline and bankruptcies following implementation of the Airline Deregulation Act, there has been relatively little criticism of the deregulation of railroads. For one thing, the trains are still running. There have been no major bankruptcies and large-scale abandonments since the liquidation of the Rock Island and Milwaukee railroads. Of today's rail giants, most are making modest earnings, that, what with the miserly interest rates available in the 1990s, exceeds the rate of return from financial institutions. On the other hand, profits are nothing to write home about, and one major carrier, Southern Pacific, was terribly debt-ridden until turning around in 1994. SP may well vastly restructure and cut back its operations by the end of the century.

Short line railroads have taken care of the branch line problem, and Amtrak has relieved the railroads of the passenger headache. Rails have been able to hold on to their traditional traffic and have expanded in intermodal carriage due to their partnership with trucking and shipping lines. Relaxation of ICC control over everyday business decisions has enabled carriers to meet the competition and respond to commercial realities. Railways are able to make rates and contracts that meet market conditions; they are able to leave markets and make alliances with short lines and regional railroads. Best of all, they have, for the most part, been able to upgrade the main lines and handle traffic in a safer and more efficient manner than during the 1970s.

As with every economic change, there is a dark side. Professor Dempsey has written of the oligopoly emerging in railroading and its anticompetitive aspects.[12] There is a large human cost as railroad division points are bypassed, as country towns and grain elevators dependent upon rail service no longer have access. In a nation hard-pressed to find good middle-class jobs, it is impossible to underestimate the effect of the disappearance of well-paid steady work with a rail carrier, with a good benefit package and the prospect of providing for one's family. There are fewer miles of track and fewer people employed, and in many places the railroad is disappearing from the public consciousness.

Deregulation has resulted in the preservation of a rail industry that seemed about to disappear two decades ago. But the loss of oversight of many functions means that public control over important transportation arteries is slipping away. Railroads abused the public trust in the nineteenth century. We, the authors, hope that they will be good stewards of the public convenience and necessity in the twenty-first.

NOTES

1. Dan Cupper, "For High-Speed Rail, A Practical Twist," *Trains*, September 1993, p. 30.
2. "Competition Mounts for Amtrak Contract," *Trains*, September 1993, p. 16. *See also* Dan Cupper, "ICE Train Makes a Splash," *Trains*, November 1993, p. 14.
3. Don Phillips, "Don't Bet the Farm on High-Speed Rail or Amtrak," *Trains*, October 1993, p. 12.
4. Don Phillips, "The Duct-Tape Railroad," *Washington Post National Weekly Edition*, October 4–10, 1993, p. 31.
5. Phillips, "Don't Bet," p. 12.
6. "Massachusetts Sees Stacsk in Its Future," *Trains*, September 1993, p. 17. *See also* "Now, RoadRailer Mixeds," *Trains*, September 1993, p. 22.
7. Bob Johnston, "Amtrak Toughs It Out," *Trains*, October 1993, p. 22.
8. Michael W. Blaszak, "When Trains Must Leave Home," *Trains*, November 1993, p. 84.
9. Fred W. Frailey, "Southern Pacific at the Crossroads," *Trains*, September 1993, p. 48.
10. "Ferment in the Dominion," *Trains*, November 1993, p. 17. *See also* "Toward Open Access," *Trains*, September 1993, p. 18.
11. Denver D. Tolliver, William E. Thoms, and Kenneth L. Casavant, *Regulation of Local and Regional Railroads: A National Survey of Perspectives and Practice*, MPC Report 93–24 (Fargo, ND: Mountain Plains Consortium, North Dakota State University, 1993).
12. Paul S. Dempsey, *The Social and Economic Consequences of Deregulation* (Westport, CT: Quorum Books, 1989).

Selected Bibliography

Arouca, Dennis A., and Henry H. Perritt, Jr. "Transportation Labor Regulation: Is the Railway Labor Act or the National Labor Relations Act the Better Statutory Vehicle?" *Labor Law Journal* 36(3) (1985):145–72.

Babcock, Michael W., and Michael Oldfather. "The Role of the Federal Employers' Liability Act in Railroad Safety." *Transportation Law Journal* 19(2) (1991):381–99.

Cappelli, Peter. *Still Working on the Railroad: An Exception to the Transformation of Labor Relations*. Philadelphia: The Wharton School of the University of Pennsylvania, 1987.

Commission on Railroad Retirement Reform: Final Report. Washington, D.C.: Government Printing Office, 1990.

Curtis, Ellen Foster, and Michael R. Crum. "Transportation Labor Relations: Contemporary Developments, Challenges, and Strategies." *Transportation Quarterly* 42(3) (1988):359–375.

Fogel, Robert W. *Railroads and American Economic Growth*. Baltimore, Md.: The Johns Hopkins Press, 1964.

Horowitz, Morris A. *Manpower Utilization in the Railroad Industry: An Analysis of Working Rules and Practices*. Boston, Mass.: Bureau of Business and Economic Research, Northeastern University, 1960.

Keeler, Theodore E. *Railroads, Freight, and Public Policy*. Washington D.C.: The Brookings Institution, 1983.

Kochan, Thomas A., Harry C. Katz, and Robert B. McKersie. *The Transformation of American Industrial Relations*. New York: Basic Books, 1986.

Licht, Walter. *Working for the Railroad*. Princeton, N.J.: Princeton University Press, 1983.

Northrup, Herbert T. "The Railway Labor Act—Time For Repeal?" *Harvard Journal of Law & Public Policy*, 13(2) (1990):441–515.

Northrup, Herbert T., and Philip A. Miscimarra, eds. *Government Protection of Employees Involved in Mergers and Acquisitions*. Philadelphia: The Wharton School of the University of Pennsylvania, 1989.

Perritt, Henry H., Jr. *U.S. Labor and the Future of Labor-Management Cooperation.* Washington, D.C.: U.S. Department of Labor, 1989.

Rehmus, Charles M. *The Railway Labor Act at Fifty: Collective Bargaining in the Railroad and Airline Industries.* Washington, D.C.: National Mediation Board, 1976.

Richardson, Reed C. *The Locomotive Engineer, 1863–1963: A Century of Railway Labor Relations and Work Rules.* Ann Arbor: University of Michigan Press, 1963.

Saphire, Daniel. "FELA and Rail Safety: A Response to Babcock and Oldfather; The Role of the Federal Employers' Liability Act in Railroad Safety." *Transportation Law Journal* 19(2) (1991):401–13.

Stover, John F. *The Life and Decline of the American Railroad.* New York: Oxford University Press, 1970.

Thoms, William. E., and Frank J. Dooley. *Airline Labor Law: The Railway Labor Act and Aviation After Deregulation.* Westport, Conn.: Quorum Books, 1990.

Thoms, William E., Frank J. Dooley, and Denver D. Tolliver. "Railroad Spinoffs, Labor Standoffs, and the P&LE." *Transportation Law Journal* 18(1) (1989):57–83.

U.S. Railroad Retirement Board. *Railroad Retirement Handbook, 1991.* Chicago: U.S. Railroad Retirement Board, 1991.

Wilner, Frank N. *The Railway Labor Act & the Dilemma of Labor Relations.* Omaha, Neb.: Simmons-Boardman Books, Inc., 1991.

———. "The Railroads' Retirement System: Its Past, Present and Future." *Transportation Practitioners Journal* 56(3) (1989):216–260.

Index

About the Authors

FRANK J. DOOLEY is an Assistant Professor of Agricultural Economics at North Dakota State University. For many years he was a researcher for the Upper Great Plains Transportation Institute in Fargo, N.D., and he has written extensively in the area of rail economics and law. A lawyer as well as an economist, Dooley is co-author of *Airline Labor Law* (Quorum Books, 1990).

WILLIAM E. THOMS is Professor of Law at the University of North Dakota and headed its institutes of aviation law and Canadian-American law. Thoms has done extensive writing in the field of transportation law. He is the author of *Reprieve for the Iron Horse* (1973), and co-author of *Law and Economic Regulation in Transportation* (Quorum, 1986), *Airline Labor Law* (Quorum, 1990) and *Pilots, Personality and Performance* (Quorum, 1992). With Paul Dempsey and Robert Hardaway, he is co-author of *Aviation Law and Regulation* (1993).

ISBN 0-89930-631-4

90000>

HARDCOVER BAR CODE